# PATRONAGE AND COMMUNITY IN MEDIEVAL CHINA

SUNY series in Chinese Philosophy and Culture

---

Roger T. Ames, editor

# PATRONAGE AND COMMUNITY IN MEDIEVAL CHINA

*The Xiangyang Garrison, 400–600 CE*

ANDREW CHITTICK

STATE UNIVERSITY OF NEW YORK PRESS

Published by
State University of New York Press, Albany



Printed in the United States of America



For information, contact
State University of New York Press, Albany, NY
www.sunypress.edu

Production, Laurie Searl
Marketing, Fran Keneston

**Library of Congress Cataloging-in-Publication Data**

Chittick, Andrew.
Patronage and community in medieval China : the Xiangyang garrison, 400–600 CE / Andrew Chittick.
p. cm. — (SUNY series in Chinese philosophy and culture)
Includes bibliographical references and index.
ISBN 978-1-4384-2897-0 (hardcover : alk. paper)
ISBN 978-1-4384-2898-7 (paperback : alk. paper)
1. Xiangyang Fu (China)—History. 2. Xiangyang Fu (China)—Politics and government. 3. Xiangyang Fu (China)—Social conditions. 4. Xiangyang Fu (China)—Social life and customs. 5. Patronage, Political—China—Xiangyang Fu—History—To 1500. 6. Community life—China—Xiangyang Fu—History—To 1500. 7. Social systems—China Xiangyang Fu—History—To 1500. 8. Garrisons—China—Xiangyang Fu—History—To 1500. 9. Jiankang Fu (China)—History. 10. China—History—220–589. I. Title.

DS793.H75C465 2009
951'.212—dc22 2009003936

10 9 8 7 6 5 4 3 2 1

# CONTENTS

# LIST OF MAPS

# ACKNOWLEDGMENTS

For my earliest work in local history materials related to the Xiangyang area I am indebted to the help of my advisors at the University of Michigan, including Chang Chun-shu, Ken DeWoskin, and most especially Ray Van Dam, whose help in navigating the scholarship on the Roman empire (especially on patronage issues) and interested outsider perspective on early Chinese history sparked many of the questions and suggested the approaches that informed my later research. More recently I have greatly benefited from the invaluable support, encouragement, and advice of numerous colleagues in the Early Medieval China Group, most notably Keith Knapp, Scott Pearce, and Albert Dien. My colleagues in the Southeast Early China Roundtable have been an invaluable sounding board for many of the ideas that went into this book; I am very appreciative of their intellectual and social companionship over the past decade. I have also appreciated financial support from the Council for Scholarly Communication with China for study in Hubei back in 1995–96, and from Eckerd College for faculty development funding, a hexennial leave, and more recently a partial research leave in order to finish up this manuscript. I am thankful to Nancy Ellegate and others at SUNY Press for their cheerful and prompt efforts to speed the process along. Lastly, I must acknowledge Ruth Pettis for her joyous friendship and her gorgeous work on the maps and the cover design, which were inspired by artwork from tombs in the Xiangyang area. Despite all that assistance, there doubtless remain errors and shortcomings in this book, all of my own doing.

# ONE

# INTRODUCTION

This work seeks to explain the development of an important provincial society, the Xiangyang 襄陽 region (in modern northern Hubei province), and the terms on which its members interacted with representatives of the southern court at Jiankang 建康 in the fifth and sixth centuries CE. It responds to the shortcomings of models of aristocracy and oligarchy, which have been applied to the social system of early medieval China, by demonstrating that a model based on patronage is far more helpful in understanding the tremendous instability of the political system, and the process of recruitment and assimilation of provincial leaders. It is the central thesis of this work that patronage is the most useful model with which to understand the general political organization of the southern dynasties.

The work further seeks to understand the effect of patronage on local society and local culture. On this issue it responds to prior efforts to characterize local society as a fairly integrated community, one in which local elites developed a protective, nurturant community ethos, and for which local men felt a significant sense of loyalty and identity. This idea is put to the test and found wanting. Instead, the evidence suggests that local society was extremely fragmented, with loyalties directed at narrowly defined familial ties or social subgroups. This fragmentation was perpetuated and accentuated by the patronage system, which persistently drew men's loyalties up and out of their communities and into the affairs of imperial patrons; it also transmitted the fierce succession rivalries of the imperial court into local affairs.

Despite this fragmentation, the culture of the Xiangyang region nonetheless had distinctive features which made it quite different from the culture of Jiankang, though the latter is often taken to be representative of "the south" in general. These features include the routine use of physical violence in one's career and personal life; the importance of revenge and personal honor; the lack of much classical education, even of basic literacy, among society's leading members; and an oral culture based on song, dance, and musical accompaniment. This regional culture lacked formal literary expression, and was not a basis for an abstract, impersonal identity or loyalty. Nonetheless, it affected the mutual perception between local men and Jiankang elites, who came from a very different cultural milieu. In depicting a provincial culture of this type, this work challenges prevailing notions of what "southern" culture was, notions that are overwhelmingly based on the writings of men from the Jiankang elite and their cultural satellites.

## ARISTOCRACY AND OLIGARCHY

The society of early medieval China has proven difficult to generalize about.[1] The period has been described as "aristocratic," but there has been considerable debate about how to characterize this "aristocracy," or whether one really existed at all. At one end of the spectrum, scholars have highlighted officeholding and status bestowed by the state as the hallmarks of the ruling class; the term *oligarchy* has also been applied to this formulation, especially for the Tang dynasty elite.[2] Evidence from the eastern Jin (317–420) and southern dynasties (420–589), however, shows that very few families proved able to retain high status and wide-scale political power for more than a few generations; this rapid rate of turnover does not support the idea of a small, self-perpetuating social and political elite that the term *oligarchy* implies.[3] Inheritable titles and officeholding alone were apparently not sufficient to stabilize the social order into hereditary classes to any great degree.

In the case of the southern dynasties, the difficulty with these formulations stems from the fact that the terminology addresses far too narrow a conception of what early medieval "society" was. Scholars have tended to focus exclusively on the cluster of family lines that were based at the southern capital, Jiankang. Men of these families were noted for their official service and their education and scholarship in classics, histories, and Buddhist materials; the most prestigious of them frequently supplied consorts to the imperial household. Most of these family lines initially secured their status immediately following their migration south to support the eastern Jin court at Jiankang following the collapse of the western Jin court at Luoyang in the early fourth century. Some "southern lineages" that were already prominent in the Yangzi delta area were begrudgingly admitted to this circle over the following century. The core of this urban official class was well established prior to 420, though some, notably the Lanling Xiaos 蘭陵蕭, were relative latecomers. Though there was substantial turnover at the highest levels, this core group of families had considerable longevity in official service for well over two centuries.[4]

Under the southern courts, however, the imperial throne and the top ranks of the military were commonly occupied, not by representatives of these "aristocratic" lineages, but by lower-class men from more distant provinces.

Such men were classed as *hanmen* 寒門, literally "cold gates," a term that suggested a household that lived in relative deprivation and poverty, and was used to signify any family that was not of the top rank of the officially privileged, genteel (*shizu* 士族) class. The term was especially appropriate for men from frontier provinces, since the term *han* could also signify the "barbarian" north and the frontier, from whence came the cold winds, both literally and metaphorically. Provincial men were not necessarily poor, however, nor was their social status always low; though they were looked down upon by the capital elite, they eventually came to hold most of the reins of actual power. In fact, men from the aristocratic lineages of the capital have been characterized as little but "props on a stage," who served at the behest of these provincials and lent them some cultural legitimacy.[5] In order to understand the political and social system of the southern dynasties, therefore, we must broaden our concept of the ruling class beyond the confines of the Jiankang elite, and attempt to write history from the perspective of these frontier *hanmen*, their provincial societies, and how they interacted with the court.

Once we adopt this broader concept of the medieval social order, the shortcomings of the more narrowly formulated models of aristocracy and oligarchy become glaringly apparent. Perhaps the most distinctive feature of the provincial *hanmen* is their extraordinarily rapid turnover in the halls of power. Fighting men from the provinces rose quickly to great heights of authority, and often fell from grace even more rapidly. The relatively fixed, stable social order predicted by the model of an aristocracy or oligarchy is clearly not helpful for understanding this process. We must find another model.

## COMMUNITY AND IDENTITY

The concept of local community suggests a much more promising approach to the study of provincial society. The other end of the spectrum of debate about the medieval "aristocracy" adopts this focus, emphasizing the social role of elite families in their local communities. Scholars have characterized these families both economically, as dominating local areas through ownership of extensive manorial estates, and ideologically, as promoting an ideal of close-knit community leadership through ethical modeling and charitable giving, thereby developing a "warm and protective" relationship with the local populace.[6] The economic side of the model is widely accepted, though evidence in this study suggests that, at least in the Xiangyang area, local families were not very extended nor necessarily very well entrenched.[7] The ideological side of the model, however, has been criticized for being too accepting of elite propaganda, and underemphasizing the likelihood of class struggle within such communities.[8]

A more serious problem with the ideological side of the model is that the evidence from early medieval texts does not support it very well. Though selected passages in medieval texts do portray local elites as engaging in local charitable and leadership activities, the broader corpus of local writing in this period does not emphasize this role.[9] The development of local history, for example, shows that local elites portrayed themselves, not as local leaders and patrons, but as detached from any concrete leadership role in local society. Medieval biographies of "retired gentlemen" who were resident in their communities (rather than at court) celebrate their disengagement from virtually all social or political concerns and their avoidance of local commoners. These accounts acknowledge only limited local ties to close family members; the most important, most deeply felt relationships are identified as being with equally erudite and disengaged men from far distant regions.[10] This evidence suggests that local elites did not seek to build their reputations through celebrating their fulfillment of civic leadership obligations, whatever their local activities may have been in practice.

An alternative approach to the ideology of local community is available from studies of modern nationalism and identity. These emphasize community as something that is "created" or "imagined" by human will in order to influence political behavior. This "imagining" draws on a variety of differences between one local society and another—in language, dress, physical appearance, residence, employment habits, cultural activities, shared history, etc.—which are accentuated by local elites in order to develop a stronger sense of cultural and political identity among their potential followers.[11] Cultural differences that had existed as a relatively nonpoliticized "soft" boundary of sentiment or habit can thereby evolve into a "hard" boundary, a commitment that commands loyal action and even sacrifice.[12] Such communities are by definition exclusive: their members are more likely to associate and ally with other members of their community, and reject, or at least subordinate, relationships with people from outside the community. The clear delineation of outsiders, and restrictions on accepting them as "members," is a central element in what constitutes a "hard" community identity. Texts that advocate and celebrate the values of such a community are likely to describe the corresponding restriction of political choices for community members as morally proper and "loyal."

Scholars have adapted these ideas to characterize the premodern development of Chinese cultural and national identity as a whole. Chinese culture has been characterized a type of universal "religious community," comparable to (for example) Islam; the development of a more restrictive Chinese national identity is then portrayed as developing out of this universal identity in response to external pressure, first from nomadic peoples beginning in the Song period (960–1279), then from Euro-American powers in the nineteenth and twentieth centuries.[13] Studies of the early medieval period have traced this "imagining" of a distinctive Chinese cultural identity back to the legacy of the Han empire, a legacy whose shadow fell heavily on the many lesser regimes that followed and sought to emulate it.[14]

Such universalist approaches to Chinese identity are of limited use for understanding *local* community, however, since they do not consider the ways in which the Han legacy became fragmented, and accommodated the development of important sub-identities. With the demise of the Han court and its domination of literary production, men from different geographical regions were more free to select from the Han corpus those elements that most emphasized and flattered their own homelands, and in this way could cast themselves as a unique "subset" of the classical whole. These locally particularistic interpretations of the Han tradition had the potential to be conceptualized as distinct cultures in and of themselves, and to serve as an important source of identity and affiliation for local elites, especially if promoted by institutions with substantial resources, such as regional kingdoms or local administrative units. Development along these lines is clearly visible, first as a result of the division during the Three Kingdoms period (220–280), and even more in the centuries-long division between northern and southern regimes (317–589).[15] Applied in this way, the "imagined community" model offers a promising approach to conceptualizing the ideological side of provincial community and identity in the early medieval period.

Compared to some other regions (notably Wu and Shu), the evidence from the Xiangyang region suggests that it was not a center for this sort of ideological production. Local writing from the Xiangyang region up through the late fourth century tended to subordinate local cultural identity to the larger Han universalist tradition, by anchoring local lore in classical references and antiquarian nostalgia; it also expressed a desire to see state representatives and other educated outsiders patronize the area and bring about a revival of the civilized traditions they had once maintained.[16] These materials promoted a soft, inclusive model of cultural identity that idealized the cultural production of the universal Han empire, reflecting the passive, disengaged, culturalist orientation of the late Han elite more generally.[17] By the end of the turbulent fourth century the members of this local "late Han elite" had all either died, sunk into obscurity, or emigrated to more congenial social and cultural centers such as Jiankang or Jiangling 江陵, the Jiankang court's primary administrative outpost in the middle Yangzi region. The legacy of their local writing remained as an antiquarian corpus to be clipped, edited, and rearranged at the behest of imperial agents and other outsiders with universalizing intentions.

The demise of Xiangyang's late Han elite opened the way in the fifth and sixth centuries for the development of a different sort of local society, which is the focus of this study. Centered on the military garrison that developed at Xiangyang, it became a critical source of military clients for powerful men from Jiankang and elsewhere. The population was extremely diverse, including many different immigrant settler groups, as well as locally born families engaged in military service or trade. The most challenging aspect of this society is that its members were largely illiterate; thus, despite its apparently vigorous oral and performative traditions, it did not develop any literary expression of an "imagined" shared history or culture.

For the modern-day researcher, the lack of literary production by local men means that their society can only be understood through the written observations of interested, but often unsympathetic outsiders. These sources are nonetheless quite valuable, and include accounts of the careers of local men; accounts of imperial princes or other officials who served as commanders of the garrison, or in their entourages; records of local oral song culture; records of local legends and stories; records of regional seasonal festivals; and archaeological evidence from local tombs. The evidence suggests that, by the mid-fifth century, the Xiangyang area had developed a distinctive cultural environment, characterized by violence, revenge, and a vibrant oral song culture. Sources from the sixth century reinforce this picture and add further evidence of the narrowness of familial ties, the importance of elite-sponsored public spectacles, and the relative indifference to Buddhism (at least in its scholarly, court-sponsored form). This distinctive local cultural mix existed in a state of significant tension with the quite different culture of Jiankang, a tension that is attested to both in imperial memorials and in local accounts of supernatural phenomena that outwit and drive away the evil agents of the southern regime.

The existence of this distinctive local culture does not mean that local men identified with this culture or with their birthplace in a way that determined their political actions, however; the evidence instead suggests that the "soft" boundaries remained soft. A certain amount of social cohesion, even exclusivity, does seem to have persisted among significant subgroups, especially clusters of immigrant settlers, and within quite narrowly conceptualized family circles. The very narrowness of these loyalties, however, exemplifies the lack of a wider conception of community identity. Evidence for broader local political cohesion peaks during the regime of Liu Jun 劉駿 (Song Emperor Xiaowu 宋孝武帝, r. 453–465). Subsequent to that time, though there is evidence that local men were occasionally resistant to political and cultural pressures emanating from the imperial court, the overwhelming majority of evidence shows that local men lacked a sense of abstract identity with "Xiangyang" that was anywhere near strong enough to determine their political behavior, their choices of allegiance, or their loyalty. They routinely served on opposing sides of wider civil conflicts, and showed no coordinated effort to work on behalf of local interests within the larger context of the southern regimes. Their "imaginations" were engaged elsewhere, on more proximate ties and narrower estimations of personal advantage. Thus, the model of the "imagined community," though suggestive for many other developments in medieval China, does not get us very far in this case.

## PATRONAGE AS A SYSTEM

An approach that holds more promise for understanding the development of the political structure of provincial society at Xiangyang proves to be the idea of patronage, not just as a particular, personal relationship, but as a system of social relations. The operation of patron-client ties has already proven to be an especially fruitful approach to understanding the official culture of the eastern Han empire (25–220 CE).[18] Work on the southern dynasties has further demonstrated the importance of personal patronage ties in the relations between military garrison commanders and their men, and in the resultant rise of the provincial commoner class that largely displaced the aristocratic capital lineages in positions of substantive power.[19]

This body of research can be broadened to develop a model for the entire social system of the southern dynasties, one that offers tremendous insights into the nature of provincial society and its relations with the imperial court. Though patronage is commonly conceived of merely as a dyadic relationship between two individuals that is subordinate to, even parasitic on, a more formal social system, it can also be seen as the primary form of social relationship, one that structures the entire social order and its allocation of resources (especially official positions). This model predicts a society in which personal relationships are paramount; in which vertical ties routinely undercut and disrupt the development of stronger horizontal or "community" ties; in which issues of personal loyalty and trust are a matter of great concern, both in individual career choices and in the written literature; and in which society overall can be characterized as pluralistic, fluid, competitive, and inherently unstable.[20]

As a dyadic relationship, patronage is defined as a one-to-one bond between two individuals characterized by the following four elements:

1. personal, face-to-face contact;
2. *inequality*: the patron is of higher status, with more access to resources, than the client;
3. *reciprocity*: something is exchanged, i.e., loyal support for a job or a fief;
4. *voluntarism*: client and patron choose one another and are able to change allegiance.

Relationships of this sort are universal throughout human societies, but there is substantial variation in the extent to which they are routine and sanctioned as a means of exchanging resources.[21] For example, in societies with highly developed aristocratic or bureaucratic systems of status, patronage relations often have a subordinate and illegitimate role, and are denigrated as "corruption." Yet patronage relations can sometimes (as in ancient Rome) play a very legitimate role as a means of resource and power distribution within a more formal institutional matrix.[22] In these cases there is typically a well-developed (though not always explicitly stated) code of behavior for patrons and clients, including the responsibilities clients have to their patrons, the means by which they may shift from one patron to another, and whether they may have multiple patrons at once. Loyalty is a central issue, for while it is always in the patron's interest to restrict client choice by demanding a high degree of loyalty, it is often in the client's interest to retain freedom of choice in order to improve their bargaining position and thereby demand more from their patrons. Since patrons are ordinarily the more powerful and better educated members of society, they are the ones most likely to delineate ideals of loyalty, reflecting their own interests in criticizing breaches of loyalty and advocating the restriction of client choice to a single patron.[23]

As noted previously, scholarship on early medieval China strongly supports the idea that patron-client relations were important in determining political behavior, even though they were not always viewed favorably by political commentators. The terms used to describe clientelage relations are fairly continuous from the late Han all the way into the southern dynasties: they include terms such as guests (*ke* 客or *binke* 賓客), followers (*zuoyou* 左右), former officials (*guli* 古吏), students (*mensheng* 門生, usually reserved for educated clients), or simply "old contacts" (*jiu* 舊).[24] Such relationships were widely understood, but also considered somewhat less than ideal and often marginalized; thus, traditional Chinese historical writing does not necessarily use these terms regularly or consistently. Instead, personal ties of gratitude (*en* 恩) seem to have been implicit in almost any situation where a man accepted a job, a favor, or otherwise developed any type of unequal and reciprocal personal relationship with another.[25]

Because personal clientelage ties are by their very nature not systematically delineated in written materials, the most important tool for determining their role is prosopography, the mapping of networks of personal relationships.[26] In this research I have tracked evidence of marital ties, friendships and private associations, and especially career ties, about which there is the most surviving information. I have also looked for contexts in which such relationships could have formed, which has led me to institutional history, not just for what it tells us about formal social structure, but for what it tells us about informal ties, about which people were most likely to be thrown together and have opportunities to develop personal patronage relationships. I have paid particular attention to how men made choices of whom to serve and when to shift allegiance; I am less concerned with how loyalty was promoted as an abstract ideal, typically by patrons, than with how loyalty was observed in actual practice by men who were clients. In particular, I have sought to identify the extent to which loyalty to an ascribed or adopted identity—to family, local community, religion, or other ideology—may have guided men's choices, potentially limiting their choice of patrons, or at least gaining them censure when they chose "inappropriately."

Conceptualizing patronage not merely as a single relationship, but as the primary system of political relationships and resource allocation, allows us to further identify two broader characteristics of society. One of these is the prevalence of voluntary relationships over ascribed ties in determining political behavior, which inhibits the development of stable, regenerating, or inherited structures of power.[27] Such instability is the most prominent feature of the political system of the southern dynasties, one which the models of aristocracy and oligarchy cannot account for; by comparison, the patronage model predicts it. The evidence of Xiangyang men's particular experience confirms the model in much greater detail, for their career paths were highly personal and unstable. Ascriptive ties, especially to family, appear to have been much less significant than has been presumed based on studies of northern families, or the southern elite at Jiankang. Though ties to close male kin, primarily sons, brothers, nephews, sometimes first cousins, and occasional affinal kin, were clearly significant, there is little evidence of affiliation with more distant agnatic kin, or of the keeping of genealogical records tracking ancestors back for generations. In one particularly clear case, a Xiangyang man was introduced to a man of the same choronym and surname in the north and asked if they were related. The northerner was proud of his own illustrious surname, which he could trace back a dozen generations, but the Xiangyang man had no idea of his distant ancestors, and had to learn them from the genealogies his northern relatives had scrupulously maintained. In other words, the circle of ascriptive family ties he grew up with was relatively narrow; voluntary personal associations had been of far more significance to his career.[28]

The other important characteristic of a patronage system is the prevalence of vertical ties of solidarity over horizontal ones such as social class, status, ethnicity, or local or ideological identities. Horizontal ties would not be wholly absent, but they would be inhibited by the open competition for resources from patrons outside the community, and the resultant destabilizing effects of these vertical ties on community solidarity.[29] In other words, the potential for developing exclusive, politicized ties to an "imagined" community identity would be ceaselessly undercut by men's perennial quest for patrons from outside the community. Again, the evidence from Xiangyang supports the patronage model, for ties of place were exceptionally tenuous. The strongest "local" tie appears to have come through military service in the local garrison, but the evidence suggests that this was less an abstract ideological tie than a concrete personal one; men who fought side by side on military campaigns developed substantial personal bonds, which were then called upon for political purposes. Men's loyalties in any case were not primarily to their local associates and peers, but to their patrons, often imperial princes or other imperially appointed commanders of the garrison, who had the potential to deliver substantial wealth and prestigious appointments. In numerous examples of civil conflict, men served their patrons fiercely, fighting other men from their own locality to the death in order to maintain their clientelage bond.

Far from being an "imagined community" with a sense of shared identity and solidarity, Xiangyang society would be better described as highly fragmentary, as I emphasize particularly in chapter 3. Men's identity appears to have been very narrowly circumscribed to close relatives and personal associates; wider solidarities, to some "imagined" local community or cultural tradition, or to a dynasty or an ideal of universal cultural values, were largely absent. This is hardly surprising, given that most men from Xiangyang were illiterate; the "empire of the text" that existed in the Han classics, commentaries, and histories was largely beyond them, as was the option of fixing and propagating more proximate abstract identities through local history writing.[30] Indeed, as I argue in chapter 4, even local icons of bygone days were probably unknown to them; lacking strong extended family traditions, and without the ability to read local histories, or even local commemorative markers, they would have been of little significance. Such unconcern with "local" tradition may have been even more pronounced among immigrant settlers, who would have brought memories and traditions from diverse, even alien cultures, which they may have chosen to protect and preserve by avoiding more proximate associations.

In this highly fragmentary social world, personal clientelage ties to powerful patrons were the only means by which larger alliances could be forged. Powerful local men had personal clients and military retainers (*buqu* 部曲) of their own; they in turn developed allegiances to imperial princes and other outside agents who recruited them as personal clients.[31] This process joined men from different subgroups of local society, as well as men from other regions, into ad hoc personal coalitions of civilian staff and fighting men that survived as long as their patron did, and dispersed just as rapidly when he met his downfall. Beginning with Liu Jun (Song Emperor Xiaowu), men who sought to take the throne at Jiankang frequently relied on clients from the Xiangyang region; they were especially prominent in the regime of Xiao Yan 蕭衍 (Liang Emperor Wu 梁武帝, r. 502–549), but also in the regimes of Xiao Daocheng 蕭道成 (Qi Emperor Gao 齊高帝, r. 479–482) and Xiao Cha 蕭察 (later Liang Emperor Xuan 後梁宣帝, r. 555–562) and his heirs.

## REGIMES, REGIME CHANGE, AND OTHER NOMENCLATURE

The patronage model allows us to reconceptualize how we write about the political system of the imperial court itself. We must begin with the fact that virtually every substantive emperor of the southern dynasties took the throne through a violent coup, and each emperor's eventual demise was promptly followed by a civil war. In order to win the civil war, each would-be successor had to have developed a personal network of battle-worthy clients, usually provincial *hanmen*, that were loyal to their individual patron. The clientelage network built up prior to and during the civil war was then swept into power when its central patron assumed the throne; its members survived and prospered, however, only so long as their patron/emperor did, unless they were able to develop personal ties to a new patron who could emerge victorious from the *next* civil war. In other words, each "emperor" essentially ruled a military dictatorship whose members lacked a stable means to perpetuate themselves in power into the next generation.

Chinese historical convention emphasizes the continuity of "dynastic" bloodline; thus, the period from 420 to 589 is identified with the four "dynasties" of Song, Qi, Liang, and Chen 宋齊梁陳. In practice, however, the inheritance of the throne was only marginally through bloodline, and rarely through a formal, designated inheritance procedure. The fact that only one designated heir, Xiao Daocheng's son Xiao Ze 蕭賾 (Qi Emperor Wu 齊武帝), actually survived to establish a stable regime in the years stretching from 420 to 550 (after which Xiangyang was no longer a part of this system) shows that, far from a guarantee of succession, designation as the imperial heir was virtually a guarantee of execution. Conceiving of this system as "dynastic" merely reiterates the fiction perpetuated by imperial history offices, obscuring more than it reveals. Rather than a "dynasty," these ad hoc assemblages of personal military clients would be better described as "regimes," a term that emphasizes the personal and shifting nature of imperial rule during this period.

The personal nature of these patronage networks also demands a more consistent terminology for referring to individuals. In classical texts, and in most modern history, men who took the imperial throne are referred to by their dynastic names; thus, Xiao Yan is much more widely known as Liang Emperor Wu, even though for the first thirty-seven years of his life he had no such title, nor was he expected to. It makes no sense to refer to Xiao Yan as "Liang Emperor Wu" at any point prior to his ascent to the throne; yet it also does not work well to suddenly start calling him by a different name once he became emperor, for it creates a disjunction in our perception of the individual and his clique, when in practice Xiao Yan retained a similar network of personal associates even after he attained the throne (as evidence of his Xiangyang clients demonstrates). The same problem of shifting nomenclature exists for imperial princes, who are commonly referred to by their oft-changing fief names (i.e., Xiao Yi 蕭繹 is known as the Prince of Xiangdong 湘東王, as well as Liang Emperor Yuan 梁元帝); for other high officials, who are often referred to by their family name and the title of their highest office (often a posthumous one that they never held while alive); and for the common use of style names, ordinarily adopted at maturity. I have tried to eliminate this multiplicity of nomenclature by using a man's family and given name throughout, regardless of what offices and titles he attained, up to and including the imperial throne; thus, I call Xiao Yan by that name throughout his career, even while he is emperor. The only partial exception to this is my use of the title "Prince" instead of the surname when referring to members of the imperial lineage, so as to signal their familial relationship to the emperor; thus, I refer to the aforementioned Xiao Yi as "Prince Yi."

Most of my other choices of nomenclature are conventional. I use pinyin transliteration throughout (and modify quoted materials accordingly) and translate Chinese official titles following Hucker's *Dictionary* unless otherwise noted. My one other unconventional usage is for dates. Chinese texts demarcate the years by the name of a dynasty and a reign title, followed by the lunar month and sometimes the day, which is indicated by a sexagenary cycle of specialized terms. In most cases I omit the specific day, and I translate the year into the Gregorian calendar year. The Chinese year has twelve or thirteen lunar months (an extracalary month is added occasionally to keep the system aligned with the solar cycle), but they do not correspond to modern months: the first lunar month, for example, may begin anywhere from late January to late February. I find translating this as "Month One" or "first lunar month" to be both cumbersome and unilluminating. Instead, I follow a common Chinese conception of the system by taking the lunar months as a reference to the seasons: the first three months correspond roughly to spring, the next three months to summer, and so forth. Thus, I translate the first three lunar months as "early spring," "mid-spring," and "late spring." This system offers better narrative flow and effectively communicates the time of the year, without sacrificing precision from the original Chinese.

## AN INTRODUCTION TO THE XIANGYANG REGION

The Xiangyang region was chosen as a case study for several complementary reasons. First, its situation on the frontier with northern regimes meant that it was perennially under military threat, and also inhabited by a large number of immigrants; as a result, issues of identity and loyalty are especially significant. Second, Xiangyang as a region played kingmaker several times during the southern dynasties, most importantly in the coup that put Xiao

Yan on the throne as Emperor Wu of the Liang dynasty. Since Xiao Yan was the longest-reigning, and in many ways the archetypal, southern monarch, understanding his relationship with this provincial area is a critical issue. Third, Xiangyang was pivotal in the eventual collapse of the Jiankang regime, since its surrender to the Chang'an regime in 550 set off the chain of events that caused the loss of the entire central and upper Yangzi region from Jiankang's control. Fourth, there are limited but valuable resources on Xiangyang local culture, including evidence from the "western lyric" tradition (*xi qu* 西曲), anecdotes preserved in local histories and festival calendars, a variety of Buddhist tales, and a few archaeological sites, that can help to flesh out the political history. In order to round out this introduction, therefore, I offer an introduction to the Xiangyang region's geography and history down to the end of the fourth century CE.

The Xiangyang region might be called one the East Asian mainland's "internal frontiers." It is situated on the climatological divide between the wheat and millet-growing north and the rice-growing south, which runs east from the Qinling range through the northern edges of the region and on into the valley of the Huai River. The region is a fairly distinctly demarcated alluvial plain hemmed in on all sides by hills and mountains (see Map 1). Its chief feature is the route of the Han 漢 River (which in this region is also called the Mian 沔), which flows out of the long narrow Hanzhong valley (in the southern part of modern-day Shaanxi). The river skirts the plain on its southwest side, then runs due south, making as if to join immediately with the Yangzi near Jiangling, but instead veering east and wandering through several hundred miles of swampland to join the Yangzi at what is now Wuhan, the modern capital of Hubei province.

The high peaks of the Wudang 武當 and Jing 荊 mountains lie immediately to the south and west of the river's course through this central section, and are drained by several fairly short alpine streams. The majority of the region is north of the river, drained primarily by the Tang-Bai 唐白 system, one of the Han's major tributaries.[32] These rivers in turn have their origins almost two hundred kilometers to the north, in the eastern reaches of the Funiu mountains 伏牛山. This low-lying yet pivotal watershed divides off the region from the upper reaches of both the Ying 穎 River, which flows east into the Huai, and the Yi 伊 and Luo 洛 rivers, which flow north to join the Yellow River just past Luoyang. The hills permit easy passage between all three drainage basins, confusing some early geographers as to which rivers ran in which direction.[33] Where the Tang-Bai system joins with the Han River there are several outcroppings of low foothills that force the Han to execute an elongated bend that swoops first to the northeast, then loops back to the southwest before turning southeast again. This bend is wide and shallow, dominated by a flat sandy island called Fish Dike Island (*yuliang zhou* 魚梁洲), and offers excellent places for fording the river. This critical juncture point came to be the location of the town of Xiangyang (see inset, Map 1).

In the early Spring and Autumn period (722–481 BCE) the region was dominated by the state of Chu 楚, whose ancient capital Ying 郢, also known as Yan 鄢, was most likely located near Yicheng 宜城, about forty miles south of the Tang-Bai junction.[34] The region's excellent strategic position as a gateway

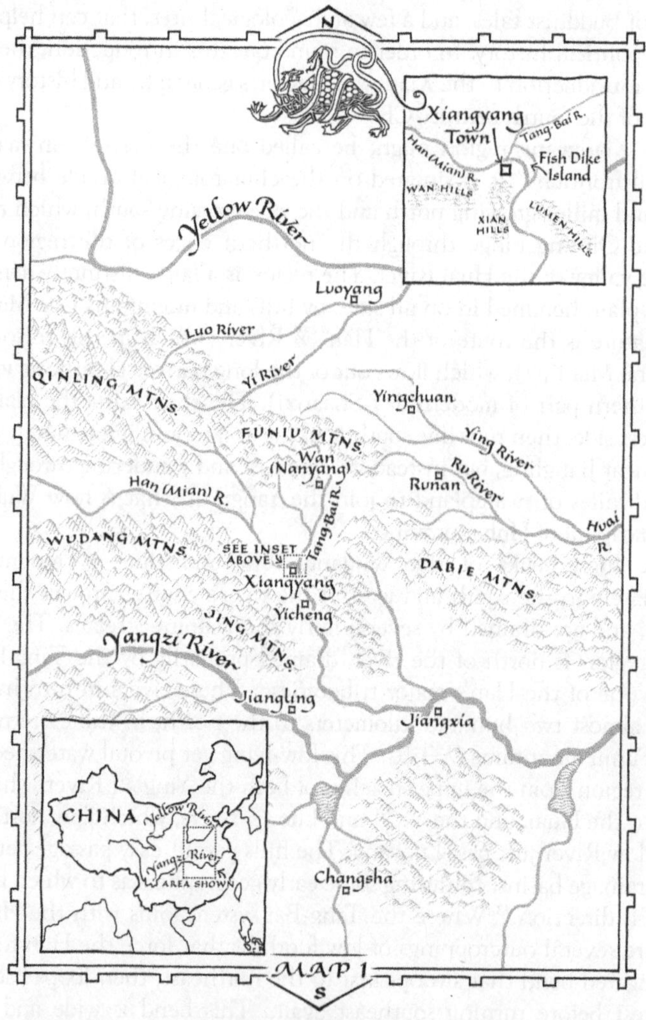


Map 1. The central Yangzi area (inset: the Xiangyang region)

to the Yellow and Huai river valleys made it a desirable route of expansion, and it was fully integrated into the Chu administrative system for more than four hundred years until the campaigns by the northwestern state of Qin 秦 in the late Warring States period (403–221 BCE) led to Chu's collapse.[35] Because of this early history, the geographical divide also gained political, cultural, and linguistic significance, and the entire region has traditionally been identified as part of the south.[36]

With the Qin conquest, the region north of the Han River was organized as Nanyang commandery 南陽郡. Its seat, Wan 宛, about seventy miles up the Bai River from its juncture with the Han, was the commercial hub of the northern part of the plain, and in the Western Han period (202 BCE–9 CE) developed strong links to the prosperous nearby commanderies of Runan 汝南 and Yingchuan 穎川, in the upper Huai valley, and Henan 河南, on the Yellow River. South of the Han River stretched the huge commandery called Nanjun 南郡, or "southern commandery," which included all of the Jiang-Han plain down to the Yangzi river and beyond, and had its seat at Jiangling, on the Yangzi. By the end of the Western Han, Nanyang had become one of the most populous commanderies in the empire, controlling thirty-six counties with almost two million inhabitants; the town of Wan itself probably boasted a population of well over a hundred thousand, and had become a major commercial and political center.[37]

In the rebellions to overthrow the rule of Wang Mang in 23–25 CE, leadership in the Nanyang area came from a branch of the Han imperial house based in the southeastern part of the commandery. A member of this branch, Liu Xiu 劉秀, ultimately established himself as Han Emperor Guangwu (漢光武帝, r. 25–57 CE), thereby restoring the Han imperial house. Many of his closest advisors and supporters hailed from the Nanyang area, and the town of Wan came to be regarded as the "southern capital." With the primary capital relocated from Chang'an to Luoyang, an easy 120 miles north of Wan, the entire region was much closer and better connected to the center of imperial power than ever before.[38]

Up until this time, the town of Xiangyang itself had been of little account, the northernmost county seat in the sprawling, rather uncivilized "southern commandery." Over the course of the next two hundred years, however, the population of this southern realm grew sharply, and the wealth and patronage that flowed into the Nanyang area seeped across the border to benefit the local elites of Xiangyang, Yicheng, and other towns south of the river. Their assimiliation into the Han imperial system made even faster gains with the decline of the Han imperial court at the end of the second century. A distant member of the imperial clan, Liu Biao 劉表, set up an independent regime based at Xiangyang which claimed authority over all of the central Yangzi area (Jing province 荊州, roughly equal to modern Hubei and Hunan). He patronized hundreds of wealthy and well-educated émigrés from the capital elite to engage in scholarly work and support his bid to once again "re-found" the Liu clan's fortunes. Though this campaign ultimately failed, local men gained contacts with educated and powerful men from all over the empire, and many of them wound up in service to one of the three rival imperial courts that struggled with one another through the subsequent Three Kingdoms period (220–280 CE).[39]

The rise to importance of the vast Yangzi watershed, and the heightened emphasis on military activity, brought Xiangyang to center stage in this period, for it was a pivotal transition point for the movement of men and goods between north and south. Material shipped by waterway from the south came up the Yangzi and Han rivers and then had to be offloaded at Xiangyang for the overland trek to Luoyang or other points on the Yellow River watershed. Goods moving wholly by land also had to cross the Han River at the fords at Xiangyang. As a result, military forces from the south needed to protect the region in order to have a place to offload men and material and prepare for overland campaigns to the north, or defend against them. Northern regimes needed to control the region to prevent this eventuality, and to have a place to prepare naval expeditions against any southern regime. The Cao 曹 regime (under Cao Cao, 155–220, and his successors, who ruled the Wei 魏 kingdom, 220–265) developed Xiangyang and the Fan fortress 樊城, just across the river on the north side, as their key defensive position in northern Jing province. They fought many battles in the area, first with the fledgling regime of Liu Bei 劉備 (161–223), then with the regime of Sun Quan 孫權 (182–252) and his successors in the Wu 吳 kingdom (229–280) based at Jiankang (then called Jianye 建業). The Sima 司馬 regime (eventual founders of the western Jin 晉 dynasty, 265–316), which succeeded the Cao regime in the north, followed this pattern, using Xiangyang as a primary staging area for their successful conquest of the south in 280 CE.[40]

The literate elite at Xiangyang enjoyed the patronage and protection afforded by this imperial attention throughout the third century, even as the private military forces they depended on became increasingly prominent, especially in surrounding hinterland areas. The civil wars and general chaos and collapse of the Jin court in the early fourth century led to a swift collapse of the arrangement, however. In the years 310–311, as the Jin capital at Luoyang was being sacked, Xiangyang town itself experienced a violent rebellion of immigrant armed groups, followed by an invasion by the rapacious armies of Shi Le 石勒, a plague epidemic, and a sweeping fire that killed thousands and put an end to several of Xiangyang's most eminent family lines.[41]

Over the next several decades, virtually all of the educated elite in the Xiangyang region either died, fell into obscurity, or moved away to more promising locales. The new "eastern" Jin capital, at Jiankang on the Yangzi delta, was far away, and Xiangyang came to be regarded as a semi-barbarian frontier outpost. A few fortunate local men managed to work their way into the lower rungs of the Jiankang elite; many more, especially from the once-eminent Nanyang region north of the river, resettled in Jiangling and aided in the slow rebuilding of a Jing provincial administration. Meanwhile, the Xiangyang region itself experienced waves of immigrants fleeing the chaotic conditions in the north. By the end of the fourth century, the makeup of Xiangyang's population was almost totally transformed.[42]

Despite these tremendous changes, the Xiangyang region retained its geo-strategic significance as a pivotal transfer point on the frontier between north and south, as well as a fertile and potentially populous region. Regardless of the makeup of that population, it was an area that, from a military standpoint, no regime could long afford to ignore. The story this work seeks to tell is how the southern court at Jiankang dealt with the area, and, more importantly, who the men in the area were, and how they dealt with the southern court.

TWO

# DEVELOPMENT, 400–465

At the beginning of the fifth century, the Xiangyang region was considered one of the southern regime's most "backward" areas. Surviving texts offer no evidence of any locally born men who occupied positions of power at Jiankang, or even ones who were prominent locally. Since the fall of Fu Jian's Chang'an-based regime in 383, the area had also been flooded with northern immigrants. As a later account observes, during this period "the old-time people were very few, and new households very many."[1] Though some of these immigrants were from proud lineages of former high status in northern regimes, the eastern Jin court at Jiankang was so scornful of them, and so disorganized and faction-ridden, that within a decade a substantial number of them left again to return north.[2]

The policies adopted by Liu Yu 劉裕 (Song Emperor Wu 宋武帝, r. 420–422), the founder of the Liu-Song regime, explicitly encouraged northern immigrants to settle in the region and opened up new opportunities for them, and for local men from low-status backgrounds. Over the long, relatively stable reign of his third son, Liu Yilong 劉義隆 (Song Emperor Wen 宋文帝, r. 424–453), these groups were further swollen by settlers who migrated or were forcibly relocated from surrounding upland areas. This diverse social mix found some common ground through commandery and provincial military service, as the men were actively employed in local campaigns to gain territory and slaves. The society they created in Xiangyang was characterized by an emphasis on personal honor, the use of violence, and the celebration of vengeance. Unlike the rarefied social and cultural world of Jiankang, there was little or no emphasis on literacy, much less classical scholarship; the hallmark of the region was instead an oral culture of song and dance.

The primary connection between these two social and cultural worlds was the opportunity for Xiangyang men to develop clientelage links with agents of the Jiankang regime. Members of the imperial Liu family, who had been born and bred in a similar military background in the Northern Garrison at Guangling 廣陵, were active patrons of Xiangyang men, and worked to identify the most influential, talented and fierce of them and gain their personal loyalty. As a result, some of them played a pivotal role in the coup that put Yilong's third son, Liu Jun 劉駿 (Song Emperor Xiaowu 宋孝武帝, r. 454–465), on the throne. The ensuing decade marked their arrival onto the stage of imperial politics, as well as the pages of imperial history.

## LIU YU'S NEW POLICIES: IMMIGRATION AND RESIDENCE DETERMINATION

During the Yixi 義熙 reign period (405–418) of the eastern Jin regime (317–420), the Jiankang court was dominated by Liu Yu, who slowly built the military and administrative machinery necessary for his eventual seizure of power. The failure of the abrupt coup attempt by Huan Xuan 桓玄 in 402–404 had taught him to lay his groundwork carefully, and he consciously modeled his slow and systematic approach to usurpation on the successful efforts of Cao Cao (155–220) and Sima Yi (179–251). Following the precedent of the western Jin regime (265–316), he also gave regional military commands to his brothers and sons; despite the potential for a repeat of civil strife like the "War of Eight Princes" (300–306), this approach promised a higher degree of loyalty than the eastern Jin precedent of leaving such commands in the hands of powerful rival clans. He also initiated several important new policies: he promoted men of low birth who demonstrated achievement, especially in military matters, in order to dilute the influence of privileged court clans; he sought to eliminate some districts-in-exile in order to undercut the power of older immigrant households, while creating new districts for his own favorites; and he reorganized the status ranking systems for some local clans. These changes had a direct impact on the development of Xiangyang society and its relations with Jiankang in the early fifth century.

The first of these administrative reforms was the effort to undertake what was called a "residence determination" (*tuduan* 土斷), a form of administrative reorganization designed to bring more people onto the official registers, so that they could be made to pay taxes and labor duties. Beginning in the eastern Jin period, the court ordinarily dealt with immigrant groups by creating new administrative districts for them, named for the districts from which they had emigrated. The leader of an immigrant band would be awarded the office of governor or magistrate of the district, and his followers would be considered as "residents" of that district. Since such groups were given tax and labor relief, they usually went unregistered, or experienced only an irregular, sub-official registration on so-called white registers, which were maintained by local officials and not sent in to the imperial capital. Though their productive resources would still not flow to the court directly, they would also not be captured by entrenched local families; instead, they would remain in the control of immigrant leaders, who would, hopefully, return the favor of being given an official title and a salary (sometimes even a heritable salary-fief) by remaining allied with the court. From the perspective of the court, therefore, the granting of "district-in-exile" status was clearly a privilege, though the advantages would have gone primarily to the leadership (who got the titles and other rewards, and were empowered to broker the relationship), not necessarily to the rest of the immigrants.[3]

The "district-in-exile" policy encompassed a wide variety of situations. In some cases, the leaders of exiled groups were wealthy, well educated, and powerful, and rapidly gained office in the eastern Jin administration. More commonly, the court's expectation was that the leaders would have authority over their own followers, who would be made available to serve on military campaigns. In Xiangyang, for example, Wei Gai 魏該 had been given the title of Inspector of Yong province-in-exile 雍州 in 317 and, over the next decade, employed his followers to dominate the region but also to aid the court in their struggles with other regional powerholders.[4] The policy was even adapted for groups that were not northern immigrants; for example, Yicheng commandery-in-exile 義成郡 was created in 332 and purposely sent in to the Xiangyang area from another part of eastern Jin territory to help the Jin court establish friendlier forces there. As a result, the designation gained a rationale far beyond the idea of temporary or exiled districts, and the peculiar, privileged administrative status of these districts took on a life of its own.[5]

In theory, a "residence determination" was an attempt to bring people from these districts onto some kind of registration list so they could be taxed by the court, if not immediately, then at some later date. It might involve the abolition of the immigrant jurisdictions altogether. Selective efforts to accomplish this had been tried repeatedly under eastern Jin rulers with only limited success; the most effective attempt had been by Huan Wen in the 360s. Liu Yu's own effort was launched in 413; his concern, expressed in a lengthy memorandum to the throne, was to remove the privileged "district-in-exile" status from the many families who had long since migrated south and clearly had no intention of returning north. Quite probably they also no longer offered much military striking power, and were simply the dependents of well-established settler families, whose allegiance to Liu Yu could not be counted upon. Evidence suggests that Liu Yu's reforms were moderately successful.[6]

Reform in the Xiangyang region, however, had to await further military events. The area was under the thrall a man named Lu Zongzhi 魯宗之, the leader of a band of immigrants that had emigrated from the Guanzhong area after the fall of Fu Jian's regime in 383. Liu Yu had given Zongzhi the title of Inspector of Yong province in 404, and he remained a semiautonomous regional warlord until Liu Yu personally led a campaign to oust him and a rebellious Jing inspector, Sima Xiuzhi 司馬休之, in 415.[7] Liu Yu then appointed his brother Daolian 劉道憐 to run the Jing command, and installed his mother's brother, Zhao Lunzhi 趙倫之, at Xiangyang. Only at this point could he extend his plans for administrative reform to the area.

Liu Yu's reforms in Xiangyang did not correspond to his public pronouncements, however, for he had other objectives in the region. The most important was to sponsor the immigration of new groups to Xiangyang that could dominate the region in his own interests. This effort was facilitated by a campaign to take advantage of the collapse of the Yao clan's "later" Qin regime in Guanzhong, which followed immediately from the Xiangyang campaign. Liu Yu and his armies occupied Luoyang in the winter of 416 and entered Chang'an by the fall of the following year, but his supply lines were stretched thin, and he was concerned about his control over the Jin emperor, so he retreated back to Jiankang. The weak force he left behind was soon compelled to flee, and the Guanzhong area fell into civil war. Thereafter it was occupied by forces from the Tabgatch (in Chinese: Tuoba 託跋) regime, which deported many leading families to their capital of Pingcheng 平城 in the far distant north.

Though the Guanzhong campaign was a failure from the aspect of territorial gain, it was a success from the aspect of recruitment. Liu Yu used the campaign to engage personally with powerful Guanzhong families and persuade them to submit to his regime, rather than the Tabgatch, and resettle in the south, with Xiangyang a primary target. Wei Hua 韋華, for example, came from a very prestigious Guanzhong clan in Duling 杜陵 county in Jingzhao 京兆 commandery, a suburb of Chang'an. He had served in high office under Fu Jian, emigrated to Xiangyang after the fall of Fu's regime in 383, and then, finding the southern regime weak, divided, and lacking in vision, had led many of his compatriots back to Guanzhong to serve the Yao regime in 398.[8] In 416, while serving as a provincial inspector for the Yao regime, Hua was persuaded to surrender to Liu Yu's advance forces and resettle in Xiangyang again, apparently for good this time, as part of a Jingzhao commandery-in-exile that had been established there in the 380s. Other branches of the Wei lineage are known to have remained in Xiangyang since their first emigration, and may have facilitated his return. Liu Yu also offered a high-ranking post to Hua's son Xuan 韋玄, a man of great reputation who had taken up the life of a recluse in the hills south of Chang'an, but he declined, and was killed in the civil war soon after. Xuan's sons, however, migrated along with their grandfather and settled in Xiangyang.

Numerous other Guanzhong clans followed in the wake of the Weis, and were also accommodated with specially designated immigrant jurisdictions. Members of a lineage of the Du 杜 surname, from the same county as the Weis, relocated to Xiangyang around this time, as did members of the Wang family of neighboring Bacheng county 霸城王. Xi Heng of Anding commandery 安定席衡, northwest of Chang'an, resettled in Xiangyang with his family and followers. A group of more than three thousand families from the Lantian 藍田 area, southeast of Chang'an, followed a man of Samarkand ancestry, Kang Mu 康穆, who had served the Yao regime; they settled around the Xian hills, just south of Xiangyang, and were granted district-in-exile status as Lantian 藍田 county in Huashan 華山 commandery. Kang Mu was also offered an important local office as inspector of Liang and Qin provinces (the latter an immigrant jurisdiction), but he declined and soon after died; his sons, however, served successively as commandery governors for Huashan. The record indicates that they were "nominated at the behest of the immigrant population," suggesting that they essentially ruled their followers autonomously, with little but a stamp of approval from the Jiankang court.[9]

Immigrant groups' preferential treatment in local administration did not necessarily translate into influence at the capital, where they are known to have experienced substantial prejudice. Du Tan 杜坦, one of the Jingzhao Dus who had migrated to Xiangyang, followed Liu Yu back to Jiankang and served as a general and inspector of several provinces. His family claimed eminent descent from Du Yu, one of the founders of the unified Jin empire, and they had been pillars of northern society for generations. Despite this pedigree, an anecdote in Tan's biography indicates that he was looked upon lightly by the court as a "late-crossing northerner," that is, someone who had served the "barbarian" courts of the north for several generations before coming south, and was therefore somehow "uncivilized."[10]

The use of immigrant jurisdictions as a part of the resettlement policy at first seems to fly in the face of the "residence determination" that was still ongoing during this period. What it shows is that "residence determination" was not simply an effort at administrative rationalization. Instead, it was used selectively, to undermine the power and privileges of preexisting immigrant groups who were no longer loyal or useful, while clearing the way for new groups to gain similar privileges. This explains why, despite repeated efforts at "residence determination" in the fourth and fifth centuries, the problem of immigrant jurisdictions never appears to have been "straightened out," for this was not the real objective of residence determination campaigns in the first place.[11]

## LIU YU'S NEW POLICIES: ADMINISTRATIVE REORGANIZATION

The policies undertaken by Zhao Lunzhi, who was now Liu Yu's leading agent in Xiangyang, offer further evidence of the multitargeted nature of Liu Yu's reforms. Xiangyang had become a jumble of long-time residents (none of whom had ancestors with any status at court), immigrant settlers of several generations' standing, and new immigrants. Zhao Lunzhi was given a mandate to impose order on the many and various families that lived in the region: first, by deciding which families really deserved elite status as "second-class households" (*ci men* 次門), meaning ones that were exempt from corvee and tax obligations (the imperial family being the only "first-class" household); and second, ordering the rankings of these exempt households.

An example of this process is the Zong 宗 family, which had emigrated from Henan to settle in the region some time in the early fourth century, and had been classified as an exempt "second-class household" of Ye 葉 county, in Nanyang commandery, in a prior residence determination (probably Huan Wen's). Under Lunzhi's reclassification, however, they were designated as "subject to corvee" (*yi men* 役門), a much lower rank.[12] This episode demonstrates that, at the same time new preferred groups led by the Weis and Kangs got their own commanderies-in-exile to administer, older immigrant families who were no longer favored were having their prior privileges removed.

In addition to this reorganization, Lunzhi undertook the reformulation of the lines of command amongst the immigrant commanderies. The seven commanderies-in-exile lodged in the Xiangyang area at this time had been classified under three different provinces, following the organization of provinces and commanderies from western Jin times. Because these commanderies were otherwise divorced from the Jing provincial administration, they had in practice been left under local military command. When Lu Zongzhi controlled that office, Liu Yu's regime had given formal military command authority over these groups to the office of the Jing inspector, who thereby had sweeping command over all forces in the west and northwest sectors of the southern regime. Under Zhao Lunzhi, the situation was reversed again, and the various immigrant commanderies in Xiangyang were brought under the direct command of the Yong inspector for both military and civilian purposes, centralizing authority in a single local office, and creating a higher-level civilian administration for the immigrant commanderies than had existed previously.[13]

Over the next several years the military command authority of the Yong inspector's office was further expanded to include six non-immigrant commanderies in northern Jing province, the entirety of neighboring Liang province (farther up the Han river), and its immigrant districts of north and south Qin province as well. These neighboring provinces ordinarily had a separate inspector who ran their civilian administration, but his position was militarily subordinate to that of the Yong inspector. In addition, the office of Commandant for Pacifying the Man (*ning Man xiaowei* 寧蠻校尉) was established and added to this portfolio, mirroring the office of Commandant of the Southern Man that had long been the prerogative of the Jing inspector at Jiangling, thereby giving the Yong inspector command over local hill peoples who had resettled and come under the imperial court's authority.[14] As a result, the position of Yong inspector was better organized and substantially strengthened, and it increasingly served as a counterweight to the perennial power of the Jing inspector.

In the wake of these reforms the Xiangyang region entered two decades of relative stability, and the court was able to send its own men to serve the post of Yong inspector and local military commander-in-chief.[15] Though several of them are noted for being quite corrupt, the period saw substantial investment in water-control and agricultural development, and there were no major military campaigns that would have strained local resources.[16]

This peaceful interlude was facilitated by the conjunction of three factors. First, the rule of the Tabgatch stabilized the situation in the north, reducing the disruptive influx of immigrants. The location of the Tabgatch capital in the far north also diminished the immediate proximity of the military threat on the northern frontier, at least for a while. Second, the Jing province command achieved an unusual level of peace and stability during this period, which spared Xiangyang the trouble of being dragged into conflicts between Jiangling and Jiankang. The rebellion of Xie Hui 謝晦, a disaffected member of the cabal of Liu Yu's associates that had helped enthrone Liu Yilong 劉義隆 (Emperor Wen 文帝, r. 424–453), was the last such contest for thirty years.[17] Third, the region saw a temporary cessation of aggressive campaigns against the people who inhabited the surrounding upland regions, referred to in the historical literature as "Man and Yi" people. This policy was maintained by Liu Daochan 劉道產, who assumed the regional command in 431 and remained in the post until his death eleven years later.

The official biography of Daochan offers a vibrant picture of Xiangyang local society during his tenure:

> He was good at governing the populace, and in Yong district his achievements of governance were particularly manifest; those Man and Yi people who had been in rebellion and would not accept "transformation" all submitted peacefully and came alongside the Mian [Han River] to live. The leading families all delighted in their occupations, and the households of the populace prospered in their livelihoods; from this came the songs of Xiangyang music, beginning with Daochan. . . . Daochan's benevolence and goodness spread over the western region and they grieved his passing; the Man people all mourned deeply and wept as they followed his entourage to the mouth of the Mian River.[18]

This passage, in some ways a stock-in-trade description of a benevolent governor, nonetheless gives us several important pieces of information about Xiangyang's development during this time. The significance of Man and Yi "rebellions" will be addressed in the next section, and the development of a distinctive musical style in Xiangyang will be taken up in a section following that. Here we may simply note that, despite years of migration from the north, there was still sufficient uncultivated land in the Xiangyang area to allow for further resettlement and agricultural development on a substantial scale, thereby giving Daochan the flexibility to entice the Man and Yi through economic means.[19]

The policies of Liu Yu's regime shifted the range of opportunities available to men from Xiangyang. The reordering of the clan rankings, the new emphasis on promoting men of lower-class or late-arriving immigrant background, and the increased emphasis on military talent all offered new routes of advancement to men who had previously been neglected by the Jiankang regime. The regular cycling of members of the imperial clan into provincial commands, and their willingness to take on local men as clients, also ensured that local men had more opportunity to gain access to the rich resources of the court and the Jiankang elite, and did not have to be dependent on regional strongmen. In the wake of Liu Daochan's rule we find the first evidence that local men were taking advantage of these opportunities.

## PRINCES AND PATRONAGE: THE EARLY CAREER OF LIU YUANJING

If Liu Daochan's tenure in Xiangyang can be seen as a heyday of peaceful integration, the subsequent decades were a period of almost continual warfare. Since Xiangyang had become noted for its fighting traditions, this offered a substantial opportunity to local men, particularly if they could win the support of powerful patrons among the imperial clan, and gain upward mobility through military service in a prince's personal retinue. By far the most impressive such career was that of Liu Yuanjing 柳元景 (406–465).

In the third and early fourth century Liu Yuanjing's paternal ancestors had held high rank in the administration of the western Jin court at Luoyang. Their ancestral home was in Jie county in Hedong commandery 河東解縣, up the valley of the Su 涑 River just north of the great bend of the Yellow River, about one hundred miles east-northeast of Chang'an. After Luoyang and Chang'an were sacked and the court fled south in the 310s, Liu Yuanjing's fourth-generation ancestor, Liu Chun 柳純, served the struggling new eastern Jin regime as a commandery governor in eastern Sichuan. He was killed in 323 CE for opposing the coup attempt of Wang Dun, and his son Zhuo 柳卓 settled his household in Xiangyang, perhaps as part of a South Hedong commandery-in-exile that was established in 337 CE.[20] Zhuo's grandson Ping 憑 never held office higher than governor of Fengyi 馮翊, an immigrant jurisdiction lodged at Xiangyang. Many immigrants had career tracks that remained localized and concentrated in immigrant jurisdictions, and Ping's career was probably of this sort, even though he was by now a third-generation settler in the area. Nonetheless, the office of commandery governor was a highly ranked and well-remunerated position, and Ping's family was certainly prosperous, for he raised seven sons. Ping trained them all in military pursuits; Yuanjing, his eldest, is recorded as having been "skilled at horsemanship and archery" and went with his father on campaigns against the Man peoples, perhaps during Zhao Lunzhi's rule, when Yuanjing would have been in his early teens.[21]

Yuanjing gained a reputation for being brave and talented, though rather taciturn, and was admired by Xie Hui, who intended to give him an appointment but was purged before he could do so. When Liu Daochan first came to Xiangyang in 431 he eagerly sought to employ him, but Yuanjing's father had recently died and Yuanjing, then twenty-five years old, refused the appointment due to mourning. The emperor's younger brother, Liu Yigong, Prince of Jiangxia 江夏王義恭, was at that time serving as Jing inspector, and having heard of Yuanjing's reputation summoned him to serve on his staff, which he did as soon as he was free of his mourning obligations. Shen Yue records an anecdote in which Daochan expresses chagrin at the loss of a valuable client, saying, "I've long hoped to see him submit. Now that the honorable prince has given a summons, how can I abruptly detain him? It's a perverse idea that would demonstrate a loss of composure."[22]

The imperial command structure that Yuanjing now entered had developed into an extremely complex system of patronage jobs and personal clientelage relationships over the preceding decades, and it is worthwhile to pause and consider the range of subordinate positions which the nineteen-year-old Prince Yigong had under his nominal command. Prince Yigong held several different powerful appointments simultaneously. First, he was inspector of Jing province, which meant he had an extensive civilian staff serving under him at Jiangling, including men whose job it was to inspect the governance of each commandery in the province. The men in this civilian staff were typically drawn from a cluster of families, based around Jiangling, who served as an urban bureaucratic elite, similar to the elite at the imperial court at Jiankang, but obviously much less prestigious. Much of this elite was from educated immigrants who had resettled in Jiangling from the Nanyang region just north of Xiangyang, which had a long tradition of well-educated and high-status lineages stretching back to the eastern Han. Prince Yigong also would have had a provincial military force drawn from lower-class local families who were subject to labor service. Men in his position sometimes also concurrently served as governor of a local commandery (for example, Liu Daochan also served as governor of Xiangyang commandery), in which capacity they would have had an additional civilian staff, again drawn from a core group of families at the administrative seat, and a smaller commandery military force. Of particular importance was the inspector's role in recommending men for appointment to prestigious commandery governorships and county magistracies under his jurisdiction; though the court was theoretically not obligated to follow these recommendations, their approval was ordinarily a foregone conclusion.

The most important nexus of power in local administration came from a prince's personal military staff. Princes always concurrently held a rank as a general, under which auspices they maintained an extensive military staff. These staff positions, usually called adjutant (*canjun* 參軍), were further delineated by specific functional titles and by the rank of general the prince held at the time; Prince Yigong, for example, was Fujun 撫軍 ("controls the army") general. Unlike the local civilian and military staffs, the prince's personal military staff followed him over a substantial period of time. Princes added to their personal staff as they moved from posting to posting, hand-picking unusually talented men from the inspectorate or commandery military garrisons or civilian staffs, and working to cement bonds of personal loyalty with them. When a prince moved to a new posting he might choose to appoint some of his trusted personal staff members to the highest local offices, leaving the less-trusted locals to lower positions; the relationship between these groups was therefore often a source of tension, as we will see later.

Prince Yigong was at the apex of several other significant administrative hierarchies. Because he was Jing inspector, he also had an additional title as Southern Man Commandant, controlling the military service households of Man peoples who had been captured or otherwise pressed into service, and here again there was a significant sub-bureaucracy, which could be drawn either from the prince's own personal retinue, or from the local pool of willing sub-bureaucrats and military men; as noted above, the Yong inspectorate had also been granted a similar special office. The prince also had overall command authority over military affairs throughout eight provinces, meaning that anyone who held a military command in that region was ultimately answerable to him in the coordination of military campaigns. Since inspectors of lesser provinces, as well as commandery governors, all routinely had either a generalship or a military staff posting, they all fell under the prince's authority to a greater or lesser extent. Finally, it was not unusual for imperial princes to be given titles in the central administration, sometimes concurrently with a provincial post. Here again there would have been a substantial number of subordinate staff positions, potentially including further military forces. Since anyone summoned by Yigong for an appointment to any of these many possible positions owed a client's debt of gratitude to him, the opportunity to develop an extensive clientelage network was great indeed.

Liu Yuanjing wound up serving for the next sixteen years directly under Prince Yigong, who was seven years his junior, and they remained close associates for life. For the first seven years or so he was the general in command of the forces of Jiangxia principality, the prince's personal fief, but when the prince received a promotion to be Minister of Works (*sikong* 司空), one of the three highest positions in the central government, Yuanjing was shifted to a position on his personal military staff and relocated to the capital. He stayed in personal military staff positions through the prince's further promotions to the office of Minister of Education (*situ* 司徒) and then Defender-in-Chief (*taiwei* 太尉), stretching over another five or six years, until Yuanjing was about forty years old.

Yuanjing's service to Prince Yigong throughout this period was critical to the advancement of his career. A colorful anecdote in his biography suggests some of the difficulties encountered by men from the provinces when they first came down to the capital:

> Yuanjing's youth was poverty-stricken and harsh. One time he came down to the capital and had reached Dalei (an upriver defensive garrison). At nightfall he was quite cold, with much of the traveler's lament. By the bank there was an old man who claimed he was good at prognostication, and said to Yuanjing, "Your aura is one of great riches and honor; your status will reach the Three Dukes." Yuanjing thought he was joking, and said, "If a man can live without hunger and cold then he is extremely lucky; how can he hope for riches and honor?" The old man said, "In the future you will remember this." When [Yuanjing] became honored he sought out the man, but did not know where he was.[23]

Despite his relative poverty and lack of connections, Yuanjing's time at Jiankang would have given him the chance to develop relationships with far more powerful and influential figures than would have been the case if he had stayed in local positions in Xiangyang. He is known to have had the invaluable opportunity to meet and impress the emperor, Yigong's elder brother Yilong.[24] He had also certainly married and started a family by this time; he would eventually have ten sons and an unknown number of daughters, whose initial opportunities to make favorable connections would have been even greater than his own.

## XIANGYANG MEN ON CAMPAIGN, 442–454

While Yuanjing was building his life in Prince Yigong's entourage, the situation at Xiangyang underwent significant changes. After Liu Daochan died in 442, the Song military began an extended series of campaigns in the area, first against the Man peoples, then a major northern campaign in 450. Yuanjing was sent back to participate and eventually lead these campaigns, a defining experience that would set the stage for his leading role in the coup that placed Prince Yigong's nephew, Liu Jun, on the throne.

In his section on the Man people in the *History of the Song*, Shen Yue explains the anti-Man campaigns of 442–448 as a response to banditry, and characterizes the relationship between the Song regime and the Man as follows:

> For those of the Man people who submitted, each household paid several *tou* (bushels) of grain, and otherwise were free of miscellaneous taxes. But Song people's tax and corvee was extremely harsh, and many of the poor who could not bear the demands fled to join the Man. The Man had no corvee, and the powerful also did not pay official taxes. They joined into gangs and hordes in movements of several hundreds of thousands of men, and since the [forces of the] province and commandery were weak, they would rise up as bandits and thieves with a great many kinds [of people] with unknowable population.[25]

Shen Yue's account is clear evidence that the Man rebellions should not be conceived of primarily as an ethnic conflict, since the epithet "Man" included people from diverse backgrounds who had fled into the hills in order to avoid tax and corvee obligations. There was clearly a significant intermixing of population, as lowlanders fled to the hills and uplanders chose to settle closer to imperial administrative centers, and many people would have had relatives and friends on "the other side." The increased interchange between lowland farm country and upland herding or swidden country under Liu Daochan would have given upland peoples, of whatever ethnic background, more interaction with the Song administrative and military system, which would have facilitated their understanding of organizational and leadership structures for coordinating more substantial military efforts. Rather than characterize these "Man rebellions" as an ethnic war, it makes more sense to view them as a struggle between different, ethnically mixed groups of people, some of whom benefited from the Song imperial system and worked to preserve it, others who, due to economic and/or political pressure, fought against it.[26] This latter group, as Shen Yue's discussion makes plain, are all lumped under the catchall epithet "Man" and treated in the historical record as less "civilized" than those groups who were more compliant.

The official causes for the conflict are also suspect. Song military campaigns against the Man were vigorous and sustained, striking deep into mountainous territory, and capturing hundreds of thousands of prisoners.[27] This belies the assertion that they were a mere response to "banditry"; rather, the campaigns clearly had the objective to capture new slave labor forces to serve in the imperial military, and to acquire new territory for settlement. This implies another important development: the lowland areas around Xiangyang (as well as along the central Yangzi River) were becoming more fully settled, and land in somewhat shorter supply, than had been the case a generation earlier.[28]

After several short-term successors to Daochan worked to organize this campaign, the court in early 445 sent out Liu Jun, the Emperor's third son and at that time entitled the Prince of Wuling 武陵王駿, to take over the Xiangyang command. As his biography notes, he was the first imperial prince to be put in charge of the Xiangyang garrison since the Jin throne had moved to the south in 317, and his appointment was thought to signal the increasing attention being paid to the Xiangyang region, at least as regards military affairs.[29] Though Prince Jun was only fifteen years old at the time, it was not his first major provincial military command; he had held an equivalent position in South Yu province for the preceding five years. Nonetheless, so young a prince was ordinarily accompanied by an experienced and loyal military staff that could safely be entrusted to run the local administration, and to ensure that the young prince stayed out of harm's way. It was no doubt with this concern in mind that Prince Yigong, who as Defender-in-Chief was in charge of all military affairs, sent his trusted client Liu Yuanjing out ahead of his nephew to take up his first independent military command, as Guangwei 廣威 ("broadly awe-inspiring") general and governor of nearby Sui commandery.

Prince Jun turned out to need help much sooner than probably even Prince Yigong had anticipated. Recognizing that this high-level appointment signaled a new military offensive in the area, Man forces stepped up their attacks in anticipation of Prince Jun's arrival, cutting the water and land routes leading into Xiangyang from the south. As a result, Prince Jun's entourage was forced to halt at Big Dike (*dadi* 大堤), outside of Yicheng, about forty miles south of Xiangyang. The staff officer in charge of Prince Jun's primary forces, Shen Qingzhi 沈慶之, was a seasoned veteran, a fifty-five-year-old man of quite low background who had spent his entire career in military staff positions, from fighting Sun En's rebellion when he was not even fifteen years old, through prior experience fighting the Man in the Xiangyang area under Zhao Lunzhi (in the 420s) and again in recent campaigns. Qingzhi led the prince's forces against the Man and succeeded in breaking the blockade. Liu Yuanjing coordinated his own commandery's troops to attack the Man, relieving the pressure on his commandery and helping to turn the tide against them.[30]

Over the next several years Yuanjing fought together with Shen Qingzhi and other long-time military staff members in campaigns against the Man. When Prince Jun was reassigned to Xu province in 448, Yuanjing went with him as the officer in charge of his Anbei 安北 ("secures the north") military staff, essentially the position Shen Qingzhi had held previously. This shift to Prince Jun's personal entourage must have been approved by Prince Yigong, who was still Defender-in-Chief and had long been Yuanjing's patron; indeed, it can be seen as a "gift" (really more like a loan) of a talented client from Prince Yigong to his nephew. Yuanjing would still have had strong ties of obligation to Prince Yigong, but he was developing significant ties to Prince Jun as well.

Meanwhile, the Song military was gearing up for a major northern campaign, the first in many decades. The Xiangyang command was to be the launching point for the western wing of the campaign, and the staff and material resources of all of the provinces along the central Yangzi were sent to Xiangyang in preparation. A further administrative reconfiguration at this time consolidated the command by splitting off five commanderies from Jing province and placing them under Yong province (see Map 2). Though these five commanderies—Xiangyang, Nanyang, Xinye, Shunyang, and Sui—had long been subsumed under the local military command, they were the first "old-time" districts, as opposed to districts-in-exile, to be placed under the civilian authority of Yong province, and further demonstrated the increasing prestige of the Xiangyang area, particularly as a counterweight to the long-standing power of the Jiangling command.

In autumn of 449 the Xiangyang command was given to the emperor's sixth son, the sixteen-year-old Prince of Suijun, Liu Dan 隨郡王誕. As usual, however, the real fighting was to be done by his staff, which included Shen Qingzhi, now the head of the forces he maintained as Northern Leader of Court Gentlemen; Liu Yuanjing, head of the central forces of the Houjun 後軍 ("rear army") military staff; and the new governor of Sui commandery, Zong Que 宗慤, among many others.[31] Que came from an old scholarly Nanyang family that had relocated to Jiangling, but he had gone against the proclivities of his clan and pursued a military career; like Yuanjing, he had been taken up by Prince Yigong while he was running the Jiangling command two decades earlier.[32] Another man to join in this campaign was Xue Andu 薛安都, who was of an eminent and powerful clan from Hedong, the ancestral home of Liu Yuanjing's family. Andu had raised a rebellion against the Tabgatch and was forced to flee to the south; he had been warmly received by Prince Jun and folded into the command structure of the local garrison.[33] With Qingzhi in overall command, this group "warmed up" in late autumn and winter of 449–450 with a series of fierce drives into Man territory, building roads up into the hills, killing thousands, enslaving tens of thousands, and seizing large quantities of provisions.

After the success of these campaigns, Qingzhi was recalled back to court to aid in the eastern wing of the northern campaign, and Liu Yuanjing was placed in operational command of the western wing at Xiangyang. The campaign was launched in mid-autumn of 450, and is detailed extensively in Yuanjing's biography. In brief, his forces fought north to take the Hongnong region along

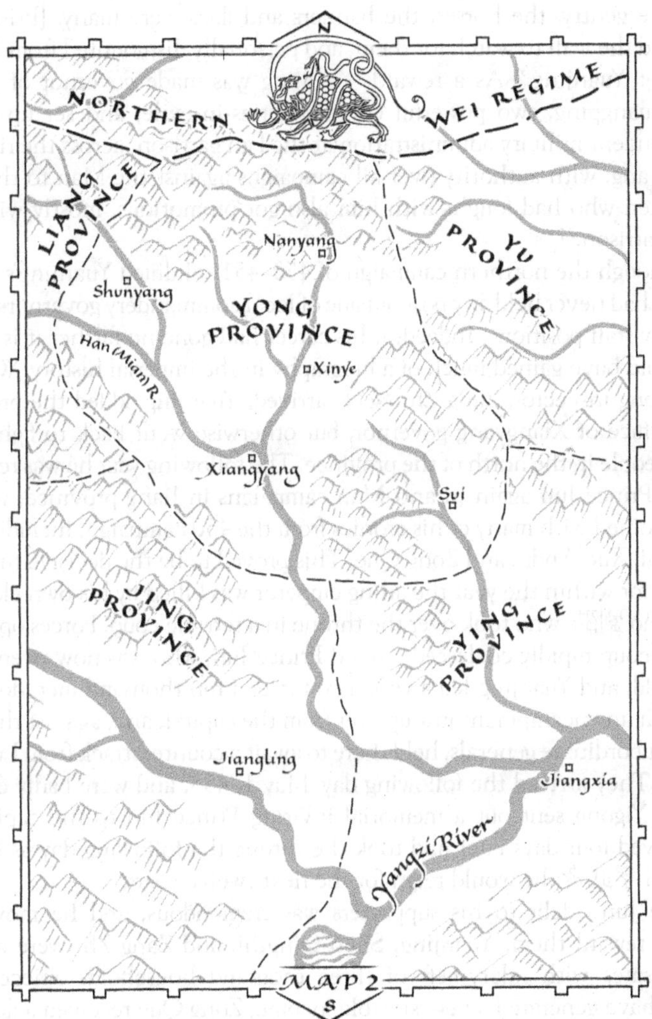


Map 2. Yong province prior to reorganization

the key route from Luoyang into Guanzhong, then moved west to seize the passes leading into the Guanzhong plain. Though Yuanjing's forces had great success, the eastern wing of the northern campaign was a total failure, and the court recalled Yuanjing's forces to Xiangyang at the beginning of the spring of the next year, after fewer than six months of campaigning. According to Yuanjing's biography, his army's achievement in fighting the fierce Tabgatch forces was highly regarded. "They all returned with great achievements, and the gentry, the horses, the banners and flags were many. [Prince] Dan climbed the wall to watch for them, and personally dismounted from his horse to greet Yuanjing." As a reward, Yuanjing was made governor of Jingzhao and Guangping, two powerful commanderies-in-exile, and set up his own independent military administration at the Fan garrison, across the river from Xiangyang, with authority over all campaigns against the Man to the north. The men who had fought with him also got promotions, mostly within the local garrison.[34]

Though the northern campaign of 450–451 solidified Yuanjing's prestige, he still had never held any post outside of local commandery governorships and military staff positions. Indeed, if his career had gone no farther it is unlikely he would have gained much of a biography in the imperial history. When the new Yong inspector, Zang Zhi 臧質, arrived, Yuanjing added the prestigious local office of Xiangyang governor, but otherwise went back to fighting the Man people in the north of the province. The following year he was reassigned to aid Prince Jun again in anti-Man campaigns in Jiang province, where he was rejoined with many of his cronies from the 450 campaign, including Shen Qingzhi, Xue Andu, and Zong Que. This proved to be the decisive turn in his career, for within the year the ailing emperor was killed by his own eldest son, Liu Shao 劉劭, who took over the throne in a terrible coup. Forces opposed to Shao's coup rapidly coalesced around Prince Jun, who was now twenty-three years old, and Yuanjing led a vanguard force of ten thousand men downriver. He built an encampment just upriver from the capital, and, against the advice of his subordinate generals, held there to await a counterattack from Liu Shao's forces. They arrived the following day, May 1, 453, and were badly defeated. Prince Yigong sent out a memorial inviting Prince Jun to the capital, and he arrived four days later and took the throne the following day as Emperor Xiaowu 孝武帝; he would reign for the next twelve years.[35]

Liu Jun's debt to his supporters was tremendous, and he moved rapidly to reward them: Yuanjing, Shen Qingzhi, and Zang Zhi were all given marquisates with salary-fiefs of three thousand households apiece, which would have generated a very sizeable income; Zong Que received a fief of two thousand households; other men received lesser rewards.[36] More difficult was the issue of what posting to give each of the men, and here Yuanjing was the biggest challenge, for he was owed more than anyone. An anecdote recorded in Yuanjing's biography frames the issue succinctly: in it, Liu Jun comes to Yuanjing and says, "The affair is settled; what is it you wish?" Yuanjing is supposed to have replied, "If you have surpassing gratitude, I would like to return to my village."[37] This did not mean Yuanjing wished to retire; it meant he wanted to be given the strategically critical Xiangyang command.

Liu Jun clearly was torn by this demand; his annals, which are somewhat confused, suggest that he repeatedly granted and then withdrew this appointment to Yuanjing over the next several months. There are at least three possible explanations for why he ultimately refused to do so, all of which may have been a factor in his decision making. First, Yuanjing had proved himself extremely useful as a defender of the capital. As if to emphasize this point, Yuanjing again demonstrated his indispensability early in 454 by fighting off a vigorous rebellion spearheaded by Liu Jun's uncle, Prince Yixuan, who teamed up with Zang Zhi and launched a campaign from his base in Jing province to oust the young new emperor. Zang Zhi, who had surreptitiously counseled Liu Jun against giving Yuanjing the Xiangyang command, perhaps anticipated Yuanjing and Shen Qingzhi would join with his rebellion, both because they were "old men" of Zang Zhi's, and because Yuanjing was disgruntled at not getting what he wished.[38] In this he miscalculated badly; Yuanjing remained tightly allied to Liu Jun and Prince Yigong.

Two other explanations, however, suggest that Liu Jun was none too confident of Yuanjing's reliability. On the one hand, Yuanjing was extremely influential over the garrison at Xiangyang, which was full of men he had served with closely over the preceding decade, including some of Yuanjing's own relatives. Events over the following decade would demonstrate just how much trouble this could cause for the throne. On the other hand, Liu Jun had good reason to suspect that Yuanjing's primary loyalty was to Prince Yigong, who had long been his patron, and who remained in the extraordinarily powerful position of Defender-in-Chief. Though there is no historical record of a "falling out" between Liu Jun and his uncle Yigong, the rebellion of his other surviving uncle, Prince Yixuan, must have given him cause to be suspicious. The violent purges of so many other imperial relatives over the next decade shows this to have been very much in his nature.

Over the following decade Yuanjing played an exceptionally cautious game of cat-and-mouse with his patron. Though he had been denied the position he most desired, he was not really free to leave the emperor's service outright, for it would have exposed him to charges of disloyalty, and compelled him to either rebel or be executed. Indeed, Liu Jun turned out to be so violent and bloodthirsty a ruler that men who served under him were known to dread going into an audience with him alone. Instead, Yuanjing and his close associate Shen Qingzhi accepted many of the high positions they were offered, but declined the very highest, the rank of the "Three Ducal Lords." Both men claimed to be doing so on the precedent of the Jin Marquis of Miling, Zheng Mao 晉密陵侯鄭袤, who had declined the same office when offered it by Sima Yan, Emperor Wu, after the founding of the Jin dynasty in 265 CE. According to his biography, Zheng Mao explained his precedent as follows: "To be one of the three lords, one must accord with the will of heaven above; unless there are such people, it would be truly harmful to the harmonizing of *qi*. I dare not risk embarrassing or disgracing the court due to my declining years. . . . To respect the legacy of a refined gentleman, one might let him refuse to serve."[39] Zheng Mao at that time had been almost eighty years old. By comparison, in 454 Shen Qingzhi was only sixty-four, and Yuanjing was a mere forty-eight. Clearly they were not declining office due to age; they were declining office due to their inability to "accord with the will" of the emperor, out of protest. It was not a strong enough protest to get them killed, but it did signal a desire to keep their distance from the throne.[40]

The more striking example of protest, however, came from the Xiangyang garrison itself, which proved to be especially difficult to govern. In Liu Jun's first eight years on the throne, three successive court appointees to run the garrison were either killed or forced out of office by the locals, and a series of mollifying efforts seemed to do little to quell the unrest. Liu Yuanjing played a key role in coordinating the efforts of his Xiangyang compatriots, but he was only able to do so as a result of a complex dynamic between court and province, one that hinged on the nature of local society itself, and the newfound power it had won as a result of the court's reliance on the garrison. We therefore need to take a closer look at how the culture of Xiangyang society had developed since Liu Yu's early reforms.

## XIANGYANG LOCAL CULTURE: HONOR, VENGEANCE, AND VIOLENCE

As noted previously, the makeup of Xiangyang local society was complex, and because no one from that society is known to have made any effort to document it at the time, evidence about it is exceedingly sketchy. Due to the rise of Yuanjing and his compatriots to national prominence, however, several biographies in the *History of the Song* offer an outsider's perspective on the kind of men that society produced, and the values they held.[41] Prominent among these biographies is the significance of personal honor, vengeance, and the willingness to be personally involved in combat and killing. Another noteworthy element among this group is the relative lack of literacy, at least for the higher literary pursuits, and the corresponding emphasis on oral culture. In this light, the development of a distinctive type of music and dance offers us a different kind of insight into local culture. Though far from a complete portrait, these sketches can nonetheless help to illuminate some of this vigorous social world.

Wu Nian 武念 is a prime example of the sort of opportunity that the Song military system offered to lower-class men from the Xiangyang area. A native of Xinye, his biography notes that he was from a household subject to corvee, meaning he had no immediate ancestors who had served in imperial office, nor who were worthy even to be named in an imperial biography. Nian worked as the leader of a division of troops for a local commandery, serving at the "Six

Gates" (*liumen* 六門) irrigation project outside of Yicheng that provided food for the army. Though of low status, his household was nonetheless wealthy and owned horses, and the Yong inspector, Xiao Sihua 蕭思話 (served 443–445) promoted him to lead a division in the Yong provincial forces. Leading his troops out to welcome Prince Jun's entourage in 445, he discovered them trapped below a cliff with a thousand Man troops on the heights above raining down arrows on them. He directed his forces to attack the Man and compelled them to retreat. As a result, he gained Prince Jun's notice and was taken onto his personal military staff. He became a mainstay in the anti-Man campaigns, and was one of Yuanjing's top generals in the campaign downriver against Jiankang. He later served on Prince Yigong's staff, and by the early 460s was back in the Xiangyang region as governor of Nanyang, a well-paid imperial appointment.[42]

Wu Nian was not the only rich man of low status in the Xiangyang area at this time who made his career through military service. The household of the Cai 蔡 clan, who originally hailed from Guanjun in Nanyang commandery, was reported to have been wealthy for a long time; their estate south of Xiangyang was impressive, all in tiled buildings.[43] Like Wu Nian's household, the Cai family owed taxes and corvee duties to the local administration, though these were later remitted. Cai Ju 蔡局, the eldest of one generation of Cai brothers, used the family wealth to employ a large number of "guests," presumably men with military or other talents who were sheltered by the family. Ju's younger brother Na 蔡那 worked for the provincial military administration; he gained a reputation as an unusually fierce fighter, and was eventually plucked up to serve on the staff of Liu Jun's younger brother, Liu Xiuren, the Prince of Jian'an 建安王休仁.[44]

Family wealth was not a prerequisite for upward mobility, however, as the example of Zong Yue 宗越 shows. Yue's family had been reclassified under Zhao Lunzhi as owing tax and corvee obligations, and Yue began his career in the Nanyang commandery sub-bureaucracy. His father was killed by a Man person, probably around 442, and Yue gained revenge by stabbing and killing the man in the middle of Xiangyang's market square. The governor of Xiangyang was impressed by Yue's valor, and rather than execute or imprison him, instead promoted him to be a division leader of commandery forces in the anti-Man campaigns. Because Yue came from a poor household, he could not afford his own horse, so he bravely fought on foot. However, the commandery gave him a bonus of five thousand cash for each victory, and he diligently saved up his money until he could afford to keep a horse of his own. Eventually he received further promotions to the provincial headquarters, and then to an independent generalship under Prince Jun. He followed Liu Yuanjing on anti-Man campaigns, served under Prince Dan, and fought downriver with his compatriots in support of Prince Jun's coup. He then got taken up onto Prince Yigong's staff and gained great merit fighting Prince Yixuan's rebellion, for which he was granted a fief worth four hundred households, much less than Yuanjing's, but still a comfortable fortune to a man raised on modest means. He also petitioned and was granted a request to be considered a corvee-exempt clan again, regaining the status his household had had prior to Zhao Lunzhi's reforms.[45]

Several aspects of these men's careers stand out in contrast with the career of Liu Yuanjing. First, all of them came from households that, whether wealthy or poor, were subject to tax and corvee duties, and had no prominent ancestors. By comparison, Yuanjing had a father who was already a local commandery governor, and so his household would have been of high enough rank to avoid tax and corvee obligations. Second, though they may have had some education, all of them served in the lower ranks of the local garrison, in actual front-line fighting positions, not command positions in the rear. There is no comparable record of Yuanjing working his way up through the ranks of commandery and provincial military forces in this way; presumably, his connections made it easier to gain the notice of men such as Liu Daochan and Prince Yigong, and jump into a staff position directly.

A parallel example can be found in the career of Xue Andu, who like Yuanjing was also from an eminent Hedong clan. Though a much more recent immigrant than Yuanjing, with no appreciable roots in the Xiangyang area, he and his uncle were immediately offered commandery governorships upon their arrival in 449, suggesting that they were much more highly regarded than lower-class upstarts like Zong Yue. After fighting side by side with Yue under Yuanjing's command throughout the coup of 453 and its aftermath, Andu emerged with a fief of a thousand households, much larger than Yue's, and a job on the personal guard of the heir-apparent, Liu Jun's eldest son Liu Ziye 劉子業. In other words, though personal connections and military merit were certainly a decisive factor in the course of these men's careers, family status, especially for northern immigrants, seems to have also played a significant role.

Nonetheless, the similarities among the careers and attitudes of these men are more striking than the differences. Each one advanced his career by demonstrating his fighting ability, and eventually made his most important career leap by gaining the notice of an imperial prince and landing a job on his personal military staff. Once they had secured a patron from the imperial clan, their main task would have been to demonstrate their loyalty and their usefulness in defending their patron and his interests. Thus, they would have been chosen by the princes for exhibiting traits of loyalty and ferocity. All of these biographies show the central role played by personal involvement in acts of violence. Zhang Jing'er 張敬兒, a man from Guanjun in Nanyang commandery of whom we shall hear a good deal more in the next chapter, is described as having personally killed dozens of men singlehandedly in one foray against the Man. Indeed, his biography describes the customs of

Nanyang and Xinye as producing good riders and archers, and Jing'er himself, like Yuanjing, was practiced at both; he is supposed to have had a particular skill at shooting tigers.[46] Zong Yue is of course noted for his commission of a brutal murder in the public square and his bloody, death-by-death approach to career advancement. Later in his career he helped to quell a rebellion in Guangling, after which he supervised the execution of every soldier in the entire garrison, several thousand men in all.[47]

The use of violence is particularly noteworthy in numerous accounts of personal honor and vengeance, and the extent to which it was tolerated and even encouraged by imperial princes and other court authorities. The most notable example is Zong Yue's revenge against the man who killed his father, in which the local governor, far from prosecuting the crime, actually took it as evidence of Yue's fitness for military duty.[48] Another account is told of Zong Que (no relation to Yue), who, though he was raised at Jiangling, served closely with Yuanjing for years. While on Prince Yigong's staff, he discovered that another member of the staff was having an affair with the concubine of his elder cousin Qi 綺, so he killed the man. Prince Yigong, instead of holding him responsible for murder, took the incident as evidence of his valor, and promoted him to serve as a top general in his fief at Jiangxia.[49] This example clearly demonstrates that traits of violence, personal honor, and revenge, shocking as they might have been to the "aristocratic" Jiankang elite, were precisely what the imperial princes were looking for in their clients.[50]

A different sort of anecdote on this issue is told of Xue Andu and Liu Yuanjing; though probably apocryphal, it captures the flavor of the code of vengeance these men lived by, and the problems it could create. According to the tale, a magistrate in the suburbs of Jiankang had a younger cousin of Andu's whipped for giving personal offense, and Andu responded by gathering together several dozen armed followers and heading off to kill the man. At the river docks he met Liu Yuanjing and told him what he was up to. Yuanjing, concerned to stop him before he got into trouble, mocked him for his hastiness and got him to step into his carriage to discuss better ways of addressing the matter. Yuanjing then pointed out that it would be considered appropriate for an official to punish a man who gave offense, and that the proper redress was to petition the government; by comparison, killing the official would go against both the state's law and higher codes of morality. The anecdote has Yuanjing exclaim: "How can you give way to passion and hastily seek to kill a man here in the capital!" Apparently such behavior was understood to be a good deal less problematic in the provinces.[51]

In this anecdote, Yuanjing is intended to represent the voice of order and reason (as well as the interests of the state), but there is no escaping the conclusion that Andu's response was a common one, approved of and sometimes (as in Zong Que's case) rewarded. Imperial princes selected personal clients on the basis of their willingness to commit acts of violence in the name of personal loyalty. These qualities were perhaps most clearly exemplified by Zong Yue, of whom Shen Yue writes: "He was a fighting man, stout and strong and not far-thinking; he acted directly on what he felt, and was incapable of being two-hearted." Zong was closely associated with two other men, Tong Taiyi 童太壹 and Tan Jin 譚金, all three of whom were noted for their fierce loyalty to Liu Jun and then to his son Liu Ziye; the latter maintained their loyalty by plying them with beautiful women and rich monetary rewards, and they in turn were characterized as his "teeth and talons."[52] For a prince to survive in the cutthroat world of imperial politics, men of this sort were a prize indeed.

## XIANGYANG LOCAL CULTURE: MUSIC AND DANCE

Notably absent in the group of biographies of Xiangyang men is any evidence of a scholarly tradition. Some of the men are known to have been outright illiterate: Zhang Jing'er, for example, is recorded as having learned his letters only late in life, and Shen Qingzhi, whose career closely tracks that of these Xiangyang men, is also identified as wholly unschooled. Illiteracy may not always have been the case; several quite serviceable memos are ascribed to Liu Yuanjing, who was clearly a cut above most of his fighting associates. But no essays, poetry, or commentaries on the classics were written by this group; they were men of action, not letters, and we should not presume that any one of them was able to read and write unless we have evidence.

The hallmark of Xiangyang local culture at this time was not written scholarship but oral performance, especially music and dance. These traditions go by the name of "western lyrics" (*xiqu* 西曲), and are closely related to, but distinct from, the "Wu songs" (*Wu ge* 吳歌) of the Yangzi delta region. Members of the imperial household patronized these sorts of performances in much the same manner that they patronized violent and vengeful behavior among their clients. Because it was not originally a written tradition, all that remains of it is a small number of literary adaptations of the lyric form by men from outside the region, either imperial princes themselves or others of their entourages, and a few descriptions of the song and dance traditions as they were adapted and performed at the imperial court.[53]

From this evidence, however, several important features of the tradition can be surmised. The western song tradition was primarily performed as an accompaniment to dancing. Groups of female dancers, sometimes slaves, wore dresses with long flowing sleeves and danced in long sinuous lines. The accompaniment emphasized percussion instruments such as bells and drums, notably a "slender-waisted" drum of central Asian origin, and had a strong rhythmic element. The song lyrics had relatively straightforward themes on illicit love, parting, separation, and work in the commercial economy. They typically had regular refrains, like a chorus, and used certain kinds of formulaic language quite distinct from the traditions of courtly poetry.[54]

The surviving lyrics in this style, though known to have been composed by men with a classical education and designed for princely entertainment, frequently adopt the persona of a merchant or boatman, suggesting their roots in the trade economy of western frontier regions. We know there to have been men of wealth, such as Wu Nian and Cai Na, whose families had built up their fortunes without serving in office; they had probably made their money in trade instead, or from the rewards gained from military careers. Men of this type would have been the ones who kept dancing girls to give performances to entertain their guests and patrons, so the lyrics naturally appealed to their experiences and their tastes.[55] As imperial princes mixed with men of such background and took them into their personal entourages they absorbed this cultural influence, and lyrics in this style, albeit with a significant admixture of more traditional literary tropes, began to be written down.

One of the earliest surviving examples of a lyric written in this style is closely linked to the political history of the Xiangyang region. Legend has it that while the teenaged Prince Dan served in Xiangyang (449–451) he heard troupes of local women singing what was known as the "Xiangyang music," and, inspired by them, wrote a verse in their style.[56] Though his literary adaptation of the lyrics of these songs cannot be taken as a direct product of Xiangyang oral culture, it nonetheless offers us a taste of what the region might have been like in that time:

At dawn depart from Xiangyang town, by evening lodge at Big Dike inn.
All the girls of Big Dike bloom voluptuous, startling young men's eyes.
Going upstream one's job is poling, downstream row a pair of oars;
Four-cornered dragon streamers encircle the pole in the river's midst.
Jiangling's three thousand three hundred *li*, midpoint of the west pass road,
But whether it is clear or blocked—how can you figure how long it takes?
Men praise Xiangyang music, but the music made is not that of my country.
Guided by stars, braving the wind, I'll sail back to my Yang province.
Lustrous unrestrained girls like creeping vines tangle around the long-lived pine.

Though their loveliness perseveres in spring, when the year is cold they are no use to me.
The yellow goose joins heaven to fly, anxiously pacing the middle way.
The cartwheels turn in my guts; whom must my love be with now?
Yang province rushes wrought in circles; a hundred cash buys two or three thickets' worth.
If I cannot buy then I will return; empty hands will clutch and embrace me.
Creeping vines arise from baseness; they rely on the surface of the long-lived pine.
Yet can one slight a death by frost? The noble becomes entangled with another.
I hate to see so much lust and pleasure, stop me, don't speak to me.
I won't be a crow that flocks in the forest; suddenly I feel I am called to go.[57]

Several elements in this poem appear to mimic the oral musical tradition. The most obvious example is the use of the term *nong* 儂 to refer to the first person singular, a colloquial usage that is almost entirely absent in traditional literary poetry, but common in examples of western and Wu verse; it is used in this poem six times. Other formulaic elements, such as the reference to spring as "three {months of) spring" (*san chun* 三春) also suggest this predilection.[58] The prince's effort to cast himself as a merchant, trading goods up and down the Yangzi and Han rivers from Xiangyang to Jiangling and downriver to Jiankang, is also a conceit based on local music's concern with public life in the markets and trading houses.

The prince's poem is not especially masterful; the central theme of women "like creeping vines" that "tangle round the long-lived pine," and the overwrought wavering between remaining upright or succumbing to lust, are well-worn, even hackneyed examples of literary verse.[59] Prince Dan's choice of metaphor, however, does suggest something of his perspective on local society. He contrasts its "base" and "unrestrained" women with those of Yang province, the imperial capital, where the girls are "rushes wrought in circles," properly restrained and molded by civilization. They are also expensive, however, and difficult to "buy," and the prince suggests that, if they won't have him, he could always come back upriver and enjoy the cheaper, less uptight women of Xiangyang. The prince's exoticization and sexualization of provincial subgroups, especially those of mixed ethnicity, clearly signals his sense of cultural superiority typical of the attitude of the Jiankang elite toward the Xiangyang region.[60]

The prince's final line, referring to a "crow that flocks in the forest," is of particular interest. The image was commonly used to refer to a group of men who gathered together for the expedient purpose of rebellion or other evil deeds. Its use here suggests a deeper layer of meaning for the metaphor of the "base" women of Xiangyang: the "base" military men of the region, who tempt the prince to become "entangled" into dangerous relationships. Like the women, these lower-class men would be "reliant" upon the prince as his clients, but their private agendas and vendettas could wind up driving his own unless he could somehow resist their temptations. Prince Dan did in fact end up at the head of just such a rebellion, the one at Guangling in 459 that was so viciously purged by Zong Yue. His concern over the dangers of "entanglement" with the "base" local society of Xiangyang turned out to be prescient for others besides himself, as local entanglements led to the downfall of successive court appointees in the years following Liu Jun's ascension to the throne.

The Xiangyang area had no local scholar and chronicler who took interest in these local men and their culture of combat and song, and so our success in sketching their society must necessarily be limited. The views of outsiders—a later historian with a significant personal interest, a prince with a taste for the exotic—at least offer us a sense of how local culture appeared to others: "uncivilized" yet alluring, useful yet entangling. Whether or not local men had developed much consciousness of their own distinctive local identity is an issue we will explore in the next section.

## LOCAL SOCIETY SHOWS ITS STRENGTH: XIANGYANG UNDER LIU JUN'S REGIME

Liu Jun's refusal to allow Yuanjing to take the post of Xiangyang commander had significant and perhaps unforeseen consequences. Yong province was full of generals and commandery governors who had substantial fighting experience and who had been instrumental in putting Liu Jun himself on the throne. Many of these men had personal ties to Yuanjing through service in the anti-Man campaigns or the northern campaign of 450; several of his brothers and cousins also held important positions in the region. Yuanjing was thus in a position to play a brokering role between Xiangyang locals and Liu Jun's new regime. The mistrust in the relationship between Yuanjing and the emperor was mirrored by a decade of vigorous and often bloody struggles between agents of the imperial court and elements of Xiangyang local society. The conflicts suggest that, though the men of the Xiangyang region were sometimes able to act in a coordinated manner for their own benefit, they were a long way from having a solidly formed sense of local identity.

The emperor selected as his first candidate to run the Xiangyang garrison his younger brother, Wuchang Prince Liu Hun 武昌王渾, who was only sixteen years old. Hun had a reputation for ruthlessness and cruelty; he is reported to have once gotten angry at a staff member, whipped out a short blade and stabbed him. Perhaps the fact that he was not easily pushed around, and would respond viciously to any threats or opposition, was part of what recommended him for the difficult Xiangyang posting. In any event, soon after his arrival at Xiangyang in summer of 454 he colluded with his personal staff, declared himself the King of Chu 楚王, took on a reign name as the first year of "Eternal Light" (*yong'guang* 永光), and began to set up an imperial-style administration. It is hard to imagine him attempting this without the cooperation of at least some members of the local garrison, but clearly he did not have very much support, for his rebellion made no real progress. Imperial history dismisses him as insane. In any event, the court demoted him to commoner status and then sent out an emissary ordering him to commit suicide. He did, and was buried in Xiangyang after barely more than a year in office there.[61]

Following this fiasco, the court sent a much more heavyweight candidate: Wang Xuanmo 王玄謨, a man of eminent pedigree who had been a leader of the eastern wing of the 450 campaign, fought alongside Liu Yuanjing during the defense of Jiankang in 454, and was fresh off a tough assignment putting down a rebellion in Yu province. Xuanmo was in his early seventies, and had earned a reputation as a cruel hardliner, willing to have his subordinates beaten even for minor offenses. He was reported to never relax or smile; it was said that his eyebrows were "incapable of stretching."[62] Again, these qualities presumably recommended him to Liu Jun, still seeking to bring the Xiangyang garrison to heel.

Xuanmo arrived in the winter of 455–456, and over the following year concluded that the local administrative and tax situation in Yong province was a complete mess. At the time, Yong province had four commanderies with territory, controlling about thirty-five subordinate counties, but it also housed at least ten commanderies-in-exile, with more than thirty additional subordinate counties; families classified under the exiled jurisdictions, some of whom had lived in the area for many generations, were not on any imperial household registers and offered no tax or corvee labor. As a result, Xuanmo decided in spring of 457 that he would undertake a far-reaching reform. His memorial to this effect states: "The immigrant commanderies and counties lack borders and territory, new and old are mixed up and disordered, and tax revenues are not timely. I request a complete residence determination." Xuanmo's primary objective was to abolish most of the immigrant counties, and all but one of the immigrant commanderies, and then consolidate the remaining counties under the jurisdiction of the remaining commandery. This new commandery was to have only four subordinate counties, and was probably to be given jurisdiction over territory north and west of Xiangyang, where most of the immigrants resided.[63] Xuanmo also sought to make sure that all households were entered on the ordinary household registers, and insisted that all from Rank Nine and up (essentially all households, including many which had formerly been exempt) should pay tax obligations.[64]

The local gentry were bitterly opposed to this plan, for many obvious reasons. First, of course, they did not wish to pay taxes. Second, they did not wish to be placed on the household registers of the imperial court; they preferred only local registration, or none at all, which kept the size of their households (including dependents, retainers, slaves, etc.) off the books, making it difficult even to propose any tax or corvee obligations.[65] Third, they did not wish to see the elimination of so many administrative jurisdictions, most of which had been created during or since the founding of the Song to award various migrant groups privileged titles in local administration and greater opportunities for government-salaried service. In Wang Xuanmo's proposal, there would have been only one well-paying and prestigious commandery governorship to hand out to a local man, instead of four or more, and correspondingly fewer patronage positions in the commandery sub-bureaucracy, fewer *xiaolian* nominees to send to the central court, and so forth.[66]

According to the account in Xuanmo's biography, opposition to these reforms united the local community: "[P]oor and rich were caused to talk to one another, and none in the territory were not enraged." Rumors began to be circulated that Xuanmo sought to rebel against the throne, an especially dangerous accusation, given the fate of the previous Yong inspector, and the fact that Xuanmo had barely survived a similar accusation only three years' previously, losing his position in the process. To add threat to the rumor, Liu Yuanjing, who is described as having had "authority" in the region, instructed his younger brother Sengjing 柳僧景, who was governor of Xincheng commandery, to join together with the governors of three other local commanderies to put forth their troops to "purge" Xuanmo's supposed "rebellion." Though we don't know the names of these other governors, they were probably old cronies of Yuanjing's from the anti-Man campaigns or the northern campaign of 450, since most men holding governorships would have been involved in those campaigns. Xuanmo, alarmed at this show of force, rapidly put a stop to the reforms and sent a highly conciliatory memorial to the emperor explaining his blamelessness in the affair. Liu Jun, who is recorded as having been wryly amused by Xuanmo's embarrassment, sent him a pointed rejoinder and recalled him in early 458 for an assignment at the capital.[67]

The upshot of Xuanmo's effort at "residence determination" was utterly different from what had originally been planned. Instead of eliminating and then consolidating immigrant jurisdictions, the court worked out an alternative scheme in which each of the existing immigrant commanderies was preserved, and in fact gained jurisdiction over one or two old-line counties with actual territory. These counties were split off from their former commanderies and made into the official administrative seats for the newly designated commanderies, giving them actual physical jurisdictions. Some immigrant counties were also reclassified as subordinate to "real" commanderies, and were perhaps also given territory. The details are complex and impossible to reconstruct with much confidence, but the overall direction of the settlement is clear: Yong province, which had previously had only four commanderies with actual territory (having lost command over Sui several years earlier), wound up shoehorning at least fourteen commanderies into the same space, and perhaps twice as many counties (see Map 3). As a result, the region had

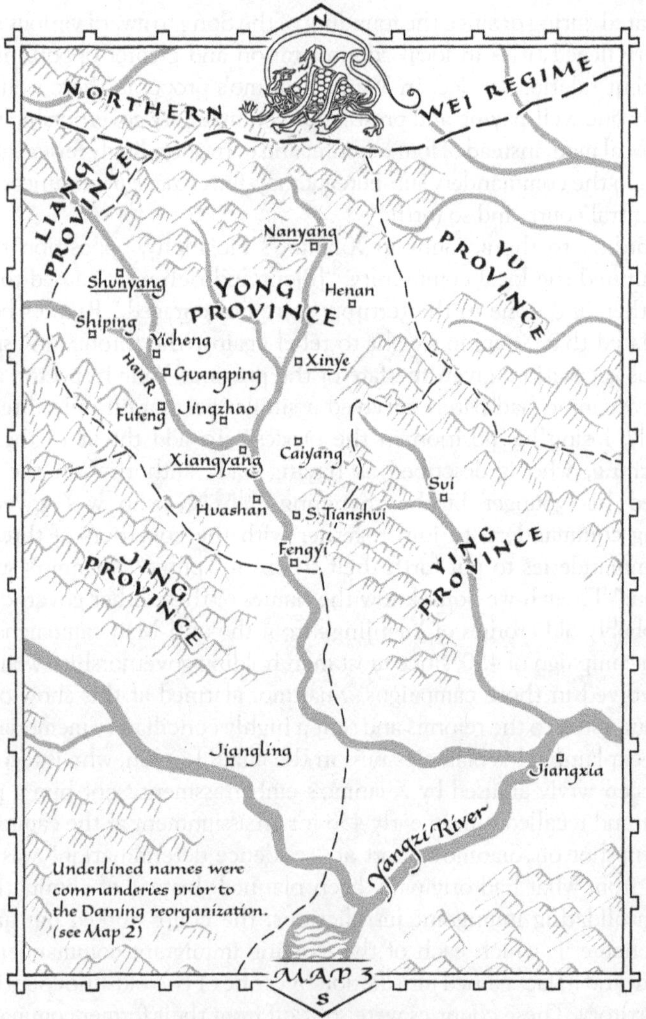


Map 3. Yong province following reorganization

a much higher administrative density than any other in the empire, and correspondingly more local patronage jobs to be doled out; its districts also on average had a rather small registered population, thus correspondingly fewer tax and corvee obligations to meet. There is no evidence that any immigrant households were actually added to the imperial registers in this process. In other words, the "reform" was no longer anything like an administrative rationalization; it was a settlement based on pure political negotiation. The extent to which the settlement did not reflect the court's wishes, but instead worked to the advantage of the prominent clans of Xiangyang, demonstrates the power of their bargaining position.[68]

In the wake of this failure, the emperor sent out as local commander another one of his younger brothers, this time the Prince of Hailing, Liu Xiumao 海陵王休茂, who at fourteen was being sent to his very first provincial command. Shen Yue's biography of the prince asserts that the garrison's affairs were in fact managed by its Assistant Commander (*sima* 司馬), Yu Shenzhi 庾深之, who was a local from nearby Xinye commandery; he and the local generals did as they pleased, routinely refusing to follow the prince's commands. The biography, which seeks to cast primary blame on the prince and his personal followers, asserts that the prince was angered by the local garrison's autonomy and, goaded on by his personal subordinates, ordered the execution of Shenzhi and many of the garrison's top staff in the early summer of 461. Whatever the root cause of the conflict, there can be no doubt that a kind of civil war broke out between the local garrison forces and Xiumao's personal staff. At one point, when Xiumao had led his troops out of the city, an official inside shut the gates and refused to allow him back in, leading to a bizarre situation in which a commander had to besiege his own garrison. After gaining reentry and killing the men responsible, Prince Xiumao was beheaded by another faction of the garrison forces. His mother and wife, both of whom had apparently come out to Xiangyang with him, were also executed, as were all of the men who had sided with him.[69]

Now leaderless, the men of the garrison went ahead and nominated a leader for themselves. Their choice, Liu Gongzhi 劉恭之, had been a commander of Xiumao's central forces, but presumably not actively supportive of his coup.[70] Apparently, a chief recommendation for Gongzhi was that he was the brother of Liu Xiuzhi 劉秀之, who had been a well-respected magistrate of Xiangyang county under Liu Jun back in the 440s. Xiuzhi had been very successful at repairing the dikes of a local irrigation project at that time, and had gone on to serve as a local commandery governor and then the inspector of adjacent Liang and Qin provinces, where he also gained a reputation for taking good care of the economy. He had been on Liu Jun's side throughout the campaigns of 453 and, after serving elsewhere, had recently been posted back to the capital.[71] The court quickly relented to the wishes of the Yong garrison leaders and sent out Liu Xiuzhi himself to take over the provincial command.

Liu Xiuzhi's four-year tenure at Xiangyang brought relative peace to the region for the first time in almost two decades. Though nothing specific is mentioned about Xiuzhi's years there, a posthumous memorial after his death in 464 suggests that he followed the same lenient, economic-oriented policies that he had in his prior provincial commands.[72] Other evidence suggests that the court also took a much more lenient line with the region at this time. For example, in the autumn of 461 the court issued a general amnesty for the province, essentially pardoning the locals for executing the emperor's brother on their own initiative.[73] The following year a memorial forgave all of the province's unpaid taxes prior to 460.[74] This latter amnesty implies that the province had ceased paying taxes at least since the chaos of Wang Xuanmo's residence determination, and perhaps since Liu Jun's ascent to the throne.

The de-escalation of the court's tense relationship with the Xiangyang garrison stands in marked contrast to the precedent set at the Guangling garrison in 459. Following the successful defeat of a rebellion under the emperor's younger brother, Prince Dan, imperial forces under Zong Yue systematically rounded up and executed all of the young men in military service, several thousand in all. The Guangling garrison, the headquarters of the Northern Army, had been the basis for Liu Yu's rise to power and the founding of the Liu-Song regime, but this bloody, brutal reprisal left it so weakened that it ceased to be a major player in the military affairs of the southern regime. The men of the Xiangyang garrison who rebelled against Prince Xiumao in 461 would certainly have been aware of the possibility of an equally harsh reprisal. Seen in this light, their opposition to Prince Xiumao's insubordination, and their nomination of a new leader that would please the court as well as themselves, may have been an effort to protect their reputation for loyalty to the court, and thereby preserve their lives.

In the decade following Liu Jun's ascent to the throne, local society at Xiangyang demonstrated a more cohesive effort to assert its own interests against the wishes of the imperial court than at any other time under the southern regimes. Led at first by Liu Yuanjing, his family, and his associates and former subordinates in the Xiangyang garrison, the community at Xiangyang helped to undercut three successive imperial agents who sought to dominate the region, extract its resources, or undermine the basis for its power and privilege. There can be no question that the years of relative peace since the founding of the Song, and the bonding experience of the successful campaigns against the Man, the north, and the Jiankang throne, all helped to generate this social cohesiveness. Though there is no record of this society written by one of its own members, its powerful song traditions offer limited but suggestive evidence of a developing sense of cultural distinctiveness as well.

Yet it would be greatly overreaching to say that the people of this society had developed a politicized local identity sufficiently powerful to sustain and defend it against the efforts of the Jiankang court. Most importantly, the region was not able to generate and support its own leadership. In the aftermath of Prince Xiumao's rebellion, the men of the garrison nominated an outsider to lead them, and quickly accepted Liu Xiuzhi as commander. This suggests that their primary motivation was not to be ruled locally, or to have some sort of autonomy, but instead to demonstrate sufficient loyalty to maintain good relations with the court, yet without surrendering the tax and administrative privileges to which they had become accustomed. The careers of local men demonstrate that they believed the route to power and prosperity lay in binding themselves in service to men more powerful than themselves, men from outside the region, agents of the Jiankang regime. This had been the key to Liu Yuanjing's ascent, and even as he appealed to be sent back to lead his homeland, he accepted that the way to obtain that leadership role required the authority and approval of men from somewhere else. The appeal of these vertical ties, and the apparent lack of any strong sanction against them, any sense that working for someone from elsewhere might involve "selling out" the local region, seems to have been prevalent even during this highwater mark of community activism. There may have been local men who felt otherwise, but they did not write history, nor did they raise a local following powerful enough to force themselves onto its pages.

## CONCLUSION: THE PERILS OF POWER

The policies of the Song regime opened up a world of opportunity to the men of Xiangyang. During the period of Liu Yuanjing's rise to prominence, the diverse inhabitants of the region had developed a relatively distinctive military and oral subculture. Initially, local men served only in local military and civilian offices; the luckiest of them attracted the attention of an imperial patron and took on low-level positions on their personal military staffs. With Liu Jun's accession to the throne, however, Yuanjing and other Xiangyang men became substantively involved in imperial-level politics for the first time. The evidence from his reign period shows that they coordinated their actions with their home region in order to defend their prerogatives and demand further preferential treatment from the court.

This entanglement was both profitable and perilous, as the career of Liu Yuanjing amply shows. Yuanjing's association with Liu Jun made his career and his fortune, for he enjoyed tremendous eminence during Liu Jun's reign, and had the unassailable standing to be able to repeatedly decline the very highest of titles on principle. His position was also very lucrative; by drawing on the income of his three thousand household fief, as well as the salary from his high-level offices, Yuanjing was able to build a tremendous estate outside of Jiankang, large enough to house his nine surviving sons (one had died young), several of his six brothers, and an unknown number of nephews, cousins, and other relatives. The estate also had a substantial garden, which produced a surplus that could be sold in urban markets, though (so the story goes) Yuanjing was too upright and high-minded to allow his family to profit from so mercantile an endeavor.[75]

When Emperor Xiaowu died in 464, Yuanjing was fifty-eight years old; he had lived and worked away from Xiangyang, mostly at the capital, for all but six of the prior thirty-two years, virtually his entire adult life. There is no evidence that Yuanjing ever returned to Xiangyang after the coup of 453, but it is clear that he remained strongly tied to local society through his family members, as well as his personal association with many members of the garrison. His sons and nephews may have had a somewhat different experience, however; largely raised at the capital, they were able to associate with a much more educated, wealthy, and influential class than had been possible at Xiangyang, and their access to books and teachers offered them the opportunity to pursue careers outside of the military. They were well on their way to becoming emigrants to Jiankang.[76]

Yuanjing, Prince Yigong, and others are said to have breathed a sigh of relief when Liu Jun died, for they had survived his dangerous and vengeful reign. Now elder statesmen aiding the reign of Liu Jun's eldest son Ziye, who was only fifteen years old, they let their guard down; Shen Yue reports that they stayed up nights drinking and singing songs, probably the very same Xiangyang music they knew from their fighting days in the provinces. Ziye, however, proved to be even more bloodthirsty than his father, and drew on his father's most loyal and low-born retainers, including Zong Yue, to conduct a series of vicious purges. In the autumn of 465, after the young sovereign had ordered a particularly objectionable execution, Yuanjing began to plot with others to stage a coup that would elevate Prince Yigong, now fifty-two years old, to the throne. Within two weeks, however, the plot was discovered, and Yuanjing was summoned to court. Knowing he would be executed, his brother and his followers urged him to call up his men and fight, but Yuanjing would not. Yuanjing and Prince Yigong were executed, along with everyone associated with them, including eight of Yuanjing's surviving nine sons, two of his brothers, and all of their sons; only family members stationed far from the court at the time were able to survive.[77] Such were the perils of power in that age.

# THREE

# FRAGMENTATION, 465–500

While Xiangyang society and its influence can be said to have reached an early zenith under the leadership of Liu Yuanjing, the generation following his execution shows evidence of substantial fragmentation. Several factors contributed to this process. The first, quite simply, was the fruits of success in the patronage system, which drew men's allegiances upward, toward their patrons, rather than sideways, to their local compatriots. As a result, factional struggles among members of the imperial household were quickly relayed down to the local level. This can be seen in the succession struggles of 465–466, in which local men who had developed clientelage obligations to imperial agents in the 440s to 460s were allied on every side, sowing intense discord and leading to brutal local purges.

The outcome of that civil war, however, allowed a particular faction of local military men to eliminate their rivals, and they subsequently formed a somewhat elite group that had both deep roots in the garrison's rank and file and the trust of members of the imperial family. Under their dominance, the garrison had peaceful relations with the court, and continued to supply fighting men to the imperial administration through the Song-Qi transition in 478. Following the sudden, capricious execution of the most important member of that group by the second Qi sovereign, however, local men's involvement in imperial affairs experienced a sharp dropoff, and the region once again became a source of trouble and friction.

A second, more permanent cause of fragmentation in the local community was the presence of large numbers of relatively aloof immigrant households. These families, many of whom had been in Xiangyang for generations, formed social "clusters," which were perpetuated by exclusive marital ties and cultural attitudes and further delineated by their privileged administrative districts. Because men of these immigrant clusters were often from families with long pedigrees in the north, they had further reason to disdain the illiterate fighting men who dominated garrison politics. They often stayed within the politics of their immigrant districts, though they were sometimes drawn onto the retinue of an imperial prince, or into the civilian administration of Yong province.

A third source of fragmentation was the temptation to emigrate away from Xiangyang. The patronage system offered the prospect of status and wealth primarily through face-to-face social contact with powerful men, and the opportunities for this were clearly far greater at Jiankang than at Xiangyang. The more successful men routinely spent much of their adult careers following imperial princes to provincial postings, but the pinnacle of achievement was to relocate to the capital, as Liu Yuanjing was able to do. His nephew Shilong and his sons would complete the process of emigration, which was also a process of "gentrification," gaining acceptance into the rarefied cultural milieu of the capital. Immigrant households with high-status backgrounds and educated familial traditions would have had an advantage in this process. Local military families also sought wealth and high-status positions from their patrons, and there are some examples of them parlaying these into capital residences, but their road to gentrification was much rockier. The evidence suggests that most of them did not take much advantage of it, even when the opportunity presented itself. They rightly perceived that, for those with little family status or education, military prowess (and picking the right patron) offered much greater opportunity for dramatic gains in wealth and influence.

## XIANGYANG MEN IN THE CIVIL WAR OF 465–466

The façade of relative unity maintained among the men of the Xiangyang garrison during Liu Jun's regime disintegrated in the vicious struggle for imperial succession that developed in the wake of Liu Ziye's purges. Men who had grown up fighting in the garrison found themselves on both sides of the subsequent civil war, their allegiance following their personal patronage relationships and their opportunistic calculations of personal advantage, rather than any sense of loyalty to the garrison or to their compatriots in it. As a result, factional struggles at court were rapidly translated down to the level of the local community, exacerbating local tensions and tendencies to social fragmentation.

Liu Ziye's purge of Prince Yigong, Liu Yuanjing, and others in autumn of 465 set off a cavalcade of infighting that would last for more than a year. Ziye was highly reliant on a group of lower-status fighting men, known as his "teeth and talons." Though some of these, such as Zong Yue and Xue Andu, had gotten their start in the Xiangyang garrison, they remained loyal to Liu Ziye even after his vicious execution of Yuanjing and his family. Other men, however, were repulsed by Liu Ziye's brutality and sought to support a different member of the imperial house, in a pattern well established in prior imperial succession battles. By midwinter, Ziye's uncle Liu Yu 劉彧, one of the many younger brothers of Liu Jun, had enough support to stage a coup and execute the desperate emperor, enthroning himself as Emperor Ming 宋明帝 (r. 465–472). He promptly set about executing some of Ziye's closest supporters, including Zong Yue; Xue Andu fled to the Tabgatch regime in the north.[1]

Liu Yu's consolidation of power was far from easy, however, for a widespread campaign to resist him was launched under the auspices of Ziye's ten-year-old younger brother, Jin'an Prince Liu Zixun 晉安王子勛, the inspector of Jiang province. He was joined by many of his brothers who were in provincial commands at the time; because Liu Yu had on his side most of his own brothers, the sons of Liu Yilong (Emperor Wen), the conflict is characterized as the "War of the Uncles and Nephews." Part of the motivation for the rebellion of Zixun and his brothers may in fact have been to oppose the diversion of the inheritance of the throne away from their father's patriline. More critical, however, was the collusion among a broad spectrum of men who had been appointed by Ziye and feared for their positions and their lives under Liu Yu's rule, and hoped for greater personal advantage under the weak Zixun.[2] The rebellion rapidly settled into a stalemate centered on the defensive works at Zheqi 赭圻 and Quewei 鵲尾, on the Yangzi River about halfway between Jiankang and the rebel capital at Xunyang.

The evidence shows that men from Xiangyang did not exhibit much cohesion during this crisis. Their choices of allegiance cannot be explained by bonds of regional identity, or even a clear familial tie, but instead followed that of their immediate patrons, or for other personal reasons. As a result, they were key players on both sides of the rebellion. On the rebel "nephews" side, their most important patron was Yuan Yi 袁顗, a man from a well-established court clan who had been appointed Yong inspector and Xiangyang garrison commander under Ziye's regime. He had previously served in Prince Zixun's entourage, and had also spent time in Xunyang, the nexus of the rebellion; thus, despite Liu Yu's effort to woo his allegiance with a promotion, he willingly joined under Prince Zixun's banner. He brought with him as a subordinate one of the leading figures of the Xiangyang garrison, Liu Hu 劉胡. Hu, a Nanyang native, is recorded as having had an ugly, dark, and pockmarked face, like a barbarian (*hu* 胡); given the multiethnic stew of his homeland, this is probably meant to signal that he was of mixed blood. Like so many of his compatriots, Hu had risen through military service to the commandery and the Xiangyang garrison, fought in the anti-Man campaigns, and served on the staff of various imperial princes before joining Yuan Yi's staff and returning to the Xiangyang region as governor of Fengyi commandery. His decision to follow Yuan Yi's lead and join Zixun's side in the civil war makes sense only as a testament to his personal loyalty to Yuan Yi, since he is not known to have had any prior acquaintance with Prince Zixun or any reason to prefer his lineage to Liu Yu's. Liu Hu's reputation for ferocity in battle quickly recommended him as the commander at the front line of the rebel advance.[3]

On the "uncles" side headed by Liu Yu were a variety of men from similar backgrounds as Liu Hu that had been picked up as clients by various members of the imperial clan. Wu Nian, for example, had served Liu Jun's regime in several different capacities over the preceding decade, and was sent by Liu Yu's court to be governor of Nanyang as a counterweight to Yuan Yi; he was betrayed by an emissary from the rebel side, captured, and beheaded. Other Xiangyang men who had served Liu Jun's regime and transferred their allegiance on to Liu Yu's network included Cai Na, Zhang Jing'er, Jiao Changsheng 交長生, and others.[4]

A particularly interesting case illustrates the strength of personal allegiance over familial ties. Liu Yuanjing's nephew Shilong 柳世隆 (443–492) had been raised by Yuanjing at the capital, then sent out to his natal region to serve as governor of Shangyong commandery under the command of Yuanjing's cousin, Liu Yuanhu 柳元怙, who was the inspector of Liang and Qin provinces. As a result, he had avoided the grisly fate that befell his brethren who remained at the capital. Liu Yuanhu elected to join the civil war on Yuan Yi's side, and sent a substantial force to aid the rebels under the command of Liu Deng 柳登, most likely a relative.[5] Shilong, however, decided to oppose the rebel movement, and led his commandery troops to try to retake Xiangyang town from Yuan Yi's allies. When he was defeated, he fled into the hills for the remainder of the conflict. In his biography, Shilong's decision is credited to his sense of personal gratitude to Liu Yu, the man who "avenged" the execution of his uncle Yuanjing.[6] Whatever the truth of this claim, the same devotion did not seem to motivate Liu Yuanhu, or others of the Liu family who chose the other side. The situation demonstrates the important role of personal voluntarism, and the relative weakness of family solidarity, in men's choice of allegiance.

An anecdote recounted by Shen Yue further illustrates the tension between patronal and local loyalties. According to the account, when Liu Hu first came to the Quewei garrison, he sent a letter (the text of which is, unfortunately, not recorded) to Cai Na, Zhang Jing'er, and the other men who hailed from Xiangyang that were fighting for Liu Yu's side, appealing to them to come over to the other side. When they refused, he followed up with a request to have a personal meeting; in their second refusal, they mocked him, demanding that he surrender.[7] That Liu Hu would have directed an appeal exclusively to his Xiangyang compatriots suggests that he anticipated their regional loyalties and their longstanding personal ties to himself and other men from the garrison would be stronger than their ties to their imperial patrons. That they refused his offer, however, suggests that loyalty to a patron depended on calculations of personal advantage as much or more than any emotional bond to shared local origins.

Another anecdote about Liu Hu further shows how rivalries that developed through such personal loyalties to imperial patrons could impact local relationships. After his entreaties at Quewei were rejected, Liu Hu is recorded as having seized many of Cai Na's brothers and sons, who were still in Xiangyang, and systematically executed them, hanging their heads up at the gate of the garrison. This led Na to fight much more fiercely, and must have sowed great emnity between these two households.[8] The fragmentation and dissention between powerful local families may not have been caused exclusively by such actions (recall that the Cais were especially wealthy, which may also have made them a target), but there can be little doubt that the prolonged participation on opposing sides of an intensely personal and hard-fought civil war between various members of the imperial clan sowed discord among members of the garrison.

Resolution to this feuding was made possible only by the military victory of one side, and the subsequent merciless and vengeful purging of the leaders of the other side. Once Liu Hu's forces at Quewei were finally defeated, Prince Zixun's rebellion rapidly unraveled, and all of the key participants were executed, including Prince Zixun, every one of his surviving brothers (the sons of Liu Jun), Yuan Yi, and Liu Hu, and their families. From the perspective of the politics within the garrison, this allowed the winning faction under Zhang Jing'er, Cai Na, and the others to eliminate Liu Hu and any other men of the garrison who had followed him, and who might have openly disputed the dominance of the winning group. The years following this bloodletting appear to have brought renewed stability to the personal hierarchy of authority within the garrison.

## THE EVOLVING STRUCTURE OF RELATIONS BETWEEN COURT AND GARRISON, 466–483

Though the men of the Xiangyang garrison did not show much internal cohesion in the civil war of 465–466, they did demonstrate their utility in the wider struggle for power. Over the ensuing decades the winning faction was able to broker this utility, not only into richer rewards for themselves, but also toward gaining higher office and greater control over the affairs of the garrison itself. Their success is reflected in a distinctive pattern of appointments to the top offices at the garrison: the top office of Yong inspector and commander-in-chief went to a figurehead court appointment, while a top position on the local staff and/or an adjacent commandery governorship was assigned to one of the Xiangyang native fighting men who had demonstrated his loyalty to the emperor in the civil war. The pattern suggests a de facto understanding that the loyalty and discipline of the garrison needed to be maintained and guaranteed by a general with local roots who had worked his way up through the ranks, even as an imperial prince or other high-status court appointee held de jure authority in the region.

This pattern had already emerged under Prince Xiumao, when local affairs were in practice run by Yu Shenzhi, a local man, while the prince served as a figurehead. Following local leaders' notable exercise of restraint in resolving Prince Xiumao's rebellion, the court began to appoint men from Xiangyang into higher positions throughout the region. While Liu Xiuzhi was at Xiangyang, Liu Yuanjing's brother Shuren 柳叔仁 and his cousin Yuanhu served consecutively as the inspector of Liang and Qin provinces.[9] Under Liu Ziye's rule, the top spot of Yong inspector and Xiangyang commander-in-chief went briefly to Zong Que, who, though not a native of the region, had local ancestral roots and had fought closely with Yuanjing and others for years.[10] Liu Yu in turn sought to control the region by appointing Wu Nian, a man who had truly come up through the lower ranks of the garrison, to take on the Nanyang governorship and counter the power of Yuan Yi and Liu Hu during the civil war.

Once Liu Yu's regime was firmly established the strategy became standard practice. The first local man to benefit from the arrangement was Zhang Jing'er, a local native who had emerged from the civil war as one of the leading figures of the Xiangyang region. He had fought vigorously under Liu Hu in anti-Man campaigns in the early 460s and, like Hu, gained a reputation for bravery and ferocity. He was picked up by Shi'an Prince Xiuren 始安王休仁, Liu Yu's younger brother and head of the anti-rebel campaign, and in this capacity found himself opposing his former commander in the faceoff at Quewei. By winning this campaign, Jing'er apparently gained Liu Yu's appreciation and his confidence, for when he requested to succeed Wu Nian as governor of his home commandery of Nanyang, Liu Yu granted the post and sent him out to manage things for his eighteen-year-old brother Xiuruo, the Prince of Baling 巴陵王休若. Jing'er engaged in fairly continuous campaigns to pacify his troubled home region in the emperor's name, including further fights against "Man" rebellions and a challenge from two of the sons of Xue Andu, who had thrown their allegiance to the northern Tabgatch regime.[11] He also took advantage of his newfound authority to undo the re-registration of his household that had been determined under Wang Xuanmo, and place his family on the registers of Guanjun county instead.[12] Though it is not clear precisely what advantage this was to him or to his household, the action demonstrates his ability to use the power of local office for his own benefit. The death of his mother around this time caused him to retire from public office, but he still lived in Xiangyang and probably remained quite influential.

Jing'er's replacement as the locally based "boss" of the garrison was Jiao Changsheng, who took on not only the office of assistant commander (*sima* 司馬), but was also made Commandant for Pacifying the Man, the first time in generations that office had not been held concurrently by the Yong inspector, now a minor court figure named Zhang Yue 張悅 (no known relation to

Jing'er). When Changsheng died in 469, the nature of his position was tacitly acknowledged by his posthumous title as Yong inspector.[13] Meanwhile, Zhang Yue was replaced by Liu Yun 劉韞, a distant member of the imperial household, while Jiao Changsheng's portfolio as de facto head of the garrison was given to Cai Na, another of the Xiangyang locals whose loyalty to the imperial house had been well tested in the civil war.[14] To some extent, he and Jiao may also have had some loyalty to Jing'er, and been appointed on his recommendation; there is no direct evidence for this, but Jing'er's prior command over these men in the civil war and his close ties with the throne suggest that he may have played a key behind the scenes role in making the arrangement work smoothly.

Liu Yu proved every bit as bloody a ruler as his predecessors; after eliminating every one of Liu Jun's offspring, he went on to eliminate four of his surviving five brothers over the next few years of his reign, before dying at the age of thirty-four in 472. His eldest son, then nine years old, was installed as emperor in the most orderly succession of the entire Song era, primarily because the cabal of men who had fought for his father maintained a firm grip on power and were pleased to have a minor child on the throne. Two men stood out as especially important in this cabal. One was Shen Youzhi 沈攸之, a cousin once removed to Shen Qingzhi, who had been one of Liu Ziye's "teeth and talons," but had successfully avoided the purges of Liu Yu's takeover and rapidly risen through Prince Xiuren's staff to become his top general and a leader of the military campaigns of the civil war. Since then he had held a series of critical provincial military postings, culminating in the Jiangling command just after the emperor passed away.[15] The other was Xiao Daocheng 蕭道成, a descendent of one of the empresses of the founder of the Song dynasty, who had served as magistrate of Jiankang for much of the period of Liu Jun's rule, and helped suppress a rebellion sympathetic to Prince Zixun's cause. Under Liu Yu he had risen to dominate the northern frontier armies in the Huai valley before returning to court to engineer the succession following the emperor's death.[16]

These two men each sought to develop a powerful clientelage network in order to oust the other and monopolize control over the enervated throne. The first major test of these rivals was the campaign to eliminate the last remaining imperial prince from Liu Yu's generation, Liu Xiufan, the Prince of Guiyang 桂陽王休範, who was accused of plotting rebellion in midsummer of 474. Shen Youzhi would appear to have had the advantage in recruiting Xiangyang fighting men for this purpose. He had served in a command position in the 465–466 war, with many men from Xiangyang as his associates and subordinates. As commander of the Jiangling garrison and inspector of Jing province, he was able to get one of these subordinates, Zhang Xingshi 張興世, appointed as head of the Xiangyang garrison. Xingshi, a low-born military man from Jingling (between Jiangling and Xiangyang), was the first such man to take on the top spot at Xiangyang; he had been a client and follower of Youzhi's ever since the civil war. When the competition to purge Prince Xiufan began, Xingshi immediately sent his Xiangyang forces downriver to join Shen Youzhi's.[17]

Xiao Daocheng did not have anything like so substantial a support network in the area, but he managed to gain one very significant client, Zhang Jing'er, who was lured out of retirement to serve Daocheng at Xinting, the court's primary defensive garrison just upriver from the capital. It is not clear how Daocheng managed to gain Jing'er's allegiance; there is no evidence of any prior association, though Daocheng had served in the Xiangyang area for a considerable period back in the 440s and may have made Jing'er's acquaintance then.[18] In any event, before Youzhi's forces could advance into battle, Zhang Jing'er and a personal associate from the Xiangyang garrison, Huang Hui 黃回, masterminded a plot to offer false surrender to Prince Xiufan and then behead him at an opportune moment. This put a quick end to the uprising, preventing Youzhi from gaining any prestige or military advantage from the purge.[19]

This action naturally gained Zhang Jing'er a substantial debt of gratitude from Daocheng, and he immediately sought to cash in the favor by requesting from Daocheng the same premiere posting as Zhang Xingshi, the one Liu Yuanjing had requested a generation earlier: Yong inspector and commander-in-chief of the Xiangyang garrison. The following anecdote further confirms what we already identified in the pattern of appointments: the top post at the Xiangyang garrison was ordinarily reserved for men of better status than Jing'er.

> Xiao Daocheng thought lightly of Jing'er's status, and did not want to give him so important a garrison as Xiangyang. Jing'er sought it without success, and so surreptitiously pushed him along, saying: "Shen Youzhi is at Jing province; do you know what it is he intends? If you don't send Jing'er to guard him, I fear it will not be to your advantage." Daocheng laughed but said nothing.[20]

Daocheng at this time was seeking to do what many had done before him: eliminate his rivals, monopolize the imperial patronage network, and eventually force the young emperor to abdicate in his favor. Shen Youzhi remained the most significant military threat to these ambitions; by appointing Jing'er to the Xiangyang garrison, Daocheng could gain a vital counterweight to Youzhi's entrenched position at Jiangling. In the end, Daocheng decided to take a chance on Jing'er's loyalty by awarding him the appointment, and threw in the title of Marquis of Xiangyang with a two thousand household fief to sweeten the deal. Jing'er richly rewarded Daocheng's patronage by spending the next two years building up the garrison and reporting to Daocheng on Youzhi's activities, all the while reassuring Youzhi of his intentions. When Daocheng had the young emperor killed and replaced with his younger and even more pliant brother in 478, Youzhi did indeed rebel, and Jing'er promptly marched his forces down to Jiangling and executed him.[21] Within the year Daocheng took over the imperial title for himself, as Emperor Gao of the new Qi dynasty 齊高帝.

The contrast with Liu Yuanjing's experience is instructive. When Liu Jun refused to appoint Yuanjing to the Xiangyang command, he created a somewhat disgruntled and distant subordinate, and a perpetually rebellious garrison. In the intervening generation, the increasing prominence of men from Xiangyang in the civil wars between imperial princes allowed their loyalty to be more fully tested and relied upon. The difficulties with controlling the garrison were largely resolved by appointing a man from the garrison to manage it, in fact if not in name. Xiao Daocheng had learned both lessons well; by relying on Jing'er, he gained a man who had the personal connections to command the garrison effectively, as well as (at least for the time being) sufficient loyalty to Daocheng to exercise that command in his patron's interest.

Though Jing'er was of a much less pedigreed background than Yuanjing, the parallels between their experiences are mostly stronger than the differences. For both men, the rise to the heights of power involved both great profit and extreme peril. Jing'er built himself a sumptuous estate west of Xiangyang town, but his beautiful second wife did not care for it, so he relocated to the capital. There he took to raising his five sons and began learning his letters, starting with simple texts such as the *Analects* and the *Classic of Filial Piety*. His fief was increased to four thousand households and his honors eventually reached the highest rank of the "three ducal lords," which Jing'er, unlike Yuanjing, accepted immediately, without engaging in any polite refusals. Despite this, when Daocheng died in 482 and was replaced by his eldest son, Xiao Ze 蕭賾 (Qi Emperor Wu 齊武帝, r. 483–493), Jing'er was concerned, for he had not developed the personal bonds of trust with the son that he had with the father. Sure enough, the son soon became suspicious of Jing'er's power and his loyalty and, just like Liu Ziye before him, summoned his father's old general for execution in the summer of 483. All but one of Jing'er's sons was also killed, and no more is heard of his lineage.[22]

The execution of Zhang Jing'er was a critical turning point in the relationship between the garrison and the court. Jing'er had been the leading figure from the garrison for a generation; the capricious action against him and his family could very readily have caused a serious rebellion among the notoriously unruly Xiangyang rank and file. Jing'er's biography notes that several dozen Xiangyang local generals left in protest to join the Man people, the perennial opponents of the Jiankang regime.[23] At the time, the Yong inspector was the emperor's fourteen-year-old younger brother Xiao Qiang, Prince of Poyang 鄱陽王鏘, who was in his very first command position. He had been accompanied to his post by Zhang Gui 張瓌, an experienced official from an eminent capital family, who served as the top military aide, governor of Xiangyang commandery, and general manager of the affairs of the garrison and the province. The pivotal local figure, however, was Cao Jingzong 曹景宗, the son of one of Xiao Daocheng's supporters who, following his father's death in 479, had returned to Xiangyang to take on the leading position in the local garrison staff, in the manner of Zhang Jing'er and others in the preceding generation. In 483 he was serving as the head of the central division of Xiao Qiang's army, the governor of Fengyi commandery, and the chief of all anti-Man campaigns.[24]

Jingzong appears to have played a key role in keeping the peace among the men and quelling any prospect of rebellion. He saw to it that the body of Jing'er's son Daomen 張道門, who had also been executed, was brought back to Xiangyang for a proper burial, an action that commended him to the locals.[25] His conduct exemplifies the way in which local men's allegiance was focused upward, toward patrons who could give them higher-status jobs and rewards, and not sideways, to their close local associates. Jingzong and his father had served together with Zhang Jing'er in the Xiangyang military garrison for many years, and Jingzong had grown up with Zhang Jing'er's sons. By comparison, he would have barely known Prince Qiang or Zhang Gui; he could only have hoped that, by serving them well, they would appoint him to a higher position, perhaps take him away when they moved on to another post, and eventually give him renewed access to the capital and the kind of wealth and prestige that Jing'er and Jingzong's own father had enjoyed. Thus, when the throne executed Jing'er and his entire family line, Jingzong did not rebel, but instead used his local prestige and authority to maintain order and bury the dead. He thereby demonstrated respect for Zhang Jing'er, but no opposition to the tyranny his execution exemplified.

## GENTRIFICATION AND EMIGRATION

By the beginning of the Qi period, men from the Xiangyang area had been prominent in imperial politics for more than a generation, and a second generation had come of age. Men from this next generation, such as the offspring of Liu Yuanjing and Zhang Jing'er, had enjoyed increased opportunities: they traveled to the capital, gained honorary imperial titles, and worked their way up through the patronage system more rapidly than they might have otherwise. As Zhang Jing'er seems to have realized, to fully capitalize on these opportunities they needed to learn to function in "polite" Jiankang society, which required gaining a modicum of cultural literacy and ritual polish. In general, however, men from the Xiangyang military families did not "gentrify" to any great degree, and instead maintained the military traditions of their fathers. Part of the reason may have been limited opportunity: the decades following the execution of Zhang Jing'er were a period of stagnation for most Xiangyang military men, and they did not gain the kinds of fiefs and positions at court that would have allowed them to relocate to the capital. It was probably also the case, however, that local men realized that, while "gentrification" might help to secure wealth and status once you had them, only military success and the right choice of patron could help you ascend.[26]

The career of Liu Yuanjing's nephew, Liu Shilong, stands out as a paradigm of what successful gentrification looked like. His father, Yuanjing's younger brother Shuzong 柳叔宗, would have been raised in Xiangyang back in the 430s, and when his son Shilong was born in 443 he was probably serving under Shen Qingzhi in the anti-Man campaigns; thus, Shilong's childhood was most likely also spent in Xiangyang.[27] Shilong's father died while he was young, and when his uncle Yuanjing moved down to the capital in 453 he took his precocious ten-year-old nephew with him, doting on him more than he did his own sons. During this period of residence in Jiankang, which lasted about five years, Shilong had a personal audience with the emperor, Liu Jun.[28] So, though recorded as being from Xiangyang, by the time he was capped at fifteen he had already become something of an expatriate, enjoying a "finishing school" experience in the capital that virtually no one else from his region would have had.

This combination of local roots and capital polish made Shilong a good candidate to be sent back to the Xiangyang area, and his first position was in the entourage of Prince Xiumao, who was sent out to head the garrison in 458. Sometime prior to Xiumao's rebellion, Shilong was brought back to the capital to work for another prince, but he was then sent back to the region again as Shangyong governor (under the command of his father's cousin, Liu Yuanhu), where he tried and failed to defend Xiangyang against the forces of Prince Zixun's campaign in 465.[29] Though we cannot say why he was unsuccessful, it is clear that his official career up to this time had emphasized the logistical and administrative side of warfare, rather than outright combat. Unlike Yuanjing, whose upbringing in the frontier conditions of Xiangyang had revolved around horse riding, archery, and military campaigns against the Man people, Shilong's youth shows no evidence of any substantial fighting experience.

Shilong emerged from hiding after Zixun's rebellion to take a minor post at the capital again and develop his relationships with other men at court, connections he probably had made previously. The 470s found him back in military staff positions, this time in Ying province, where he got to know Xiao Ze, the son of Xiao Daocheng. Shilong was a leading figure in organizing the defense of the Ying garrison against Shen Youzhi's forces in 478, and was rewarded for this accomplishment with a two thousand household fief and a series of high-level appointments in the central court, as well as several stints as inspector and commander-in-chief of various eastern provinces. From then until his death in 492, he was based in Jiankang, where he had a fine estate, raised his fifteen sons (and an unknown number of daughters), and developed a reputation for conversation and his skill on the zither. He is famously quoted as having said, "Checkers ranks first, pure conversation ranks second, and the zither ranks third."[30] All this was a far cry from the military life in the provinces that his father and grandfather had led.

The early careers of Shilong's sons demonstrate the completion of this lineage's transformation. All of them were raised entirely at the capital, where they were introduced into high society to great acclaim, gaining the acquaintance of men from such eminent court clans as the Langye Wangs and the Chenjun Xies. They gained early reputations for their skills in scholarship, literature, poetry, and music; none was noted for military ability. All of them started their careers with appointments at court or on the personal staffs of the most eminent princes, such as Xiao Ze or Xiao Ziliang 蕭子良, Ze's second son, who sponsored an extensive literary salon. Their subsequent postings through to the end of the Qi period would best be described as prestigious and secure, but not especially powerful. Unlike their father, their early careers show no association with Xiangyang whatsoever. In short, Shilong's branch of the Lius had essentially emigrated to Jiankang and become a court clan, and can no longer really be considered a Xiangyang local clan.[31]

The Lius had advantages early on in this ascent, including a fine family pedigree and an early success in officeholding with Liu Yuanjing, whose reputation was sterling. Less eminent Xiangyang military men did not have anything like the same kind of success in integrating themselves and their families into Jiankang elite society. Zhang Jing'er seems to have made the most effort in this direction, for he relocated his household to Jiankang and worked on learning his letters, reputedly in order to be more appropriate to the noble titles he held. Presumably he also sought to gain an education for his sons, perhaps intending his family to follow a road similar to Shilong's. Unfortunately, because he and all but one of his sons were purged by Xiao Ze in 483, we cannot say whether his strategy would have borne fruit.

Zhang Jing'er was not the only local man to gain opportunities at court through his association with Xiao Daocheng. Cao Xinzhi 曹欣之 had been a low-level division leader in the Yong garrison, but due to unspecified "achievements" in the rebellion of Prince Xiufan in 474 he received a very good fief of five hundred households. His career then took off; within a mere two years he was serving as inspector of Xu province, a powerful and very well-remunerated office. He had at least ten sons; he introduced his eldest, Jingzong, at the capital when he was around twenty years old, arranging for him to get a minor position as a court gentleman in the census section of the imperial secretariat. This was quite a good start for a young man from the provinces whose prior experience was mostly in hunting, archery, and killing Man people on raids. When Xinzhi died in 479, however, Jingzong went into mourning and returned to Xiangyang, taking on the lead position in the garrison and keeping the peace after Zhang Jing'er was executed in 483. Despite that notable effort to appeal to his superiors, he spent the next twenty years of his career at Xiangyang, with no further opportunities at court.[32]

Opportunities also came directly to Xiangyang, in the form of imperial princes sent out to run the garrison. Xiao Ze's eldest son, Xiao Changmao 蕭長懋 (posthumously known as Emperor Wen 齊文帝, though he died before he was able to inherit the throne), came to garrison Xiangyang in 479 and accepted several Xiangyang fighting men as his clients. These included Cai Na's son Daogong 蔡道恭, along with his brother (or perhaps a cousin) Daogui 蔡道貴; Kang Xuan 康絢, the son of the governor of Huashan commandery; and several other Xiangyang men of obscure background. They followed him back to court in 480 and presumably were still on his retinue even after he was made heir-apparent in 482. Kang is known to have gained an imperial audience in 485, but thereafter retired due to his mother's death; Changmao himself died in 493. Kang and the Cai brothers are not heard from again until the late 490s, at which time they were back in Xiangyang provincial military service, their earlier foray to the capital apparently having not been parlayed into any more lasting eminence.

The stunted career tracks of these men, despite early opportunities, suggests that the climate for patronage of Xiangyang fighting men by members of the Qi ruling house was not promising, giving them little chance, and less motivation, to "gentrify."[33] Cao Jingzong was known primarily for his fighting skills, and continued to serve in front line battle positions well into his forties; though he was apparently literate, his favorite works were historical accounts of heroic fighters such as Sima Rangju and Yue Yi. Cai Daogui was flatteringly compared to Zhang Fei, a military hero, while Cai Daogong was still known as "an old-time general" in the late 490s.[34] These men certainly gained some advantage from their fathers' wealth and status, and enjoyed improved access to imperial patrons early in their careers; however, they in no way succeeded in leveraging this access into higher-level office, wealth, or social acceptance at court, as Shilong and his sons had.

They were able to deploy these advantages to good use in local society, however, as a tale about Cao Jingzong and his younger brother Yizong 曹義宗 testifies. At the end of the Qi period Jingzong had a position as a local commandery governor, and his family was considered a "powerful household" (*haoqiang zhi men* 豪強之門) of the area. A very wealthy local man surnamed Xiang 向 sought to make Yizong his in-law, sending him his younger sister and offering him a million cash. Yizong, who was quite covetous of wealth, nonetheless consulted his elder brother before proceeding; Jingzong did not object, and the marriage went through. The tale shows the extent to which the Caos had local status because they had a leading role in the garrison, and therefore had connections with imperial administration that allowed them to gain positions as squadron leaders, local magistrates, or commandery governors, positions of relatively little account from the perspective of the capital elite, but of great significance within Xiangyang local society. On the other hand, their status did not necessarily mean that they were especially wealthy by comparison with a household such as the Xiangs, who presumably made their money in trade and land ownership. The Xiangs, like the Cai and Wu households in prior generations, had great wealth but low status, and sought to buy into the status the Cao family had. It turned out to be a very good buy indeed, for the Cao family's status vis-à-vis the imperial court soon improved tremendously, and the brothers of the Xiang family became high officials due to their well-chosen affinal relationship.[35]

The careers of Cao Jingzong and others demonstrate how the patronage system encouraged local military men to develop vertical affiliations with potential patrons, men who had the greatest prospect of delivering rapid improvements in wealth and status. Though some princes did sponsor famous literary salons and patronize provincial men for their learning, men of primarily military background were unlikely to develop the erudite skills required to join them, no matter how assiduously they read the *Classic of Filial Piety*. The fact was that the most powerful men in the Jiankang regime chose clients for their fighting skills, their loyalty, and their ruthlessness, not for their poetry. As a result, men from local military families such as the Caos and Cais mostly did not gentrify. As one illiterate man of low-class background who rose to top offices in the late Qi period astutely observed, had he been book-learned, he'd have never attained such a powerful position.[36]

## IMMIGRANT CLUSTERS

Local fragmentation was also influenced by another important social pattern: the "clustering" of immigrants by the commanderies from which they emigrated, and the development of personal and affinal ties within these clusters which lasted for generations. This pattern of immigrant clustering has been identified in studies of other regions, such as Shandong, where a cluster of northern immigrants came to dominate the local power structure.[37] The clustering of immigrant groups in Xiangyang was exacerbated by the use of immigrant jurisdictions, which provided institutional reinforcement to nascent immigrant identities. Other institutional affiliations also served to reinforce social distinctions and divisions: civilian offices in provincial and commandery administration (which required an education), lower-level military service (involving actual combat), and high-level military command positions (close to imperial princes and other court figures). These affiliations are even clearer for the Nanyang immigrant cluster at Jiangling, in which association with the Buddhist church may also have played an important role. Such affiliational subgroups, and the vertical ties that allowed progress upward within them, were probably more important than geographical proximity, or "ethnic" ties, despite the tendency of these categories to overlap at times.[38]

It would be a mistake to place too much emphasis on "ethnicity" as an identifying marker for immigrant clusters. The "ethnic" epithets used by early Chinese historiographers are notoriously unreliable by modern standards, as the example of the Man people showed.[40] Immigrant groups that would be considered of Han ethnicity by modern historians frequently developed highly exclusive and clannish behaviors when they relocated to distant lands, creating "hard" distinctions that would have been comparable, perhaps even more sharply marked, than those which early texts demarcate as "ethnic." The motivations for such clustering behavior are varied and complex. One motivation may have been actual cultural differences, such as dialectical differences (many of which persist to this day) or other cultural distinctions that would have been obvious and important to people at the time, even if they went unrecorded.[41] Another motivation would have been status differentials: clans who had long pedigrees and had enjoyed high status in the north would have sought to protect themselves from the degradation of mixing with low-class local Xiangyang people, and there was no local "upper" class for them to mix with, since the educated elite of the Xiangyang region had all died or fled in the fourth century. The privileged status of immigrant jurisdictions would have also offered a segregated administrative hierarchy within which immigrant groups could protect their position.[42]

The previous chapter addressed the extent of immigration into the Xiangyang area in the early fourth century. The immigrant jurisdictions created for these groups were perpetuated for generations, and some even took over preexisting jurisdictions in the reforms following Wang Xuanmo's ouster. Some of these jurisdictions became virtual private fiefs of the leading immigrant families. The governorship of Huashan commandery, for example, was perpetually assigned to men from the Kang clan; thus, Kang Xuan, who spent a few years at court under the patronage of Xiao Changmao, was able to return to the Xiangyang area after his mother's death and once again take up his family's sinecure. The ancestors of the Kang family had migrated from Samarkand in central Asia, so this commandery may have been an ethnic enclave; on the other hand, many of its members may have come from Lantian, southeast of Chang'an, where the Kangs had settled for a substantial period before moving on to Xiangyang.[39]

The clearest example of an immigrant cluster in the Xiangyang region is the group of families from Jingzhao commandery, a suburb of the ancient capital of Chang'an, among whom the leading surnames were Wei, Du, and Wang. As noted in chapter 2, Wei Hua emigrated to Xiangyang from Duling county in the wake of Liu Yu's foray into Guanzhong back in 417–418. Though his son remained in Guanzhong, Wei Hua brought with him his two grandsons, Zuzheng 韋祖征 and Zugui 韋祖歸, who were probably not much more than small children at the time. Though neither of them has a biography in the imperial histories, Zuzheng is known to have served in the 460s as governor of Jingzhao commandery, which by then possessed real territory and was located on the north bank of the Han River opposite Xiangyang town; later (probably posthumously) he received what was essentially an honorary court title as Master for Imperial Entertainment. His younger brother Zugui's highest title was as an aide to a Ningyuan general, which, if the usual pattern of local service held true, was most probably Zhang Yue, who held that title while he was Yong inspector in 468–469.[43] Zugui had three sons, all roughly of Liu Shilong's generation, who were raised with reputations for scholarship and filiality.

The Wei family was closely associated with the Du 杜 family, another eminent lineage, which had emigrated from the same county as the Weis at about the same time as did Wei Hua. One of them, Du Ji, was already married to the sister of Zuzheng and Zugui at that time, and the union produced six sons; the most prominent, Du Youwen 杜幼文, was granted a three hundred household fief as a reward for his services fighting against Prince Zixun's rebellion, and went on to serve as inspector of Liang and Qin provinces, a position routinely reserved for men from prominent Xiangyang households.[44]

An anecdote recorded in the official biography of Wei Zugui's son Rui 韋叡 illustrates the extent to which these Jingzhao immigrant families maintained close relationships with one another for generations following their resettlement in the Xiangyang region:

> [Wei] Rui's wife's brother, Wang Deng 王憕 and his mother's sister's son, Du Yun 杜惲, had great reputations in the local region. [Wei] Zuzheng said to Rui, "How would you compare yourself to Deng and Yun?" Rui humbly refused to dare make a comparison. Zuzheng said, "Though your literary essays are of minor talent, your scholarly understanding exceeds theirs. Therefore, in accomplishments in service to the state, they will not equal you."[45]

This piece, though an obvious panegyric to Rui, reveals the existence of a tight web of associations between immigrants from Jingzhao. First, they commonly had affinal relations with one another (see Appendix A, diagram 2). Wei Zugui's wife's sister had married someone from the Jingzhao Du clan, just as Zugui's own sister had. Wei Rui's own wife, meanwhile, was from the Jingzhao Wang clan.[46] In other words, this cluster of Jingzhao immigrants defended some sense of exclusivity by maintaining marital ties to one another for several generations after they settled in Xiangyang.

Second, the anecdote demonstrates that these men thought of themselves and evaluated themselves as a group, comparable to one another, and clearly distinguished from other men of their generation from the region. It is not surprising that an illiterate fighting man such as Zhang Jing'er, who was around Wei Rui's age, would have been excluded from this company; it is more noteworthy that Liu Shilong, who was educated and quite well connected, is also not included in the comparison. The clear implication is that the men of the Jingzhao cluster of families were considered as a distinct category for comparison. Such self-identification would have been reinforced by the long-standing designation of the Jingzhao immigrant families as a separate commandery-in-exile. The commandery administration would have been dominated by these elite Jingzhao lineages—recall that Wei Zuzheng had served at one time as the commandery governor—which further allowed them to develop a sense of themselves as a distinctive entity within the larger Xiangyang region.

Despite their apparent pride in scholarly traditions, the Weis and Dus did not have the same opportunities to network with men at the capital that Liu Shilong enjoyed, and besides Du Youwen they had relatively little success in gaining notice in the patronage system of Song and Qi imperial adminsitration. Wei Rui, Zugui's third son, began his career on the civilian staff of the Yong inspector, Yuan Yi, in 465, a posting appropriate for a local man of literary rather than fighting background, but not particularly remarkable.[47] Also on Yuan Yi's staff was Rui's distant cousin Wei Ai 韋愛, who was descended from another lineage of the Wei clan that had migrated to Xiangyang in the late fourth century. Ai had traveled to court and gained an imperial audience when he was only twelve years old, but he apparently did not impress anyone, for his entire adult career was spent in Yong provincial offices.[48]

Rui's subsequent career was not especially fortunate either. Having avoided the pitfalls of following Yuan Yi into Prince Zixun's rebellion, he gained a post under his affinal first cousin Du Youwen, whose rule in Liang-Qin province was notoriously corrupt and eventually led to his purge and execution. Rui avoided the taint of this association too, but he followed up by gaining staff positions for two doomed imperial princes, first Prince Xiushi (executed in 471), then Prince Xiufan (killed in rebellion in 474). Rui eventually served under Liu Shilong, who was one year his junior, in the defense of the Ying garrison against Shen Youzhi's forces in 478. The episode made Shilong's career, but it had no great impact on Rui's, who received no noble title, fief, or high court position from it. Throughout the Qi period he served in unremarkable positions in the lower ranks of imperial administration, though unlike many his service was not limited to the western commands.[49] His elder brothers also had some opportunities to impress the court elite; the eldest, Wei Zuan 韋纂, was a records clerk for the Ministry of Education (*situ jishi* 司徒記室), and is supposed to have impressed Shen Yue, who would eventually become the leading figure among the capital literary elite.[50] However, as is so often the case with such accolades, their point is to make up for the fact that the actual offices held were not especially impressive.

Families such as the Weis traditionally made a virtue out of their failure to gain material success, claiming that their educated traditions were not adequately appreciated by uncouth regimes, and their lack of career success was due to their unsullied aloofness from everyday affairs. A later anecdote about Xiangyang immigrants suggests how they wove this sort of ethos into their own legends:

> The retired gentleman Xin 辛, given name Xuanzhong 宣仲, was a man of Longxi 隴西. At the end of the Daming period (457–464) he lodged two miles west of Xiangyang county [seat], planted many pines and bamboo, and "nested" in the peace and quiet beneath them, having no relations with the common people. In the woods he built a grass hut which was only a cramped one. He was good at playing the zither (*zheng* 箏). He shared goals with Hu Tao of Huainan 淮南胡陶 and Luo Huidu of Jingzhao 京兆駱惠度, and they became friends.[51] They would often gather to feast at these woods. Tao was able to play pipes, Huidu would sing, and the harmonious ordering of string and pipe beneath the woods was called by men of that day the "music of the three lords" (*san gong yue* 三公藥).[52]

What is notable about this account of eminent immigrant households is their sustained effort to avoid any leadership role in the local community; indeed, they make a virtue out of ignoring local affairs and "having no relations with the common people." Their ethos contrasts sharply with the much more aggressive, engaged social and political behavior of men such as Zhang Jing'er, or even Liu Yuanjing. The anecdote goes on to further celebrate Xin Xuanzhong's lack of political success:

> The Song Prince of Baling[53] Xiuruo was South Yong Inspector (466–468) and went to recruit them. Xuanzhong was just then in the woods playing the zither and paid no attention. After a bit,

> he set the zither on his mat and invited Baling to converse with him, but only of trivial recent events and the weather. At that time among Baling's clients (*ke* 客) was one who gestured with his finger, got the zither and ordered [Xuanzhong] to play. After being invited three times, [Xin] replied, "Xin is not a musician of the prince's house, so why should I be compelled this way? What makes me superior to you is that I rectify my behavior for myself. If I were to submit upon being ordered, then how would I be different from you?" His manner of answer was serene and elegant, and none could make him submit.[54]

Xin and his companions are portrayed as paragons of aloofness, men who rejected the patronage system and its demand for slavish service to the powerful. Despite this posture, it was nonetheless useful to assert that one's worth was indeed recognized by the "right sort of people," such as Shen Yue, noted for praising Wei Zuan. The tale about Xin Xuanzhong likewise goes on to take advantage of Shen Yue's reputation, claiming that Xin was approached by Shen when he was stationed in Xiangyang, in the service of Xiao Changmao. Shen supposedly discussed literature with Xin and tried to persuade him to take up a position, to no avail.

The following tale about Wei Zuzheng, circulated only after Wei Rui was a very high-ranking official, also attempts to borrow from an eminent reputation, this time Liu Shilong's:

> The Master for Imperial Entertainment Wei Zuzheng was a virtuous elder of the [Xiangyang] local region, and though [Liu] Shilong himself was of great status, he always paid him respect. Men advised Zuzheng to stop him; he replied, "What Commandants and Ducal Lords wish to do, a lesser man like me takes as his model; how can I stop him?"[55]

One further observation we can draw from these tales is that immigrant clans from different commanderies might, under the right circumstances, ally with one another in an effort to maintain their "eminent" reputation by comparison with the "common people." In fact, Wei Rui and Liu Shilong's first cousin, Liu Qingyuan 柳慶遠, did eventually establish affinal ties through their children, the only known marital linkage between these two prominent Xiangyang-area clans.[56]

In addition to recording examples of admiration from those whose opinions "mattered," it was equally important for exclusive clusters to clarify the social and cultural gulf between themselves and the military families and other nouveaux-riches of the Xiangyang area, despite the fact that the latter may have had better imperial connections and titles, or more wealth, or both. The following entertaining tale, like the one on Xin Xuanzhong, is probably derived from a mid-sixth century collection that will be discussed in chapter 4:

> The west gate of the outer wall of [Xiangyang] town was where, when Wei Rui was young, Cai Na of Nanyang, who was good at prognostication, did a reading of Rui's estate and said it would produce a Three-Lord-rank Inspector and was exalted beyond words. At that time there were ten grass buildings on Rui's estate, while Na's estate south of town had all of its buildings tiled. [Na] sought to exchange estates with Rui, but [Rui] was suspicious and did not accept.[57]

This tale seeks to cast Wei Rui in the mold of a "poor scholar" household—not quite as poor as Xin Xuanzhong, who had but one cramped building, but living under thatch nonetheless. Cai Na, by comparison, is cast in the role of the less-approved "wealthy local bravo," seeking to gain advantage by "buying" his good fortune, rather than by simply exhibiting upright behavior and letting eminence and good fortune flow to him naturally, as Wei Rui does.

Immigrant clusters with this sort of ethos existed in many different areas of the southern regime; the imperial court at Jiankang was essentially an overgrown version of one. An especially well-documented example is the descendents of families who had emigrated away from the Xiangyang area and settled in Jiangling in the fourth century. Several of these families, notably those of the Xinye Yu 新野庾 and Nanyang Zong 宗, Yue 樂, and Liu 劉 lineages, maintained affinal ties and close social relationships with one another through the late Song and Qi periods (see Appendix A, diagram 3). Many men from these families refused to engage in government service, notably Zong Bing 宗炳 and his cousin Yuzhi 宗彧之 in the early Song period, then Bing's grandson Zong Ce 宗測 and his distant cousin Shangzhi 宗尚之 in the Qi period.[58] Zong Ce was closely associated with Yu Yi 庾易 and Liu Qiu 劉虬, other "retired gentlemen" of his day from the same cluster of families.[59] The men of this group had significant scholarly output, with particular interests in Jiangling local history and in Buddhism, and they contributed substantial resources to local Buddhist institutions.[60] The perpetuation of blood, affinal, and affiliational connections between these men suggests that they maintained and even accentuated their exclusivity and their distinctive cultural traditions as Nanyang men, traditions they would have traced all the way back to later Han times. Ironically, Nanyang commandery itself had long since devolved into a frontier region, its men (such as Cai Na, Liu Hu, and Zhang Jing'er) noted for their fighting traditions, archery, horsemanship, and ruthless ferocity.

Yet the so-called recluses of this Nanyang cluster did not exist in isolation; other men from their families were active in government service, sometimes in very high positions. We have already noted Zong Que, Zong Bing's nephew (and Zong Ce's cousin once removed), who broke his family's aloof scholarly tradition by pursuing a military career, for which he was criticized by his family and community.[61] Others pursued mid-level civilian careers that carried no such stigma, including Ce's cousin Zong Kuai 宗夬; Liu Qiu's cousin ("clan-brother") Liu Tan 劉坦; and Yue Ai 樂藹, the son of Zong Que's sister and the brother of Liu Qiu's wife.[62] These men represented the leading families of Jiangling, and supplied much of the high-level personnel that staffed Jiangling provincial offices.

In the case of the Jingzhao cluster, too, we can see that the ethos of "aloofness" did not necessarily translate into an actual refusal of office by all, or even most, family members. All of the known members of the Wei and Du lineages served imperial administration at some level, just like members of the Nanyang lineages. Many of these men would surely have accepted even better positions, salaries, titles, and fiefs had they had the opportunity; they went on to do so in the sixth century. The rhetoric of reclusion was a way for them to make their failure to profit from the patronage system into a virtue, and to demand the highest possible "price" for their eventual participation. It nonetheless demonstrates how disengagement from much of local society was a calculated strategy among some immigrant groups, one that would have contributed to the fragmentary nature of the local community.

## IMMIGRANT GROUPS WITH MORE EXPANSIVE TIES

It would be a mistake, however, to presume that all immigrant groups pursued the exclusive and reclusive strategy of the Jingzhao and Nanyang clusters. Many men from local immigrant jurisdictions joined the garrison rank and file and worked their way up through military service, just as "local" men did, in which case the distinction between local and immigrant was probably not of great significance.[63] Another pattern was for immigrant families to develop expansive ties with the imperial house, and with prominent families from other regions, in an effort to become part of the "national elite." The best example of this pattern is the families which migrated south from Hedong 河東 commandery, with surnames of Liu 柳, Xue 薛, and Pei 裴.

There are many reasons for the extraordinarily diffuse and complex relationships of men with these surnames. First of all, the Hedong surnames are known to have been exceedingly widespread; the Xues are reputed by one source to have had over three thousand distinct lineages.[64] Furthermore, due to concubinage, each lineage could be exceedingly fertile. For example, Liu Yuanjing was one of seven brothers; he himself had ten sons; and his nephew

Shilong had fifteen sons.[65] In all cases there would have been a comparable number of daughters who have gone unrecorded but whose marriages would have further cemented the lineage's social network.

Second, different lineages with the same surname and county of origin often migrated to the south at different times, and to different destinations. Liu Yuanjing's great-grandfather Zhuo 卓, who was the first to come to the south in the early fourth century, also had a first cousin Gong 恭 who settled in what is now southeastern Henan, and his third-generation descendent Qi 緝 served the Song regime as lieutenant governor of Si province, in the same area[66] (see Appendix A, diagram 1). There is no evidence that these two branches of the Lius had any dealings with one another. Meanwhile, Liu Guangshi 光世, who was Liu Yuanjing's second cousin, was from a lineage of Lius that had stayed in the north; after a purge of the leading families of Hedong in 450, however, he migrated along with Xue Andu to Xiangyang, where Yuanjing was already a leading figure. Despite that tie, the two men's careers soon moved in quite different directions from those of Yuanjing and his brothers, sons, and nephews.[67] The episode suggests that, though distant cousins may sometimes have used their familial ties to help get themselves established, these relations were not necessarily more decisive than other, non-kin ties.

The careers of Xue Andu and Liu Guangshi are a good example of a third complicating factor: members of prestigious northern lineages were frequently able to gain high office from either the southern or the northern regimes when they crossed over, and thus did not necessarily "settle" anywhere in particular, but took on itinerant careers as imperial agents. Thus, though Andu and Guangshi served Liu Jun's regime in the 450s and early 460s, they fled back to the north again when Liu Yu established his regime after 466; Guangshi later crossed back over to the south again and gained appointment before finally being suspected of rebellion and executed. The political behavior of these men was not predictable by their family line; Liu Yuanjing's descendents, Guangshi's cousins, all stayed in the south throughout, while Xue Andu's cousin's son, Xue Yuan 薛淵, who had come to the south with him, chose not to follow him back to the north, but instead stayed in the south and served Xiao Daocheng and his heirs faithfully for several decades.[68]

Another example of this sort of "high-flying" pattern of association is Pei Shuye 裴叔業. Men of the Pei surname had emigrated into the southern regime at various times and settled in a variety of places, leading to numerous prosperous lineages with no clear evidence of any strong association between them.[69] Pei Shuye's father and grandfather emigrated south to Xiangyang during the early Qi regime, but Shuye's own career involved almost continuous relocation, and it is not at all clear that he had "settled" a household in the Xiangyang area in any meaningful sense of the word. He associated with Liu Sengxi 柳僧習, a descendent of the Si province Lius noted above; he also had unspecified "affinal ties" (*yinya* 姻婭) with a pair of brothers of the Hedong Liu surname, Xuanda 玄達 and Xuanyu 玄瑜, and married one of his sons to Xuanyu's daughter. He and his cluster had little difficulty gaining rich rewards and high office from the northern Tabgatch regime when they crossed back over in the late Qi period.[70]

There is no reason to believe that this rather mobile cluster of men with Hedong surnames had any particular relationship with the descendents of Liu Yuanjing. In fact, Yuanjing's line was quite well-rooted by comparison. His ancestors had been settled in the Xiangyang region for well over a hundred years (since the early fourth century), and though some branches (such as Liu Shilong and his offspring) emigrated to the capital, other members of the lineage remained prominent in Xiangyang for at least seven generations, all throughout the fifth and sixth centuries. There is no evidence that they developed affinal relationships with the more scattered branches of other Hedong surnames.[71]

Families with Hedong surnames were not the only ones to exhibit these various, complex, and expansive relationship patterns. The Jingzhao Wei surname was as widespread as any of the Hedong surnames; at least three different branches migrated south to Xiangyang in the years between 380 and 420, while numerous other branches remained in the north, offering service to the Tabgatch regime.[72] Evidence suggests that there was little or no communication between these different lineages, and certainly no consistent allegiance.[73] In other words, the existence of distant branches of a particular surname did not necessarily disrupt the cohesion of a local cluster of immigrant families, though it might smooth the transition to a new regime or a new locale when opportunity allowed it, or exigency compelled it.

In summation, the evidence suggests that immigrant lineages with high-status surnames pursued a variety of strategies, ranging from a reclusive and essentially local strategy to an expansive and often quite mobile strategy, and that different lineages of the same surname tried different strategies that were almost certainly not coordinated with each other. One element that the more successful lineages do seem to have in common, however, is their aloofness from "the common people," meaning military families. There is no evidence from the Xiangyang area that members of the more prominent immigrant households ever intermarried, or even socialized as equals, with members of local military families. This is not surprising, given the ample evidence that men who engaged in active military service were looked down upon. Despite the substantial association between Liu Yuanjing and local fighting men, forged through their common service in war, his ties to them were as a respected former commander and patron, not a social equal. Unlike the lower-class local men, Yuanjing had a family ancestry as a prominent clan from the north, a respected father in imperial (albeit provincial) service, and some education, and he did not have to work his way up through the ranks of the garrison. His drinking buddy was Prince Yigong, not one of his old army subordinates.[74]

## THE CRISIS OF THE QI REGIME

Following the execution of Zhang Jing'er, men from the local garrison did not enjoy close ties with the Jiankang court, and local figures such as Cao Jingzong, despite efforts to please the regime, held only minor and local positions. As a result, the garrison was more difficult to manage, and saw several prominent rebellions. By the late Qi period the garrison was also under continuous threat of invasion and seizure by the northern Wei regime. Given its neglect by the Qi court, this was a development that at least some in the area may have welcomed.

The relative isolation of the leading men of the Xiangyang region from Xiao Ze's court set the context for the first major rebellion in the area since that of Prince Xiumao in 461. It was begun in the spring of 487 by a man named Huan Tiansheng 桓天生, who claimed to be the heir of Huan Xuan, the notorious usurper of the eastern Jin throne who had founded an abortive "Chu" dynasty in the years 402–404 CE. The root causes and ideological appeal of Tiansheng's rebellion are otherwise obscure.[75] The rebellion was substantially aided by forces from the Man people and the northern Wei regime, however, and a major threat. The court sent out one of the emperor's closest associates, Chen Xianda 陳顯達, who finally put down the rebellion after the better part of a year and several lengthy sieges of towns north of the Han River.[76]

Chen Xianda would become the linchpin of imperial strategy in the Xiangyang region for the next decade. He hailed from Jingkou 京口, a critical garrison town just east of the capital, but his early career was otherwise much like Zhang Jing'er's: raised in an immigrant military household of no pedigree, he developed close clientelage ties to Xiao Daocheng, fought against Prince Xiufan and Shen Youzhi, and received a large fief upon Daocheng's enthronement. However, Chen managed to cultivate close ties with Daocheng's son Xiao Ze, and therefore continued to be relied upon, and to prosper, through the critical transfer of power.[77] His battle-hardened leadership at Xiangyang in times of crisis and rebellion served an important role in the otherwise estranged relations between the garrison and the throne. Yet Chen apparently did not hold the local men in especially high regard; he is known to have slighted Cao Jingzong's military accomplishments in one campaign, and at another point complained that the men of Xiangyang were "difficult to rein in and use."[78]

Soon after Chen was reassigned in 490, the Xiangyang garrison once again experienced internal upheaval. The new local commander, Wang Huan

王奐, was a member of the eminent Langye Wang clan, a devout Buddhist who had already served in many high court and provincial offices. In a crisis reminiscent of the local civil war sparked by Prince Xiumao in 461, Wang Huan developed very troubled relations with the powerful adjutant in charge of the Man Pacification office, Liu Xingzu 劉興祖. Eventually, in a rather complex chain of events, Wang had the man executed against the express command of the court. The court sent forces out to seize Wang and his hotheaded son in the spring of 493, but some of the garrison troops allied with Wang and began a spirited defense. Others led by Pei Shuye, who had been sent out by the court to join Wang's retinue, eventually raised forces to attack and defeat them, cutting off Wang's head after he retreated to his inner quarters to meditate.[79] The situation exemplified the tension between weak court-appointed commanders and militant locals that was symptomatic of periods when relations between court and garrison were troubled and lacked trusted local brokerage.

Two important developments beyond Xiangyang further contributed to a sense of mounting crisis at this time. The most immediate problem was the Qi court's descent into an especially severe succession crisis. Xiao Ze's eldest son and heir, Xiao Changmao, had died in the early spring of 493, and the emperor himself died in early autumn, only barely managing a deathbed appointment of Changmao's son as his new heir. However, the real power behind the throne was Xiao Luan 蕭鸞, Xiao Ze's first cousin, who had been a favorite of Xiao Daocheng's and had built up a powerful clientelage network among the regime's most pugnacious generals. The following year saw the enthronement of two puppet emperors in rapid succession, and several bloody purges, before Xiao Luan formally took the throne as Emperor Ming 齊明帝(r. 494–498) toward the end of the year.

During this succession battle, the new inspector at Xiangyang was Xiao Zimao, the Prince of Jin'an 晉安王子懋. As a son of Xiao Ze he was a marked man, and naturally considered rebelling against Xiao Luan's ascent. However, the real power in Xiangyang was Chen Xianda, who had been returned to the Fan garrison in anticipation of an attack from the north. Chen had developed a tight alliance with Xiao Luan; he reported on Prince Zimao's plans, got him reassigned to Jiang province, and persuaded him to go peacefully, leaving several thousand military retainers behind. Before Chen returned to the capital he made sure to install as head of Yong province one of his own protégés, Cao Hu 曹虎, another low-status military man who had served in the area fighting Huan Tiansheng's rebellion.[80]

The second, less easily resolved threat to the Xiangyang region was the Tabgatch northern Wei regime, which was in the process of relocating its imperial capital to Luoyang, less than two hundred miles north of Xiangyang. The weakness of Xiao Luan's claim to the throne encouraged the powerful ruler of the northern regime, Yuan Hong 元宏 (Emperor Xiaowen 魏孝文帝, r. 471–499), to mount a southern campaign in the winter of 494–495. Their forces were soundly beaten by the governors of Nanyang and Xinye, Fang Boyu 房伯玉 and Liu Siji 劉思忌, and forced to retreat.[81] Yuan Hong planned a followup attack on the Xiangyang region to make up for this humiliation, and in late autumn of 497 assembled a force recorded as having had more than a million men, probably the largest campaign ever undertaken in the Xiangyang area up to this time (even accounting for some exaggeration). The Wei emperor personally led the campaign against Wan and Xinye, laying simultaneous sieges upon both cities. The governors and commanders of many towns and garrisons north of the Han River surrendered, and Wei forces advanced to the northern banks of the river, menacing the city of Xiangyang on the south bank. In the spring of 498 the holdout garrisons at Wan and Xinye finally fell to northern forces.[82]

Up until this point no substantive reinforcements had come from the court at Jiankang. Cao Hu's forces, poorly coordinated with his northern garrisons (and perhaps fearful of confronting the powerful Wei army), had never really advanced into the fray, and remained backed up against the Han River in the fort at Fan, across from Xiangyang. An expeditionary force of five thousand men finally arrived, led by Cui Huijing 崔慧景, another associate of Chen Xianda's, and Xiao Yan, a distant cousin of the ruling clan. They took over the Deng fortress, the seat of Jingzhao commandery just north of the river, and were promptly surrounded by Wei forces many times their number; the men inside were reportedly frightened for their lives. They finally managed to escape, and fled back across the river to the relative safety of Xiangyang. Cao Hu's forces at Fan retreated soon after.[83] As a result, the entire region north of the Han River came under control of the northern Wei regime, putting Xiangyang, and with it the domination of the entire central Yangzi region, at tremendous risk.[84]

Unfortunately, the situation at court had once again become dire, as Xiao Luan, now seriously ailing, decided to "protect" his legacy by executing all ten surviving sons and grandsons of Xiao Daocheng and Xiao Ze. Any prospect of further military response to the Wei threat had to await the death of the emperor, which finally came in the early autumn. Once his eldest living son, Xiao Baojuan 蕭寶卷 (posthumously known as the Marquis of Eastern Chaos, *Donghun Hou* 東昏侯), had secured the throne, further effort was made to retake the territory north of the Han River. Xiao Yan was made inspector of Yong province, and Chen Xianda, now the Defender-in-Chief for the entire regime, was once again appointed to come to the region's defense. In the spring of 499 he and Cui Huijing advanced from Xiangyang and besieged the fortress at Horse Camp (*maquan* 馬圈), just south of Wan, for forty days until it finally fell. They could not hold it long, however, for Wei forces, again led by Yuan Hong in person, rapidly moved into the region and forced them to retreat. Chen lost more than thirty thousand men in the campaign, and was demoted to become governor of Jiang province.[85]

The loss of the area north of the Han River was a critical development for numerous reasons besides the obvious strategic implications. One problem was that it caused a large number of people from north of the river to flee south, leading to a substantial population of transient and restless migrants clustered in the vicinity of Xiangyang town. The area was already notoriously unruly; the influx of more immigrants, especially from the Nanyang region, which had a reputation for fierce fighting men, would only have added to the tension.[86]

A more troubling problem was that the men of the Xiangyang region already had relatively weak ties to the Qi imperial house, which would have made a shift in allegiance to the newly proximate and obviously powerful Tabgatch regime an inviting prospect. An especially high-profile change in loyalty was made by Pei Shuye, whose close association with Xiao Luan had made him the nearest thing the Xiangyang region had to a local broker with the throne. As previously noted, however, Pei Shuye had rather limited roots in Xiangyang, and his attitude toward local men was little better than Chen Xianda's; at one point it is asserted that he actually feared Xiangyang fighting men for their toughness, and sought to avoid confronting them. Nonetheless, numerous men with roots in Xiangyang, such as Xi Fayou 席法友, wound up serving under him, as did men from other Hedong lineages.[87] When Xiao Luan died in 498, Shuye was commander of Yan province, on the Huai valley frontier; fearing for his life under Xiao Luan's successor, he threw his support over to the Tabgatch regime. All of Shuye's men followed him and emigrated to the north, where they gained high offices and became quite prosperous.

Stories of similar shifts in allegiance much closer to home can be found in the examples of Liu Siji and Fang Boyu during the 497–498 campaign. Liu Siji's biography holds him up as an exemplar of loyalty: captured and killed after refusing to surrender, he is recorded as having declared at the very end, "I'd rather be a southern ghost than a northern official," a standard declaration of steadfast loyalty that had long been put in the mouths of historical figures.[88] On the other hand, Fang Boyu is recorded as having been more pliant, eventually surrendering and being taken to the north. Northern accounts record that he held a succession of significant offices in the north; southern accounts, however, minimize his service, emphasizing that he declined most of the high positions he was offered, and pined to return south.[89] Either way, there can be little question that many local Xiangyang men would have done quite well had they taken their loyalties and their followers over to the northern regime at this time.

Fortunately for the Qi court, the powerful Wei emperor died of illness, putting an end to the Wei advance and giving the hard-pressed northwest frontier some breathing room. Nonetheless, the fact remained that Xiao Luan's regime had been unable to muster forces with anything like enough strength to ward off the powerful armies of the northern Wei, and the prospects were not likely to improve under his successor. Indeed, the depravity and infighting of the Qi court under Xiao Baojuan was so severe that everyone associated with it seems to have feared for their lives, and rebellions and executions became the norm for the next several years. The same forces of distrust and rebellion that had led to the executions of Liu Yuanjing and Zhang Jing'er also eventually undermined relations between the throne and Chen Xianda. Now in his early seventies, the old general spearheaded one of the most dire rebellions against Baojuan from his new base in Jiang province in the winter of 499–500, but it was quickly smothered, and Xianda was killed. His old compatriots in Xiangyang offered him no aid; accounts suggest that they saw little hope of him succeeding and, more to the point, he had always slighted them instead of cultivating their allegiance.[90] He paid dearly for it.

## CONCLUSION

The evidence from the late fifth century shows that Xiangyang was a highly fragmented society, populated by different social groups with only limited ties to one another: uneducated military men and nouveaux riches; reclusive and exclusive immigrant clusters; lineages that had relocated away to Jiangling or other regional centers but sometimes maintained ties in the area; and a variety of imperial agents, royal patrons, and their staffs. Limited evidence suggests that men were likely to affiliate with other members of these self-identified subgroups, and even nurtured a distinctive and separate ethos, especially in the case of immigrant clusters. Along with these familial, cultural, and quasi-ethnic divisions were the affiliational distinctions among participants in different local institutional hierarchies.

Much of this fragmentation was certainly not new. As we saw in chapter 2, the population of Xiangyang was already extremely diverse and heterogeneous early in the fifth century, and the groundwork for the exclusivity of settler groups was already being laid. There is evidence from that earlier period of some political cohesion, however, first in the period of Liu Daochan's administration, then more clearly in the response to Liu Jun's regime in the 450s. Yet, as Xiangyang men's choices in the civil war of 465–466 clearly show, and Cao Jingzong's actions in 483 further confirm, men's strongest identification came to be with their imperial patrons, the most likely sources for career advancement, wealth, and prestige. These vertical lines of affiliation appear to have exacerbated the tendencies toward fragmentation already present in local society. Success in the patronage system acted as a solvent, weakening the fragile local ties that had been able to form when the region was politically more isolated.

FOUR

# ZENITH, 500–530

By the end of the fifth century the Xiangyang area was militarily much more significant to the southern court than it had been a century earlier. Though this afforded local men the opportunity to serve the staffs of imperial princes, make connections with the Jiankang elite, and occasionally gain substantial wealth and status, they were still relatively marginalized. Neither local military families nor settlers from the north were particularly well established or well connected at court. The sole exception, Liu Shilong and his sons, had emigrated to the capital, and their role in local society was probably quite limited. Nonetheless, the perennial threat of civil war between potential successors to the throne always held out the promise of tremendous career advancement for any man who could back the right candidate at the right time.

It was just such a fortuitous conjunction of events that brought Xiao Yan 蕭衍 (464–549) to Xiangyang in 498 CE, and had him assuming the title of Emperor Wu of the Liang dynasty 梁武帝less than four years later. Xiao Yan took with him to court an entourage of men from the Xiangyang region who had backed his coup from the start; they were rewarded with valuable fiefs, high offices, and positions of power within the system of provincial military commands. As a result, many men from Xiangyang vaulted from mere provincial respectability to positions of wealth and power in the imperial system. Like Liu Yuanjing two generations before, their newfound resources allowed them to build impressive estates, develop higher-level social networks, and educate their descendents among the powerful and mighty at court. Yet this transition did not prove easy; only one local man is known to have taken full advantage of the opportunity, while a half-dozen others for whom we have a record left little to show for their success by the next generation.

Xiao Yan's dependence on the Xiangyang region also meant that more imperial largesse began to flow its way. The most impressive and well-documented period is the years 523–530, when the extensive literary salon surrounding Xiao Yan's third son, Xiao Gang, Prince of Jin'an 晉安王綱, settled in Xiangyang.

This eminent group of capital literati sought to use the power of the court to effect a cultural transformation in the region, especially through the patronage of Buddhist institutions. Though their efforts may have benefited and been welcomed by some local families, others were clearly much less accommodating, and the overall effects of the policy were largely superficial. The political and cultural tensions of this relationship are evident in collections of local lore, in tombs, in poetry, and in records of local festivals.

The unusual length of Xiao Yan's reign prolonged the influence of local men in imperial affairs, but their involvement also proved to be rather ephemeral. Meanwhile, real power in the Xiangyang garrison devolved to those men who were "left behind" by Xiao Yan's coup, as well as by the more civilian-oriented recruitment policies of Xiao Yan's offspring. These local men oversaw the operations of the garrison, recruited their own local clientelage networks into small fighting bands, and defending the region's stability and prosperity in their own interests. Their story will be taken up in chapter 5; in this chapter we will concentrate on Xiangyang's decades of power and influence in the early Liang period.

## XIAO YAN ASSEMBLES THE "XIANGYANG CLIQUE"

Xiao Yan was appointed to serve as head of the Xiangyang garrison in the autumn of 498. The nucleus of men he gathered around him during the next few years would play a significant role in the imperial system for two generations, so the nature of this early clique of supporters deserves close scrutiny. What is immediately apparent is that the group was of very mixed origins. Though it has been characterized as consisting primarily of men from Xiangyang,[1] the core Xiangyang clique was a blend of Xiangyang locals and men from elsewhere who had known Xiao Yan previously and followed him to his Xiangyang post. By the time Xiao Yan took the throne, however, he had enlarged this initial group of supporters with two other important groups: a clique from Jiangling, which included some Xiangyang natives, and a much larger cluster of important court figures, including several sons of Liu Shilong, who threw their support to Xiao Yan at a critical time. In other words, the course of the coup and its outcome does not suggest a top leadership within Xiao Yan's clique that closely identified itself with Xiangyang as an integral society per se, so much as a personal clique attached to Xiao Yan, for whom Xiangyang had served as an early staging area and contributed several significant members.

Xiao Yan was a distant member of the Qi imperial house, a fourth cousin of both Xiao Ze and Xiao Luan. He had served in minor princely staff positions, most importantly as an associate of Xiao Ziliang, Prince of Jingling 竟陵王子良, during the relatively peaceful Yongming period (483–493). Ziliang had collected around him a network of influential court figures who had a tremendous impact on the cultural life of the capital in the late Qi and early Liang periods.[2] Xiao Yan shifted to the entourage of Ziliang's younger brother Zilong and was stationed at Jiangliang in 493, thereby avoiding Xiao Luan's horrible purges of Prince Ziliang and many other court notables. Once the coast was clear, Xiao Yan, like many others, went into service to Xiao Luan's regime, working on the staff of his eldest son and heir apparent, Jin'an Prince Xiao Baoyi 晉安王寶義. He engaged in a minor campaign against Wei forces in Si province in 495, then was reassigned to serve under Cui Huijing in the campaign to defend Yong province in 497. After their defeat at the Deng fortress in the spring of 498, Xiao Yan was appointed inspector of Yong province the following autumn.

Xiao Yan's biography in the official *History of the Liang* attempts to highlight his military prowess in these campaigns, but there is some reason to be skeptical of the accounts. While his official annals have a heroic anecdote about his leading role in the defense of the Deng fortress, the parallel account in Cui Huijing's biography in the *History of the Southern Qi* merely mentions that he participated in the campaign, with an appointment not as a military commander, but an office in the heir-apparent's entourage. According to this version, when Wei forces surrounded the fortress, "Cui Huijing and the others took meals in bed, acted frivolously, and all showed an extremely fearful countenance." There is no suggestion that anyone engaged in any heroics.[3] Even more revealing is the indisputable fact that, when southern forces staged their most important counterattack, the Maquan campaign in spring of 499, the forces were led by Chen Xianda and Cui Huijing. Xiao Yan, though he was already serving as Yong inspector and regional commander-in-chief at that time, and should by rights have been leading this campaign, is not even recorded as having participated in it.[4] If he had actually demonstrated his military mettle in the 498 campaign, and received the inspectorate posting as a result, one would have expected him to have been involved in the followup effort. That he was not suggests that Xiao Yan, like many of his predecessors in the top position, was not considered a military leader; he could be compared to someone such as Wang Huan, the high-status court figure with little military experience who had experienced so much difficulty controlling the garrison a few years earlier.

Also following the pattern of his predecessors in the Xiangyang command, Xiao Yan brought with him a circle of close associates to advise him and help run the garrison. The most important was his mother's first cousin, Zhang Hongce 張弘策 (455–502) nine years older than Xiao Yan and a mentor and associate from his youth. Others were men from well-established court families who had been associated with the Xiao imperial clan for decades, such as Wang Mao 王茂 (457–516), of the eminent Taiyuan Wang lineage, who had served under Xiao Yan since 495 and was appointed to be his top military aide and governor of Xiangyang. Numerous men of lower-class provincial military families had also developed clientelage relations with Xiao Yan; this included men such as Lü Sengzhen 呂僧珍 (453–511) and Zheng Shaoshu 鄭紹叔 (462–507), both of whom, like Wang Mao, had impressed Xiao Yan when he had observed earlier military campaigns. They had been invited to follow him to Xiangyang and take posts on his personal staff, Lü as a retainer for his central military forces, Zheng as top official in the Man Pacification office.[5]

These outside appointments at the top of the command hierarchy were supplemented by some local appointments. An anecdote tells the story of Xiao Yan's quest for talented local men to flesh out his administration upon his arrival in Xiangyang. According to the tale, Xiao Yan called in Du Yun 杜惲, one of the Jingzhao cluster of relatively well-educated northern settler families, and asked him to make some recommendations. His first recommendation, Liu Qingyuan 柳慶遠 (458–515), was the nephew of Liu Yuanjing and first cousin to Liu Shilong; he had served at the capital (he perhaps grew up there) but was now back in his natal district serving as magistrate of Xiangyang county. According to the anecdote, Xiao Yan laughed and said, "I already know about him; I asked you for ones I don't know yet!"[6] Qingyuan was made lieutenant inspector (*biejia* 別駕), second in command in the civilian offices of the inspectorate. Wei Fang 韋放 (474–533), the eldest son of Du Yun's first cousin Wei Rui 韋叡 (441–520), was given the civilian office of recorder (*zhubu* 主簿), no doubt also on Yun's recommendation, but also to help gain the allegiance of his influential father.[7]

The most important local contact Xiao Yan would make, however, was with Cao Jingzong (456–508). Jingzong had been a leading figure in the local garrison even prior to his critical role in soothing the waters following Zhang Jing'er's execution in 483. His extensive family, including at least nine younger brothers, maintained a reputation for military valor and better-than-average links to the imperial system. Now in his early forties, Cao had served vigorously in the defense of Xiangyang in the preceding years, but he had been slighted by Chen Xianda and remained stationed locally. He and Xiao Yan became close associates, and Xiao Yan was a regular guest at Jingzong's estate west of town.[8] Gaining Cao Jingzong's confidence was pivotal to Xiao Yan's success, for Cao had the experience, the prestige, and the influence over the rank-and-file fighting men of the garrison to hold them together and bring them in under Xiao Yan's banner.

Another important source of local support for Xiao Yan was among the governors of outlying commanderies, each of whom controlled significant numbers of commandery troops, but who came from disparate backgrounds. Wei Rui, Wei Fang's father, was serving as governor of Shangyong commandery. According to his biography, he had sought out this position because he was "unwilling to be stationed far from his home province" in such an unsettled time; once there, "the plans of western men all turned to him."[9] This account no doubt experienced some embellishment, given the later prominence of Wei Rui's career, but there can be no doubt that Xiao Yan was pleased to see the two thousand troops and two hundred horses he brought with him. Liu Dan 柳惔 (461–507), the second son of Liu Shilong, was serving as Liang-Qin inspector, even though he had been raised entirely at Jiankang and mostly served at court; he also may have found it prudent to take a post far from the capital while court life was especially dangerous and unpredictable. By comparison, Kang Xuan 康絢 (462–517) had a very different background: despite a stint at the capital in his younger days, his family had controlled Huashan commandery as a near-private fief for generations, and he had been its ruler for many years. He was able to bring three thousand soldiers and two hundred and fifty horses to support Xiao Yan's rebellion, a major contribution. Other local fighting men of immigrant background, such as Chang Yizhi 昌義之 (d. 523) and Feng Daogen 馮道根 (463–520), were mere garrison commanders, with family lineages much less exalted and prosperous than Kang's.[10]

Xiao Yan developed one other significant personal tie to the Xiangyang area. His first wife had died soon after their arrival in Xiangyang; she had borne him three daughters but no sons (though he had adopted one). Following her death he accepted an offer from a go-between and took a fourteen-year-old local girl as a concubine. She was the daughter of Ding Zhongqian 丁仲遷, about whom virtually nothing else is known; no other members of the Ding family are noted in the historical literature.[11] This strongly suggests that her lineage did not have any members with high status or official positions in the court hierarchy; they may have been local merchants, or high-ranking men from the military garrison. Xiao Yan's rather unusual decision to develop such ties to a young woman of merely local prominence may have helped secure his local support base. By the beginning of the year 501 she was pregnant with Xiao Yan's first son (and eventual heir).

There is not a lot that would otherwise bind this motley collection of people together. With the exception of Zhang Hongce, the men of Xiao Yan's clique had developed personal ties to him quite recently, none more than a few years prior to his appointment in Xiangyang. Their family backgrounds varied from prestigious to obscure, their natal places were scattered across the map of the southern realm, and their career trajectories were extremely diverse. Even the men with roots in Xiangyang came from very different subgroups: families that had already emigrated to the capital, such as the Lius; locally powerful men from immigrant subgroups such as the Weis and the Kangs; and local men with prominent roles in the central garrison, such as Cao Jingzong. The single most striking common feature among the men of Xiao Yan's clique was their age: with the exception of Wei Rui, who was somewhat older, and his young sons, all of the other men were between the ages of thirty-six (Xiao Yan himself) and forty-seven (Lu Sengzhen) in 500 CE. In other words, all of them were born during the regime of Liu Jun and reached maturity in the late 470s to the early 490s, a relatively peaceful period in which Xiao Daocheng established his Qi regime and passed along his clientelage network fairly smoothly to his son Xiao Ze. They were a generation now at the peak of their careers, and they clearly intended to make something of themselves.

## THE "JIANGLING CLIQUE" AND THE JIANKANG COUP

Xiangyang was not the only regional garrison making preparations for armed conflict. Several failed efforts to overthrow Xiao Baojuan's regime had already been launched from other regions. At Jiangling, the military and civilian staff were also gearing up for the anticipated civil war, and their efforts offer illuminating parallels to the activities of Xiao Yan and his nascent organization at Xiangyang. The eventual union of the two groups proved essential to the success of their coup, and the two cliques, joined by the Jiankang elite, formed the three legs of the tripod that supported Xiao Yan's eventual elevation to the throne.

Initially, however, there was no reason to assume that Xiao Yan's group would take the leading role in a campaign against the throne. Indeed, Xiao Yan was not even the leader of his own clique; he had to defer to his elder brother, Xiao Yi 蕭懿, who held the very high central court position of Director of State Affairs (*shangshu ling* 尚書令). While Xiao Yi was at Yingcheng, at the confluence of the Han and Yangzi rivers, Xiao Yan sent his most trusted confidante, Zhang Hongce, to discuss the prospect of a rebellion, but Yi was unwilling. Two of their younger brothers, Xiao Wei 蕭偉 (475–533) and Xiao Dan 蕭憺 (477–522), came out to Xiangyang from the capital at this time, which greatly reassured Xiao Yan; he is recorded as having said, "I have no worries now," for it meant that his brothers were securely away from the capital and out of harm's way. Perhaps more importantly, they were men whom he could fully trust in command positions. Xiao Baojuan and his minions soon became suspicious of all of the brothers, and they had Xiao Yi killed in the early winter of 500. This was a significant tactical error, for it left Xiao Yan as the eldest surviving brother, and he quickly declared his intent to rebel against the throne in midwinter of 500–501.[12]

However ambitious Xiao Yan's group at Xiangyang may have been, they could not muster enough forces on their own to stage a successful coup. There was still a potentially serious threat from Luoyang, so a significant rear guard would have to be left at Xiangyang to ensure the area's loyalty and guard against the northern regime taking advantage of the diversion of so many troops and resources. As a result, they could not afford to fight very many other imperial garrisons on their way downriver to Jiankang; they needed allies. By far the most strategic ally was the garrison at Jiangling.

The Jiangling garrison had developed along similar lines to the Xiangyang one, but it was not on the northern frontier, and had a stronger civilian, and a correspondingly weaker military, component. At the time it was nominally headed by Xiao Baojuan's twelve-year-old younger brother, the Prince of Nankang, Xiao Baorong 南康王寶融 (488–502), but he was a figurehead, too young to play an effective role in a military campaign. Instead, the key players were the various members of his military and civilian staff at Jiangling, who had been recruited under circumstances almost as diverse as those at Xiangyang. The most critical men were ones with long experience at court who had come to the garrison with the prince, such as Xiahou Xiang 夏侯詳 (433–507), an older man with longstanding ties to Xiao Luan and his sons, or Liu Chen 柳忱 (470–511), another of the sons of Liu Shilong, who had been raised at court and served on the staffs of several imperial princes before being brought out to Xiangyang in Baorong's retinue. By far the most pivotal figure, however, was Xiao Yingzhou 蕭穎胄 (461–501), the son of a former Yong inspector and, like Xiao Yan, a distant (in his case, third) cousin of the deceased Xiao Luan. Also like Xiao Yan, Yingzhou was in his late thirties, had grown up at court, been close with Xiao Ze (also his third cousin), and served on numerous princely staffs, including that of Prince Ziliang in the early 490s. As the top staff member in Prince Baorong's military administration and the governor of Nan commandery, he worked to recruit local men under Baorong's nominal banner.[13]

For our purposes, two groups within Xiao Yingzhou's "Jiangling clique" stand out: men with primarily military backgrounds, and men from the Nanyang émigré cluster. Among the generals, the majority of the leading figures had a family tradition of military service and some roots in the Xiangyang region. Xi Chanwen 席闡文 (d. 503), for example, was from an immigrant household of Anding commandery, which had settled in the hills southwest of Xiangyang. He had served under Xiao Yingzhou's father at Xiangyang, and followed the son to Jiangling as his client back in the 480s. The background of Yang Gongze 楊公則 (444–505) was similar: classified under Tianshui commandery, along the Han River southeast of Yicheng town, he had served as a general and garrison commander under Chen Xianda in the late 480s, was sent to quell an uprising at Jiangling in 490, and stayed on as a local commandery governor. Cai Daogong 蔡道恭 (d. 504), one of the many sons of Cai Na, had been languishing in a Xiangyang provincial career until he followed Pei Shuye to Yan province in 497 and somehow got picked up by Prince Baorong and brought out to Jiangling. Not all of the Jiangling generals had Xiangyang origins; Deng Yuanqi 鄧元起 (458–506) hailed from an area just northwest of Jiangling, and was brought over to Xiao Yingzhou's cause from a posting in Ying province. Still, he too had served in the Xiangyang region at one time; military men in the western regions often moved around between various commands, and Xiangyang, being on the frontier with the north, had experienced more than its share of active fighting.[14]

By comparison, the civilian staff in Jiangling was dominated by the educated men of the Nanyang émigré cluster mentioned in the previous chapter. Though all claimed distant ancestral roots in the greater Xiangyang region, in practice they had all been born and raised in Jiangling society. Three key figures of this group were Zong Kuai (456–504), Liu Tan (442–504), and Yue Ai, all of whom had served members of the Qi imperial household at a high level. Zong, for example, had been amongst the literary figures in the capital salon of Prince Ziliang in the early 490s; Yue had been consulted by Xiao Ze, Emperor Wu, following a rebellion in Jiangling in 490, and was thereafter instrumental in rebuilding the Jing provincial administration. Their official biographies each give credit to Xiao Yingzhou for recruiting them to run the Jing provincial offices and serve on Prince Baorong's military staff, and they played a key strategic role in plotting the rebellion against Baojuan. They may also have played a direct material role; Zong Kuai and his family, for example, are recorded as having contributed two thousand *hu* of grain and two head of oxen to the rebellion.[15]

Both cliques were highly diverse collections of men, in both cases probably driven primarily by the desire to gain high titles from the elevation of their group's central figure. The Jiangling clique was overall much better connected to the imperial clan and the Jiankang court, but from a military standpoint the Xiangyang clique was more experienced and better prepared. The issue is highlighted by an anecdote regarding Xi Chanwen, who together with Liu Chen is portrayed as convincing Xiao Yingzhou to throw in his lot with Xiao Yan's Xiangyang group, rather than opposing them. Central to Xi's argument is that Xiao Yan was well prepared and ready to fight, and that "Jiangling generally fears Xiangyang men," a reflection of the reputation Xiangyang generals had at the time.[16] The fact that so many of the Jiangling clique's leading generals had roots in Xiangyang cannot have been reassuring in this regard, since they had the potential to be "brought over" to the other side through old personal ties.

The united front between the Xiangyang and Jiangling cliques in opposition to Xiao Baojuan's regime was quite effective. The Jiangling clique provided the legitimacy and the expertise in courtly affairs; the Xiangyang clique provided most of the striking force. Prince Baorong became the titular head of the alliance and, with the complicity of the Empress Dowager Xuande 宣德太后 (the widow of his first cousin, Wenhui heir Xiao Changmao), gained appointment as prime minister. He promptly appointed Xiao Yan as Zhengdong ("invades the east") general; Xiao Yan's forces advanced to the critical juncture point of Yingcheng in mid-spring of 501, joined forces with Jiangling troops led by Yang Gongze and Deng Yuanqi, and began to besiege the town (see Map 4). By the next month Prince Baorong took the title of Emperor, and his administration at Jiangling was declared the "Western Court" (*xitai* 西臺), inaugurating a new reign title of Zhongxing (中興, "Restoration"). Accompanying these moves was a raft of advancements in the titles of all participants, with the highest imperial titles going to those closest to Prince Baorong and Xiao Yingzhou.[17]

In the hindsight of imperial history, as well as in more recent accounts, the merger of these two cliques is portrayed as a propaganda front for Xiao Yan to gain legitimacy and ease the removal of Baojuan before usurping the throne himself. At the time, however, the Jiangling clique surely did not intend this result. Xiao Yingzhou was the equal of Xiao Yan in terms of his birth, his connections, and his success in building a coalition of supporters. His role close to the young new emperor left him in a very good position to control the destiny of the Qi imperial house; he may have hoped to engineer his own usurpation at some point in the future. Other members of the Jiangling clique were not close to Xiao Yan and could not have counted on doing as well under a regime led by him as one led by Xiao Yingzhou. It makes the most sense to presume that they intended the western regime to maintain control of the

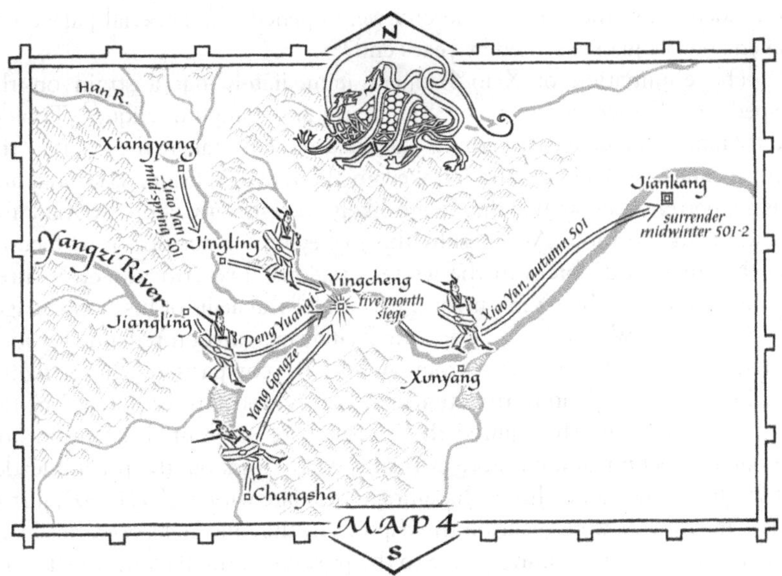


Map 4. Military campaign of Xiao Yan, 501 CE

throne. This would mean that men in both cliques must have anticipated a potentially destructive competition between Xiao Yan and Xiao Yingzhou once their immediate goal was accomplished, and would have positioned themselves accordingly.

Even with the merger of these two powerful groups, the progress of the coup against Baojuan was not assured. The Yingcheng garrison, which stood astride the only route to the capital, remained for several months in the hands of men loyal to Baojuan, and some of the western coalition argued against Xiao Yan's strategy of besieging the town, fearing that the rebellion would lose momentum. After the decisive defeat of relief forces sent up from Jiankang, however, the Yingcheng garrison fell in early autumn, and Xiao Yan and his forces, under the primary command of Wang Mao and Cao Jingzong, moved rapidly downriver, gaining allies as they went. The key to a quick end to the conflict now turned on gaining support from a significant faction of the capital elite. Xiao Yan, fortunately, had a well-developed clique of friends and supporters at court from his days in the salon of Xiao Ziliang, including such accomplished and highly regarded figures as Shen Yue, Fan Yun, and Ren Fang, as well as two more of the ubiquitous sons of Liu Shilong. Xiao Yan's connections no doubt were important, but the capital literati had also long since shown themselves to be quite unselective in their acceptance of candidates for the throne, so long as they offered relative security and plentiful patronage jobs. By midwinter the main garrisons guarding Jiankang had surrendered and the gates of the city were opened; the imperial palace was taken and Baojuan executed by year's end.[18]

The elimination of Xiao Baojuan immediately put a strain on the expedient alliance between the Xiangyang and Jiangling cliques. Though Xiao Yan commanded the armies that had actually taken the capital, the entire campaign had been undertaken in the name of Prince Baorong, and his supporters back at Jiangling were likely to resist any effort by Xiao Yan to usurp his position. As a result, the jockeying for position now focused on the "rearguard" forces in the western regions. Two critical factors tilted the advantage in Xiao Yan's favor. First, under the aegis of his two younger brothers, Xiao Wei and Xiao Dan, the Xiangyang garrison remained stoutly defended and relatively free from attack. By comparison, the Jiangling garrison was immediately threatened by a rebellion farther upriver, in the Badong region, which required the diversion of substantial attention and resources. Second, and far more critically, Xiao Yingzhou, the pivotal leader of the Jiangling clique, died at Jiangling in the late winter of 501–502, just as Xiao Yan's forces were securing the capital. In the official account his death is blamed on his "nervousness" due to the pressure of the Badong attacks, but Xiao Yingzhou was only forty years old and no stranger to such pressures. It is unlikely that his well-timed demise was a coincidence.[19]

With Xiao Yingzhou's death, the Jiangling coalition lost cohesion and was rapidly absorbed under Xiao Yan's banner. Xiahou Xiang led the remains of the Jiangling administration to submit to Xiao Wei, who then sent Xiao Dan down to take over direct control of the garrison. Prince Baorong was brought down to Jiankang to go through the motions of ceding the throne to Xiao Yan by the end of the spring; Xiao Yan then took the imperial title as Emperor Wu of the new Liang dynasty, and renamed the reign year Tianjian (天監, "supervised by Heaven"). His followers had already begun undertaking the grisly but by now widely accepted practice of killing all the male relatives of the former regime that might prove a problem, namely all of Xiao Baojuan's brothers, the young sons of Xiao Luan. Poor Prince Baorong, a mere fourteen years old, was duly executed the month after he ceded the throne.[20]

## XIANGYANG MEN AT THE CAPITAL

In the first few years of Xiao Yan's reign the ad hoc pyramid of his personal clientelage network mushroomed into an enormous and complex web of relationships between men of very diverse backgrounds, which was further stratified by the granting of valuable inheritable fiefs and high-level and very remunerative imperial offices. The initial division between the Xiangyang, Jiangling, and Jiankang cliques had some staying power (as Yao Siliang testifies by his organization of the official *History of the Liang*),[21] but once Xiao Yan had the throne and the men of these groups were thrown together into different institutions and provincial commands the structure of the network would have become far more complicated. The historical literature rarely identifies critical relationships at these middle and lower levels of imperial administration. However, we can map what men from Xiangyang actually did with their newfound wealth, prominence, and connections, and thereby gain some sense of the impact of this coup on their lives.

The most immediate reward men received for their association with Xiao Yan was a noble title and a salary-fief, which, unlike high office, was inheritable by subsequent generations and could serve as a permanent basis for comfort and status. Eighteen men received the title of Marquis (*hou* 侯) or Lord (*gong* 公) and a substantial fief that paid the tax revenue from one thousand households or more. In this elite group, the two largest rewards went to Xiao Yingzhou (posthumously) and Xiahou Xiang; below them were men from the Xiangyang and Jiangling cliques (seven men and three men, respectively) who had been on the downriver campaign, and men at Jiankang who had thrown support to Xiao Yan when he first arrived (six men). Of these eighteen men, only three had substantial local roots in Xiangyang: Cao Jingzong, Liu Qingyuan, and Yang Gongze (though he was at Jiangling when the coup began). Xiangyang locals were much better represented in a lower tier of men who gained lesser titles and fiefs worth several hundred households, including Cai Daogong, Xi Chanwen, Wei Rui, Kang Xuan, Chang Yizhi, and Feng Daogen.[22] This distribution suggests that most men from Xiangyang lacked the leverage to receive the greatest rewards once Xiao Yan was on the throne, and that their loyalty and service were purchased for relatively less than that demanded by high court officials, who had otherwise contributed relatively little to the actual fighting.

The official positions that men from Xiangyang gained bear this out as well. The highest positions in the central court were reserved for members of the imperial clan, or men from long-standing court clans. Men from the western regions were all posted to positions in the provinces, as military commanders-in-chief or commandery governors, positions that were well remunerated and prestigious, but also bore substantial command authority and personal risk. Most of the men from Xiangyang were stationed, not in their home region, but in the Huai valley commands of Yu and Xu provinces, and they soon became intimately involved in leading the defense of Xiao Yan's regime against an invasion from the northern Wei regime in 503–504, and in their own counterattack over the following several years. Their performance in these campaigns resulted either in death (in the case of Xi Chanwen, Cai Daogong, and Yang Gongze), or in further glory and a corresponding improvement in their fief income (in the case of Cao Jingzong, Chang Yizhi, Feng Daogen, and especially Wei Rui).

These men were intermittently resident at the capital when they were not in imperial service in the provinces, and the wealth and respectability that came with well-paying official posts and noble titles was quickly channeled into the development of their estates at Jiankang. Wei Rui's capital estate was large enough to house all of his extended household, including his four sons, some nephews, and all of their grandchildren.[23] Cao Jingzong is known to have had at least three estates: his old one west of Xiangyang; a substantial one at Xiakou while he served as inspector of Ying province (502–505); and an extensive one at Jiankang, which had its own hunting grounds, hundreds of concubines, and every manner of luxury.[24]

The process of fitting in to Jiankang society was much less straightforward, however. The surviving anecdotes about Cao Jingzong, in particular, demonstrate the striking disjuncture between his code of behavior and what was considered appropriate at court. For example, though Cao was literate, he is described as a sloppy scholar, too proud to ask others for help with his writing; instead, he would simply invent characters for himself. His biography is especially critical of his failure to control his subordinates, an area where some other men from Xiangyang are commended. Cao's men are reported to have plundered valuables and violated women as they came downriver to the capital in 501, and been oppressive and corrupt while they were in command of Ying province in subsequent years. Cao is described as sharing these characteristics: he enriched himself from the public purse, and failed to support his fellow generals in several instances during the campaigns of 504–507. His lack of discipline as a commander is correlated to his dissolute behavior while at the capital, where he reportedly demonstrated an enormous appetite for women, liquor, and music. He threw parties at his capital estate that involved lecherous affairs, as well as some sort of activity that involved wild screaming in order to drive away evil spirits, a practice his guests apparently did not really understand. Cao's drunkenness also caused him to act inappropriately at imperial functions; only the kindly tolerance of Xiao Yan for his old friend allowed him to get away with it.[25]

Cao was by far the most prominent and best remunerated of Xiangyang fighting men in the early Liang period, and one suspects that he became something of a lightning rod for negative tales that circulated among the disdainful literati of the capital. The biographies of other Xiangyang men contrast with Cao's by being shorter and much less colorful, thus less critical; however, their roots in a largely illiterate and martial-oriented culture are always noted. Chang Yizhi, for example, is recorded as having been "unable to recognize more than ten characters," but is nonetheless praised for being able to keep his men loyal and well behaved. Feng Daogen, nicknamed the "Great Tree General," also did not study and was only marginally literate; he too is commended for winning his troops' loyalty and good behavior, and for his plain and frugal lifestyle. Kang Xuan is noted as having been tall, imposing, and, "despite his career as an illustrious official, always practiced the martial arts"; his close bonds with Xiao Yan are exemplified by their joint participation in a palace competition of shooting from horseback, in which Kang excelled. Yang Gongze, alone of this group, is noted for loving his letters, and "always had a scroll in his hand."[26]

There is little evidence from these biographies that Xiangyang men passed along a social network or other privileges to family members. Some of the nine brothers of Cao Jingzong, for example, are noted in passing as local generals or aides in the Xiangyang-area staff, positions not sharply different from what they otherwise might have attained on their own.[27] None of these men's heirs warranted an official biography; even Cao Jingzong's son Jiao 曹皎, who would have inherited a large estate, high noble title, and a lush fief of two thousand households, failed even to buy himself a reputation worthy of record, much less earn one. In other words, the men from Xiangyang who made the leap into the court nobility in Xiao Yan's wake did not manage to raise their offspring in such a way as to command the respect of the court literati who compiled imperial history.

The exception to this pattern is Wei Rui, who, like Liu Shilong in the previous generation, was able to take advantage of the opportunity his newfound wealth and prominence at Jiankang offered him. He is noted for devoting his time and resources while at the capital to the classical education of his offspring. His elder two sons had personally participated in the coup effort of 501–502; his eldest, Fang, was part of the downriver campaign, while his second son, Zheng 韋正, stayed behind in Xiao Wei's local administration. Both men were soon at the capital in typical entry-level court offices such as court gentlemen for the imperial secretariat (*shang-shu lang* 尚書郎); Fang soon joined the personal staff of Xiao Yan's third son, Prince Gang. They also developed good relationships with men from eminent court clans; Fang, for example, was very close to Zhang Shuai 張率 (of Wujun), who was also a part of Prince Gang's entourage, and the two men intermarried their children. Meanwhile, Rui's younger two sons, Leng 韋稜 and An 韋黯, were especially noted for their scholarship in classics, histories, and Buddhist materials. Wei Fang's eldest son Can 韋粲 (495–549) also followed in the footsteps of his father, beginning his career on the personal staff of Prince Gang, in whose service he would remain for over two decades.[28]

Wei Rui's success in establishing his descendents must be seen as a combination of several factors. The single most important factor was his good foresight (and good luck) in backing Xiao Yan at the right time, which opened up opportunities that he never would have had otherwise. His education must be considered a secondary factor, which only became important once these opportunities were available. According to Rui's biography, his parents had given their sons a classical education, but it only gained them low-level careers in the service of the local province. Immediately following the coup itself, Rui's education was still not a very decisive factor; men with much less education wound up with much higher offices and larger fiefs, at least initially. Over the longer term, however, Rui's education seems to have placed him in a good position to take advantage of modest fortune and connections, better than an utter parvenu such as Cao Jingzong, or even a respected but uneducated general such as Feng Daogen. By acculturating his sons to the capital milieu, Wei Rui rapidly developed a social network with high-status capital clans that was quite beyond the reach of most other men from Xiangyang.

A possible third factor was Wei Rui's surname, which had a fine history in the late Han, Wei, and Jin periods and was conceivably of some use in gaining entry into the Jiankang social milieu. However, there is good reason to think this was not that important. Men from the equally eminent Jingzhao Du surname who attached themselves to Xiao Yan's campaign did not see the same career advancement, nor did other lineages of the Wei surname who did not participate. The Wei surname was not significant at the southern court at the time, and there is no reason to think that its prominence in the north made much difference. In fact, Wei Rui's descendents later showed themselves to be wholly unaware of their distant ancestors, suggesting that family ancestry and genealogy was not a significant part of their campaign to raise their status.[29]

Perhaps the most interesting case is that of Liu Qingyuan, who started off with much greater advantages than did Wei Rui: in addition to his education and early personal ties at the capital, he had close male relatives (the sons of his first cousin Shilong) who were deeply networked with the capital elite and held important offices. Qingyuan also played a much more pivotal role in Xiao Yan's coup than did Rui, and as a result was one of the best remunerated of the Xiangyang men. Nonetheless, his career, though admirable, is not particularly impressive. His mother died soon after the coup, compelling him to leave office and "retire" to Xiangyang. In 505 he accepted appointment as the commander-in-chief of the Xiangyang garrison and Yong provincial inspector, taking over that portfolio from Xiao Yan's younger brother Xiao Wei, who had held it ever since the coup. Yet even though Xiangyang was a critical frontier area, there is no evidence that Qingyuan was called upon to contribute to the military campaigns of the next several years. He finally came back downriver in 508, accepted a command position in the Huai valley, and lived in the capital for a few years. He was eventually reappointed to the Xiangyang command in 513, where he served for two more years until his death.[30]

What stands out about Liu Qingyuan's career is that he made no effort to ingratiate himself or his children with the Jiankang elite; he did not even bring his eldest son Jin 柳津 down to the capital with him, instead leaving him behind at Xiangyang. This is surprising, given that the reputation of Qingyuan's uncle Yuanjing and his first cousin Shilong had been carried on with great success by Shilong's sons. By comparison, Liu Jin, who did not come to court until more than a decade after his father died, is noted as being "deficient in refined traditions" and actively resistant to learning his letters.

One possible explanation for this response is suggested by an anecdote in Liu Jin's official biography. "[Liu Jin] was advised to accumulate books, and Jin said: 'I often invite a Daoist priest (*daoshi* 道士) to [recite] verses to expel demons (*gui* 鬼). How could I employ the names of these demons?' "[31] The method of expelling demons would have involved inscribing characters in petitions, or as a sort of talisman, both common practices in the Celestial Masters tradition and its successors.[32] By the early sixth century, devotees of the newer Lingbao and Shangqing orders of Daoism, which were popular at Jiankang, had come to look down upon the old-fashioned Celestial Masters tradition as decadent and unlettered, the preserve of lower-class provincials.[33] The court had also begun to adopt increasingly repressive measures against certain Daoist activities in its effort to promote a more orthodox Buddhism.[34] If Liu Jin, and perhaps also his father, were devotees of the Celestial Masters religious order, it might help to explain why they chose to remain aloof from capital affairs at this time. Their example demonstrates that not all local men who had the means and the opportunity chose to acculturate to Jiankang society; some chose to stay resolutely provincial.

The relationship of these men to the court at Jiankang suggests that, while some men of Xiangyang were able to leverage the favor they had received from the new emperor into a personal network among the capital elite, this was the exception, not the rule. For Cao Jingzong, it is doubtful whether he had an adequate cultural background to do so; he was very much the product of the military garrison and its rough code of behavior and, in his late forties, he does not seem to have been much inclined to change his ways. In the case of Liu Qingyuan, however, the situation appears to have been one of choice, a deliberate effort to resist the culture and politics of the capital. In any case, the fact that so few Xiangyang men developed their offspring's influence at court meant that, as the founding generation aged and died, there were relatively few to take their place. After Qingyuan's death, Wei Rui was nominated to take over the Xiangyang garrison, but after his death in 520 CE there were virtually no members of the founding generation remaining in imperial service. Chang Yizhi, who died in 523, was perhaps the last of them.

## XIANGYANG LOCAL LORE: THE EVIDENCE FROM BAO ZHI

It was in that same year, 523 CE, that Prince Gang, the second son born to Xiao Yan and Consort Ding, was sent out to command the Xiangyang garrison. His seven-year tenure in Xiangyang was a pivotal period in the relationship between the region and the court. Had it followed the pattern of many previous interactions, such as Xiao Changmao's tenure early in the Qi regime, it would have been an opportunity for the next generation of the imperial lineage to associate with the fighting men of the region, take on some new blood as personal clients, and bring them back to court. Though some patronage of this sort was engaged in, it does not appear to have been the focus of Prince Gang and his entourage. Instead, they sought to use imperial patronage to try to inject some of their own cultural priorities into what had traditionally been seen as an unruly and uncivilized, yet strategically critical part of the empire. This cultural campaign included political and financial sponsorship of commemorative stelae and Buddhist temples, and literary efforts to represent the Xiangyang region in a more "refined" manner. It also included efforts by at least one man among the prince's entourage to collect and record local stories. Finally, it involved the active suppression of local competitive spectacles that were considered too militarily oriented.

Xiao Yan had erected around his young son an entourage of extremely eminent scholars to give him every cultural advantage that money and prestige could buy. This group was headed by men of Xiao Yan's own generation, such as

Xu Chi 徐摛 (473–549) and Zhang Shuai 張率 (475–527), as well as slightly younger men, such as the Liu brothers, Xiaoyi 劉孝儀 (b. 487) and Xiaowei 劉孝威 (b. 495), all some of the capital's leading literary figures. The group also included Yu Jianwu 庾肩吾 (487–551), who had been part of the "Nanyang cluster" in Jiangling; his father had been a well-known recluse there, while his brother had been actively courted by Xiao Yingzhou and later came downriver to serve in the entourage of Prince Gang's elder brother, the Zhaoming Crown Prince, Xiao Tong 昭明太子統. Prince Gang's entourage also included two of Wei Rui's sons, Wei Fang and Wei Leng, and Fang's son Can, all of whom had served intermittently since the group was first put together when the prince was only six years old. By the time this entourage came out to Xiangyang, its leading men ranged in age from thirty to fifty-five and had been associated with one another for almost fifteen years; their charge, the prince himself, was only twenty years old.[35]

The presence of such an eminent group of capital literati in Xiangyang means that we have more information about the town from this brief period than any other. Previous records of Xiangyang area lore were highly antiquarian and nostalgic. The most important work in the genre was written in the late fourth century by Xi Zuochi 習鑿齒, one of the last representatives of the old late-Han gentry class still resident in the area. His work focuses on stories about men from the late Han and Three Kingdoms period, showing very little engagement with the Xiangyang of his own time.[36] Several further local history compilations were drafted in the Song period, but they were probably commissioned by imperial agents based in Jiangling and written by men with little or no direct experience of the Xiangyang region. One such work, the *Record of South Yong Province* (*Nan Yongzhou ji* 南雍州記), was compiled by Guo Zhongchan 郭仲產, who served under the auspices of Song Prince Yixuan and assembled several such local history works for provinces under the prince's military jurisdiction while he was the commander at Jiangling (444–454). Not surprisingly, the surviving fragments of this text indicate that it consisted mostly of material excerpted from Xi Zuochi and other sources, and added little new information.[37] When Li Daoyuan 酈道元, a northerner, compiled his *Annotations to the Classic of Waterways* (*Shuijing zhu* 水經注) around 520, he was dependent on these sorts of written materials for information about the Xiangyang area; as a result, the chapter of his work on the Mian/Han River as it flows through Xiangyang contains only a single anecdote dealing with any event after the year 420 CE, despite the great transformation and rising influence of the region in the intervening century.[38]

There is no reason to believe that this antiquarian history tradition was of much significance to the new Xiangyang elite, most of whom were either immigrants from elsewhere, or illiterate, or both. For example, one of the most towering figures in Xiangyang's earlier history was Yang Hu 羊祜, under whose guidance (in the years 269–278) the area became a bulwark of the Jin dynasty and the launching pad for the successful conquest of the south in 280. Yang Hu had been celebrated locally for his benevolent and capable governance, but by far the most famous tale about him addressed his desire for eternal fame:

> Hu delighted in mountains and rivers, and when the weather was fine he would have to go to the Xian hills 峴山 to drink and recite poetry all day without tiring. Once he sighed mournfully and said to his Retainer-Court Gentleman Zou Zhan 鄒湛 and others, "So long as there has been the universe there has been this mountain. Many have been the worthy, perceptive, outstanding gentlemen, such as myself and you all, who have climbed it and gazed afar. They have all passed away and are unheard of—it makes one grieve. If I am known a hundred years' hence, my spirit will still climb this mountain." Zhan said, "Your Excellency's virtue crowns the four seas and your leadership is the successor to the sages of old. Such reputation and admiration will be transmitted onwards like this mountain. When it comes to people like myself, then of course it will be as you have said."
>
> [After his death] the people of Xiangyang erected a shrine and memorial stele at the place where Hu always relaxed, and made offerings to it at the proper times. None who looked upon his stele failed to shed tears, and because of this {his successor} Du Yu named it the "Stele of Falling Tears" (*duolei bei* 墮淚碑).[39]

This stele subsequently became one of the best-known commemorative stelae in the entire Chinese tradition.[40] Knowing this, the following sardonic anecdote from Zhang Jing'er's official biography would have carried tremendous punch:

> [Zhang Jing'er] wished to relocate Yang [Hu's] "Stele of Falling Tears" and build a platform at the spot. Some remonstrated, saying: "It would not be proper to relocate the evidence of Grand Tutor Yang's virtue." Jing'er said, "Who is this Grand Tutor? I don't know."[41]

Even though this anecdote may very well be an invention, it demonstrates a perception that men of Zhang Jing'er's ilk knew absolutely nothing about the history and cultural traditions of their homeland, not even from local stelae, much less from dusty scrolls in some far-off imperial archive. The presumption is corroborated by the fact that the Stele of Falling Tears had fallen into substantial disrepair by the sixth century. It was only re-erected and reinscribed in 544 CE under the patronage of an imperial prince, using the expert knowledge of Liu Zhilin 劉之遴 (479–550 CE), one of the Nanyang cluster of relatively conservative scholars for whom antiquarian objects such as Yang Hu's stele were the focus of fervent ideological attention.[42] The Xiangyang area apparently produced no one with such preoccupations.

The influx of literary scholars under Prince Gang, however, led to a revived interest in the region's cultural history. Bao Zhi 鮑至, one of Prince Gang's entourage, undertook to write an updated version of Guo Zhongchan's *Record of South Yong Province*, which was now several generations old.[43] Though Bao's work would have compiled a good deal of older material, it was not merely an antiquarian record; its surviving fragments show that it contained substantial new material based on men and events from the late fifth and early sixth centuries.[44] By this time the area was of much greater significance to the reigning dynasty than it had been when the earlier edition was compiled. Furthermore, unlike Guo, Bao actually spent considerable time in Xiangyang, which would have improved both his motivation and his ability to gather new information.

Bao Zhi's specific and often quite sympathetic interest in the Xiangyang of his own time is exemplified by the amount of detail he provides about Xiangyang's official district (*jincheng* 金城), where Prince Gang's entourage spent much of their time. Bao discusses the buildings of the Inspectorate Academy (*cishi yuan* 刺史院), including one made of "exceptionally rare and pure" clay, which was called the "Eminent Studio" (*gao zhai* 高齋). Several other buildings surrounded it, such as the "Lower Studio" (*xia zhai* 下齋), a grand and imposing building where the Inspectors heard court cases. Behind the Eminent Studio was another hall and a servant's quarters, all of which were along the edge of a pond with a pavilion in the middle of it, called the "Pavilion for Delighting in Music" (*yuexi tai* 樂熹臺). South of this compound was another studio, made of chestnut wood, which had been a favored resting place for Xiao Yan while he was the local commander; by Bao Zhi's day it was claimed that multicolored clouds had coiled around it like a dragon at that time, presaging Xiao Yan's flight to the imperial throne. Several sources indicate that Crown Prince Tong also spent time there, a fact not attested to in official histories. By the early Tang period it was further asserted that the Crown Prince compiled his famous *Selections of Refined Literature* (*Wen xuan* 文選) there, though it is far more likely that the work was done at his tremendous library in the Eastern Palace at Jiankang.[45]

Bao Zhi's most interesting and involved tales show a special preoccupation with the supernatural efficacy of certain local places, a theme which, though not unknown in prior local works, had not been their primary concern. The remains of Xi Zuochi's work, for example, have only a few tales which mention supernatural events, and these tend to be brief, and demarcated as legendary, using introductory statements such as, "The town elders say . . ." as if to distance the author from the veracity of the tale.[46] Bao Zhi's tales, by comparison, are both more detailed and more straightforward about the power of local spirits. The following account of the Deer Gate Temple illustrates the distinctive nature of Bao Zhi's contribution, as well as the accretive effect of two centuries of updates to the account of a single location:

> The gate of the Suling Hill Temple in Xiangyang has two stone deer flanking it, so they are called the Deer Gate Hills. Mr. Xi's *Record* says: "Xi Yu served as Palace Attendant and followed [Later Han Emperor] Guangwu in touring Liqiu (ca. 28 CE). Yu and Guangwu together saw the spirit of the Suling Hills in a dream, and thus [he] was ordered to build the temple." Guo Zhongchan's *Record* says: "The pair of deer are erected as if in a fight. Woodsmen often pass beneath them, and sometimes do not see the deer; they thereby know they have a magic aura."
>
> At the beginning of the Liang Tianjian era (502–519), a man of Banghu village was hunting in these meadowlands and saw two huge deer, different from ordinary deer, so he rode his horse in pursuit. The deer plunged through a mountain torrent and headed directly towards Suling. The man chased the deer to the spirit place, then lost their location, only seeing the two stone deer in front of the temple. The hunter figured it was just that those two deer had been transformed, so he returned. That night he dreamed he saw a man wearing a single cloth turban and yellow cloth riding breeches, who said: "An envoy sent me to tend the horses; why did you chase them off? You are shameless beyond all; if you encounter misfortune, how can you expect to be saved?"[47]

The part of the account attributed to Xi Zuochi is quite condensed compared to other quotes we have of his version of the tale, but captures the essentially straightforward reporting of events that characterizes Xi's style.[48] We have no other version of Guo's version, but it apparently offered the suggestion of an active supernatural presence at the shrine.[49] Bao Zhi's tale about the hunter from Banghu village, by comparison, spins out a lively and detailed narrative story, marked by dramatic description of action and direct use of dialogue, far different from that of his predecessors.

The illustration of supernatural efficacy through the means of detailed, colorful storytelling is even more clearly demonstrated in the following striking anecdote:

> A village west of the Han River in Xiangyang has a shrine named "Lord of Local Earth [*tudi zhu* 土地主]." The gentleman of the

> headquarters truly think it has spiritual efficacy (*lingyan* 靈驗). In the last years of the Qi Yongyuan period (499–501) the Governor of Fengyi, Gong Shuang 龔雙, did not believe in spirits. He went to see this shrine and ordered men to burn it down. Suddenly a whirlwind twisted the fire and two things bulged out; they turned into two blue birds and entered Gong Shuang's two eyes. His eyes were pained by this, and his whole body had a vigorous fever; by the next day he was dead.[50]

This tale notably does not rely in any way on the antiquarian tradition of prior local histories; the shrine is an ordinary popular shrine, not linked to any historical event, nor created by imperial commission, nor noted for its connection to an elite local lineage. The emphasis here is on the immediate, contemporary power of local spirits. The timing of the tale, set during the period when Xiao Yan was plotting his coup, may not be a mere coincidence; we can only wonder whether Gong Shuang might have been an opponent of Xiao Yan's, making the tale a metaphorical comment on local politics whose significance has since been lost.

Another tale of ghostly retribution addresses the well-established tension between locals and the staffs of imperial princes:

> East of the road outside the south gate of Xiangyang's official district there is the office of subordinate officials (*canzuo jie* 參佐廨). An old legend says that it is quite evil, and that those who approach it, if they do not die, will surely take ill. When the Liang Zhaoming Crown Prince [Xiao Tong] came to the province he gave it to the garrison subordinate Lü Xiuqian 呂休蒨. Xiuqian often slept in the north end of the audience hall, and a ghost took hold of him so that he fell to the floor. He awoke after a long while. Soon afterwards Xiuqian committed a transgression and was ordered to commit suicide.[51]

The characterization of the hall for subordinates as "evil" clearly demonstrates local prejudice against the men brought in by the newly appointed commander, men who might block personal access to a potential patron and prevent the development of clientelage ties. The tale is immediately followed by another which describes a much more elaborate "haunting" of the Xiangyang garrison offices with lengthy and sustained storytelling skill. In this tale, an otherwise unknown scion of the imperial house, Xiao Teng 蕭騰, comes to serve as local commander and is repeatedly troubled by a mysterious specter who claims to be Zhou Yu 周瑜, the heroic general of the Three Kingdoms state of Wu. Xiao Teng tries various methods of eliminating this pesky spirit, including sending twenty of his retainers after it with swords, and resorting to exorcism, before finally having a Daoist priest set up an altar for performing libations and expulsions of spirits. The episode greatly amuses and flummoxes Xiao Teng's highly impressionable concubines, leading a local man on Teng's staff, Wei Yanbian 韋言辯 (no doubt one of the Jingzhao Weis) to make a wisecrack about the ghost's foolishness.[52] The entire sequence emphasizes the power of local spirits, and their incomprehensibility to the agents from the capital who come to govern the area. Whether or not these spirits are "foolish" (perhaps a reflection of Wei Yanbian's failure to understand locals any longer, once he started working for the prince), they have the ability to pester, bewilder, and outwit the authorities sent out from the capital and, in the case of Lü Xiuqian, actually bring about their death. In this case, just as in the exorcisms performed by Liu Jin, only the local Daoist libationer seems to have been able to intercede successfully.

Bao Zhi's tales reflect a local tradition that was preoccupied with the supernatural efficacy of local places, a power that had the ability to frustrate the influence of imperial agents. The pattern of antagonism between court appointments and men from the garrison was long-standing; what is new here is the written record of how this antagonism was mediated through stories of the supernatural. Though seen through the literary filter of a court-based outsider, these tales have a far more authentic ring to them than any prior evidence of Xiangyang lore.

## XIANGYANG ICONOGRAPHY: THE EVIDENCE FROM LOCAL TOMBS

The stories recorded by Bao Zhi, along with the biography of Liu Qingyuan's son Jin, suggest that the belief in evil spirits and ghosts, and the importance of local Daoist practitioners in performing appropriate intercessions with them, was an important element of Xiangyang local culture. Further evidence for this comes from two tombs excavated from the area, one near the old county seat of Rang 穰, west of Xinye (near modern Dengxian 鄧縣), and the other just west of Xiangyang town itself (at modern Jiajiachong 賈家沖). Though neither tomb can be dated precisely, stylistic evidence suggests that both were built in the late fifth or early sixth centuries, with the Dengxian tomb perhaps a bit earlier.[53]

The Dengxian tomb, which was first excavated in the late 1950s, is a brick barrel-vaulted tomb with a rectangular main chamber and an extended passageway leading into it roughly from the south; it is a type of tomb construction commonly seen in the south, though also known in the north. The side walls are decorated with incised bricks that show a variety of scenes carefully laid out in three tiers, an arrangement similar to that found at tombs from this period in the Nanjing (Jiankang) area.[54] The upper tier is decorated with images of celestial beings (in one case specifically labeled *tianren* 天人), and a variety of fantastic animals, including the animals of the four cardinal directions, both common motifs in Jiankang tombs as well. The other tiers show a conspicuous emphasis on military themes, suggesting that the tomb was for a high-ranking local military officer. The primary decorative motif in the central tier on both walls is an extensive procession, led by the horse and empty palanquin of the deceased, common symbols for a fallen military leader.[55] Arranged in the lower tier is a regular repeated motif of guardian military officials, each facing straight outward and leaning on a large sword. Some fifty pottery figurines found in the tomb also have military subjects. Finally, a hastily written graffito on one of the tiles, though difficult to decipher, appears to concern military maneuvers, including mention of armies and troops, supplies of oxen and liquor, and a sequence of months that may refer to a particular campaign.[56]

The second tomb, at Jiajiachong, was first excavated in the mid-1980s. It is laid out in very similar fashion to the Dengxian tomb, though somewhat smaller, and on a northeast to southwest axis. It is more densely decorated, but lacks the strong organizing motif of a procession. Instead, it has a tremendous variety of smaller tiles, including nearly two hundred images of servants and forty-six images of celestial beings, plus many images of fantastic animals and floral decorations. Military themes are not nearly so predominant in this tomb; for example, of forty-four earthenware figurines, only thirteen are identifiably military officials or guardian figures.[57]

The theme of supernatural efficacy is prominent in both tombs, especially Dengxian. One of the figures in the Dengxian tomb's funerary procession appears to be an exorcist or shaman.[58] Two separate scenes depict the sage Wang Ziqiao 王子橋, who is supposed to have played the mouth organ so beautifully that he brought down a phoenix from Heaven. He is paired with Lord Fuqiu 浮丘公, who is mentioned in the Han dynasty *Accounts of Immortals* (*Liexian zhuan* 列仙傳) as Ziqiao's companion.[59] Another depicts the "Four Old Men of Southern Mountain" (*nanshan sihao* 南山四皓), a variant of the graphically similar "Shang Mountain 商山." These four wise men are supposed to have fled the chaos of the Qin dynasty (221–206 BC), but were eventually coaxed back out of the hills to advise Liu Bang, Han Emperor Gaozu. Like the "Seven Sages of the Bamboo Grove," who are depicted on several tombs from this period in the Jiankang region, these images are meant to reflect the moral uprightness and sociopolitical detachment of the occupant and his family.[60] Though the Jiajiachong tomb lacks these sorts of "storytelling" images of Han-era figures, it does include nineteen small images of Buddha figures in seated meditation.[61]

Supernatural efficacy is also evident in the depiction of well-known filial piety stories. Both tombs have scenes depicting the legend of Guo Ju 郭巨, who was too poor to support both his aging mother and his infant son; in digging a grave to sacrifice his son he discovered a pot of gold, a blessing from Heaven in response to his filial piety. The Dengxian tomb also has an image of Lao Laizi 老來子, who acted like a child in order to please his parents. These were two of the more popular filial piety stories, and were frequently depicted in northern tombs.[62]

Though we cannot extrapolate much from only two tombs, their record of the visual and religious preoccupations of locals do tend to reinforce what is suggested from other sources, especially with regards to supernatural efficacy. The difference between "Daoist" and "Confucian" themes, often highlighted by other analysts, seems less important here than the importance of the "response" of supernatural forces to virtuous human actions.[63] This is particularly evident in the Dengxian tomb, in which a "Daoist" tale such as that of Wang Ziqiao (where the response is to beautiful music) is juxtaposed with a typically "Confucian" tale such as that of Guo Ju (where the response is to filial virtue).

The tales recorded by Bao Zhi also demonstrate this sort of heterogeneity, emphasizing the local origins of the supernatural response more than any particular virtues or characters. The filial piety theme, for example, is highlighted in his story of a young women of the Jingzhao-Bacheng Wang lineage (which had immigrated to Xiangyang), who was widowed at sixteen but steadfastly refused to marry, despite the wishes of her family. To demonstrate her fixity of purpose, she eventually cut off her ear and placed it in a bowl as an oath. Her dedication to chastity is supposed to have engendered two supernatural "responses," one by a cypress tree in front of her husband's grave, the other by a pair of swallows; she is noted for writing poems in response to these events. At that time (ca. 512–513) the garrison was under the command of the Marquis of Xichang, Xiao Yan's nephew Xiao Zao 西昌侯藻, a mild-mannered classical scholar, who commemorated the girl by sponsoring the erection of a pavilion and terrace atop the city wall.[64] The story of the virtuous young widow Wang, and Heaven's positive response to her, functioned rather like Xiangyang's own local equivalent to the far more widespread tale of Guo Ju depicted in the tombs. Though her commemoration was sponsored by an imperial agent, it clearly served to appeal to the sentiments of local elites—the Jingzhao Wangs in particular.

The other element in these tombs that stands out is their relatively conservative iconographic vocabulary, drawing on a repertoire that would have been largely familiar in the late Han period. Some of these traditional elements, such as the four directional animals or images of recluses like the "Four Old Men of South Mountain," were also in vogue at the time in tombs at Jiankang, suggesting some influence from the capital area.[65] Buddhist stylistic motifs such as lotus flowers and celestial beings had long since been borrowed from Buddhist art and could not be considered a marker of any fervent Buddhist dedication on the part of the occupant. The Buddha images in the Jiajiachong tomb are more indicative of such impact, yet even here they are scattered among other non-Buddhist figures in an eclectic fashion, not treated as the central organizing element of the design as they are in the much more strongly Buddhist-themed northern tombs of this period.

The tombs' conservative iconography suggests that their engagement with the aesthetic ideas of other contemporary tombs, in both the north and the south, was eclectic and pluralist.[66] This sort of attitude to religious belief is reflected in written sources as well, in the description in Wei Rui's biography of his "plain and meager" faith in Buddhism. When Xiao Yan and his sons began to promote a more zealously orthodox version of Buddhism (probably referring to the period around 517, when Daoist institutions came under sharp attack), Rui is described as having ignored their efforts and continued to follow the faith in a comparatively perfunctory manner, "just as in earlier times."[67]

## THE PATRONAGE OF COURT-STYLE BUDDHISM

The relatively laissez-faire and eclectic approach to religious traditions exemplified by local tombs, and by Wei Rui's attitude, contrasts with the scholarly and more exclusive variant of Buddhism promoted by the Liang court in this period. The effort of Xiao Yan, his sons and supporters to promote their interpretation of Buddhism, and suppress some elements of Daoism and other heterodoxies, exemplified a kind of "cultural imperialism" practiced during the early Liang period. The evidence from Xiangyang suggests that this effort, though perhaps of benefit to some locals, also exacerbated the cultural tension between the court and the Xiangyang area.

One of the first local targets of imperial patronage was the Rosewood Creek Monastery (*tanqi si* 檀溪寺). This compound had first been established by the famous monk Shi Dao'an 釋道安 in the late fourth century. Dao'an's ministry at Xiangyang had brought a group of several hundred eminent, learned northern monks to the area for a period of fifteen years, during which the region received attention and patronage from powerful members of several courts, including those at Jiankang, Chang'an, and Liang province 涼州 (in modern Gansu). Following Dao'an's departure in 379, however, there is little evidence for much further activity at the compound. The sangha's wealthiest temples and most eminent monks tended to concentrate at the capital and other major administrative centers, where the opportunity for patronage was greatest; by comparison, Rosewood Creek apparently saw little development over the next century, as monks with great talent and ambition went elsewhere.[68]

When Xiao Yan was organizing his campaign, he used the inlet where Rosewood Creek joined the Han River as the staging area for his naval operations, but there is no mention that the monastery was a factor in this decision.[69] In fact, the evidence suggests that the relationship between Xiao

Yan's group and the sangha was not a positive one, for Xiao Yan's brother Xiao Wei is noted for confiscating a bronze image from an unnamed monastery and melting it down to help finance operations; he suffered illness as a karmic result.[70] The monastery in question was probably Rosewood Creek, the only substantial Buddhist compound known to have existed in the area at that time.[71] Perhaps in compensation, Rosewood Creek was given an imperial bequest in 505 for new lands, and the temple's operations were reestablished. Seven years later a stele was added to the temple, with an inscription composed by Liu Zhilin, already known as one of the most erudite scholars from the Nanyang cluster at Jiangling.[72]

Prince Gang was an especially vigorous patron of Buddhism. There are numerous records of inscriptions that members of his entourage composed for newly built Buddhist monasteries. At least four Buddhist establishments in Xiangyang are known to have been built or dedicated at the prince's behest, including the Compassionate Awareness Monastery (*cijue si* 慈覺寺), for which Prince Gang himself did the memorial inscription, and the Equal Ranks Monastery (*pingdeng si* 平等寺), with an inscription written by one of Prince Gang's entourage, Liu Xiaoyi.[73] Xiao Gang also sponsored Buddhist scholarship while he was at Xiangyang, commandeering Buddhist texts from all over the "western lands" and assembling them into a massive collection which was eventually promulgated in 535. The preface, written by his younger brother Xiao Yi, Prince of Xiangdong 湘東王繹, notes the names, titles, and ages of thirty-eight men who participated in the project. Unsurprisingly, men from the capital dominate; more than half are from the imperial clan or one of two particularly favored lineages, the Langye Wangs and the Pengcheng Lius. Only two came from the western part of the empire: Yu Jianwu, one of the cluster of Nanyang émigrés at Jiangling, and Wei Leng, Wei Rui's third son.[74]

Wei Leng's name on this eminent list suggests that members of Wei Rui's lineage were the most vigorous local supporters of the imperial promotion of Buddhism. As noted previously, Wei Rui's official biography mentions his support, albeit rather lukewarm, for the court's pro-Buddhist efforts. While serving as garrison commander of Xiangyang (515–17) Wei Rui also sponsored the building of a Buddhist "Liberation Terrace" (*fangsheng tai* 放生臺) at Phoenix woods, five *li* south of town in the Xian hills.[75] Wei Rui's descendents were closely associated with Prince Gang; in addition to his third son Leng, Rui's second son Zheng was also on the prince's staff, as was his grandson Can. They are also known to have hosted the prince at the family estate west of town.[76] Though only Wei Leng is specifically noted for Buddhist scholarly work, the close association between Wei Rui's offspring and Prince Gang means that they must have, at the very least, been willing to accommodate his Buddhist agenda.

Other men from Xiangyang were opposed to this campaign, however. One extreme example is Guo Zushen 郭祖深, who came from a Xiangyang family of no known background. Guo had become a personal client of Xiao Yan's in the run-up to the coup, and thereafter served in relatively low-level provincial positions, where he reported on local conditions and the activities of imperial princes. Literate and knowledgeable, Guo wrote several lengthy memorials to the emperor recommending policies from a strongly authoritarian, legalist perspective. He denounced the influence of Buddhism and its institutions, pointing out how their tremendous growth in property and power threatened to undermine state authority. Guo was equally critical of Daoist practitioners and others, such as "populist teachers" and "medical quacks," all of whom were "small men that harmed the state."[77] His close ties to Xiao Yan and his regime mean that his perspective cannot be considered typically "local," but it does clearly demonstrate that some Xiangyang men were not at all invested in the development of Buddhist or other religious institutions.

The most interesting perspective on Prince Gang's effort to promote Buddhism in Xiangyang comes from the biography of the monk Facong 法聰, recorded in the Tang-era *Continued Biographies of Eminent Monks* (*Xu gaoseng zhuan* 續高僧傳). The biography emphasizes many of the same themes of local power and protection against imperial agents that we saw in Bao Zhi's writing; it appears to exemplify a response to Buddhist cultural imperialism characteristic of those without special links to the regime. Facong was a small-time local monk, a native of Xinye who, after traveling far afield, returned to settle on the south side of the Xian hills next to White Horse spring, the site of a former residence for Dao'an's community before they relocated to the Rosewood Creek compound. There he built himself a meager meditation hut which he called "House of the Resting Heart" (*qixin zhi zhai* 棲心之宅). According to the account, Prince Gang went numerous times to visit Facong, who by this time was in his mid-fifties; the prince was repeatedly amazed by Facong's remarkable power over animals, notably tigers, but also a white tortoise and a five-colored carp (incarnations of male and female dragons, respectively), as well as white deer, small birds, and other creatures. The prince's "evil subordinates," however, elicited a far more threatening demonstration of Facong's power:

> [The prince had] an evil clique of subordinates, numbering several dozen men. At night they came to plunder the things they had been shown. They met with tigers snarling, blocking their way. They also saw a giant man standing beside the mediation hall; beside him was a pine tree which only came up to his knees. He grasped a diamond club (*jingang chu* 金剛杵) for protection.[78]

This tale draws on many of the same themes as Bao Zhi's stories: the "evil" subordinates of imperial agents and their conflict with locals, and the supernatural efficacy of local places and/or people, which overcomes the threat from these agents. Facong's supernatural power to baffle and defeat the hostile forces of the prince's entourage would have been a significant part of this tale's local appeal. The story goes on to record that the prince tried to become Facong's patron; he himself contributed the funds to establish the Meditative Residence Monastery (*chanju si* 禪居寺), and he instructed Xu Chi to likewise sponsor the Magic Spring Monastery (*lingquan si* 靈泉寺). However, Facong refused to live there.

## IMPERIAL BIAS AGAINST LOCAL CULTURE

The campaign to promote the court's preferred approach to Buddhism exemplifies the prince's deep-seated attachment to the culture of the capital, and his bias against the quite different local culture of the Xiangyang region. He and his entourage were enamored of the literary culture of the imperial court, including the celebration of sensual pleasures, sexual dalliances, and leisurely delights, and they brought these preferences with them to Xiangyang. Bao Zhi records that they ensconced themselves in the buildings of the Inspectorate Academy, particularly the Eminent Studio, and engaged in literary activities, which would have included the collecting, exchanging, and perusal of classical texts, literary and poetry games, calligraphy, art, music, and board games. The group eventually came to be known as the "Eminent Studio Scholars."

This group was especially enamored of poetry. In this, at least, Xiangyang had some claim to fame, for it had been one of the wellsprings of the "western lyric" tradition that had inspired courtly adaptations for more than a century. Quatrains in western style had been written to commemorate important political events, such as the defeat of Shen Youzhi in 478, and Xiao Yan's campaign in 501 had naturally also received such treatment. Xiao Yan himself is credited with having composed western-style verses on this theme, in a series called *Stamping Brass Hooves of Xiangyang* (*Xiangyang tatongti* 襄陽蹋銅蹄), supposedly performed with a line of sixteen dancers. One example:

> a dragon-horse, a gold and purple saddle
> a kingfisher-plume, a white jade halter
> splendor accruing to the emperor
> know it to be Xiangyang men.[79]

Xiao Yan's poem seeks to show his deep appreciation for the clients who served him in the campaign, comparing them to valued bits of military equipment and decoration, the "splendor accruing to the emperor." Xiao Yan's close associate Shen Yue also composed poems to this title, responding to Xiao Yan in a posture of admiration and gratitude from his fortunate local clients:

born and raised by the waters of Wan
a retainer in the city of Xiangyang
one morning I met with his divine might
lifted my wings and gave the first call

dancing reins and flying dust
each one in his entourage shines
a man gains rank and wealth
what need is there to come home again?[80]

The poems in this exchange celebrate Xiangyang men's military glory, the emperor's pleasure at gaining their service and their loyalty, and the frank advantages this bestowed upon local men, including their willingness to emigrate. Though Xiangyang men are recognized as subordinate, they are also represented as deeply valued and respected by the emperor.

Prince Gang naturally also wished to write poems in the western style to commemorate his own tenure in Xiangyang. His preoccupations were quite different than those of the previous generation, as in this example called "Big Dike" (*dadi* 大堤):

at Yicheng we stop midway
en route we frequently linger here
divorced women skilled in embroidery
bewitching courtesans practiced in counting cash
exotic dishes detain honored guests
wine on credit, we pursue the gods.[81]

This poem, along with the others in Prince Gang's series, is reminiscent of the young Song Prince Dan's verses from the mid-fifth century, a celebration of leisure and sensual pleasures. By comparison with those early poems, or those by Xiao Yan and Shen Yue, Prince Gang exhibits little interest in the culture and society of Xiangyang. Except for the reference to Yicheng (also called "Big Dike"), his poem could have been describing a pleasure garden at the capital.

The prince was not without some understanding of Xiangyang local history, but it appears to have been largely book-learned and antiquarian, emphasizing the glories of its distant past, rather than the society that was currently there. For example, in an inscription he wrote for a local temple, he refers to the region as the cradle of the eastern Han, noting the surnames of several eminent local families from that period, but with no reference to anything more recent.[82] He also commissioned the painting of portraits of famous local governors of past years; though we have no list of which ones were chosen, distant paragons such as Yang Hu and Du Yu seem most likely.[83] Similarly, his memorials expressing concern for the locals reflect a textbook Confucian paternalism more than a substantive engagement with the details of the particular locale.[84]

One notable emphasis of these memorials is the prince's opposition to military campaigns; he expresses concern over the expense of campaigns and the burden of conscription, due to which "young men are exhausted from the bearing of armor."[85] Prince Gang's entourage, led by Xu Chi, did coordinate a military campaign to retake the area north of the Han River, which had been under northern domination for more than two decades. The campaign sought to take advantage of the utter collapse of central authority in the north at this time, including the wholesale destruction of the prosperous northern capital at Luoyang due to civil war. It resulted in a short-lived reassertion of the southern regime's control over Xinye, Nanxiang, Nanyang, and Rangcheng, among other areas, but, given the opportunities available, its objectives were quite limited.[86]

Prince Gang's distaste for military campaigns was a reflection of his more general bias against the rough and combative customs of the Xiangyang area, with which little in his genteel upbringing had prepared him to understand or sympathize. His disdain is expressed explicitly in a personal letter to his first cousin Xiao Gong 蕭恭, the son of Xiao Wei, who was sent out to Xiangyang at a later date.[87] Its first section reads:

> In this place the gentry's customs are foul and corrupt, with some of the manner of the Guanzhong region. The commoners are obstructive, only knowing to value the sword and slight death. The northern barbarians (*hu* 胡) who have submitted only concern themselves with avarice, while the hill-barbarians (*man* 蠻) on the borders do not know respect or deference. Show concern for them without making distinctions; legal statutes have no use in governing them.[88]

Prince Gang's dislike of the region was also evident upon the death of his mother, Consort Ding, in 526 CE, when he petitioned the throne to be allowed to return to the capital to mourn her. The petition was denied, and the prince was compelled to stay in Xiangyang for four more years.[89]

Xiao Yan's desire to keep his son at Xiangyang at this time was probably motivated by his understanding that the strength of his dynasty depended on his sons and heirs developing a network of military clients through personal experience in provincial commands. In this, however, Prince Gang was not very successful. Disinclined to sponsor military affairs, repulsed by the violent customs of the region, and well protected by his large personal entourage of court favorites, the prince is known to have made only one significant clientelage tie during his time at Xiangyang: Liu Jin, the son of Liu Qingyuan, who followed the prince back to Jiankang in 530.[90] Liu Jin had been one of the commanders of the northern campaign of 525, and he was of course the son of a man who had been of great importance to the prince's father. On the other hand, he was probably still not very literate or cultured; a memorandum from him appealing to the prince to stay longer in Xiangyang was ghost-written by Liu Xiaoyi, one of the prince's entourage, and Jin's subsequent career at the capital was negligible.[91] Meanwhile, most of the fighting men of Xiangyang were left behind in the garrison, awaiting a more welcoming imperial patron.

## COMPETITIVE SPECTACLE: THE LOCAL CULTURE OF MILITARY FESTIVALS

One last arena in which there is evidence of tension between the culture of the capital and that of the Xiangyang region is in the celebration of local festivals. Several distinctive festival events had become a hallmark of western garrison culture; unlike earlier such celebrations, they involved public spectacles based on competitive, mock-military competitions. Prince Gang and his entourage are known to have actively discouraged at least one of these, a kind of noisy tug-of-war competition. Another competitive spectacle involving boat racing eventually took on a literary guise, perhaps in response to pressure from the court around this time, and became an enduring hallmark of Chinese culture.

The boat races were associated with midsummer, specifically the fifth day of the lunar fifth month, known as the *duanwu* 端午. Such "double" days had been important in the Chinese festival calendar since the Han dynasty. Midsummer in general, and the "double fifth" in particular, was considered strongly inauspicious, and texts dating as early as the late Han record a variety of practices used on that day to ward off evil spirits, appease water dragons, and such.[92] The staging of boat races on this date was a comparatively late phenomenon, however; the earliest mention of it comes from the *Record of the Jing-Chu Region* (*Jing-Chu ji* 荊楚記) a brief festival calendar dating to the mid-sixth century. The following expanded account, which was either part of the original text or appended to it no later than the early seventh century, offers a vivid description:

> As for the boat races ("competitive crossing," *jingdu* 競渡) on the fifth day of the fifth month, it is commonly reckoned to be the day that Qu Yuan 屈原 threw himself into the Miluo [River], and in mourning his death, they therefore all order boats and oarsmen to "rescue" him. The boats are selected for lightness and sharpness [i.e., speed] and are called "flying ducks" (*feifu* 飛鳧). One may

> style itself the "Water Army" (*shuijun* 水軍), one may style itself the "Water Horse" (*shuima* 水馬). The provincial generals and local people all watch from the water's edge.[93]

The development of these boat races reveals several important features of the society and culture of Xiangyang and other western garrison towns. First, unlike earlier accounts of *duanwu*, which mention only activities undertaken by individual households (weaving special cloth, making special foods, hanging up protective amulets), the boat competitions were coordinated, community-wide events that clearly required significant organizational resources to mount. They could not have occurred without the leadership and financial backing of a motivated and wealthy local elite with an interest in staging a popular public spectacle. This sort of local leadership role was sharply at odds with the classical model of "disengagement" from local common people and local affairs (exemplified by the tale of Xin Xuanzhong) which had dominated the self-representation of local elites and the written records of local lore since the late Han period.[94]

Second, the festival was intentionally a *competitive* spectacle, with obvious ties to military traditions; it was essentially a kind of war game, a mock battle, possibly involving real casualties.[95] The use of military epithets for the boats, and the fact that the observers were "provincial generals and local people," strongly suggests this. Further evidence of the festival's link to military culture is offered by the account in the section on Jing province from the "Treatise on Geography" in the *History of the Sui*. After first detailing an early legend of Qu Yuan and the boats that supposedly went out to save him, the account continues:

> This was handed down through common practice, and became the performance of "competitive crossing." Their swift paddles move quickly together, sounds of oar and song echoing across, the noise shaking both water and land, those watching gathered like clouds. All the [Jing] commanderies are like this, but Nanjun [Jiangling] and Xiangyang are the most intense.[96]

The account's emphasis on Jiangling and Xiangyang is illuminating. Neither of these places was the site of Qu Yuan's suicide, nor his hometown, so they would have had no special reason to commemorate him. Their significance instead lies in the fact that they were the two most important military garrisons of the western regions, which supports the thesis that the boat competition had its origins in military exercises, which were developed into a form of public spectacle. The public, competitive, and potentially violent nature of the boat races was very much in line with the ideals and actions of the men whom we know had come to dominate garrison society, especially in Xiangyang.

Moreover, the boat competition was not the only mock-military public competition known to have been held in the western regions. Others included ball games, cockfights, and a kind of tug-of-war, which went by a variety of names such as "dragging the hook" (*qian gou* 牽鉤) or "seizing the rope" (*ba geng* 拔綆). This latter competition also involved loud cursing, called "shouting to achieve victory" (*yasheng* 厭勝), a practice that was also supposed to drive away evil spirits. It may have been akin to the loud shouting and cursing practiced by Cao Jingzong and his companions in their New Year's soirees, which had seemed so foreign to the elite of the capital region. The tug-of-war had apparently been staged for generations prior to the Liang period, and the boat competition may have been as well, though not necessarily always on the *duanwu* date, nor with any expressed link to Qu Yuan.[97]

This brings us to the third point: the putative origins of the boat competition in the ancient effort to rescue Qu Yuan from drowning. This association is most certainly a late development. Qu Yuan had substantial prestige in classical literature, for he had been one of the most revered, yet controversial poets in Han literary circles, and his wrongful exile and tragic suicide were central to his legend and his poetic legacy.[98] However, aside from some scattered references to a single commemorative shrine at the site of his suicide on the Miluo River, there is no evidence that he was widely worshipped or much regarded in popular lore prior to the sixth century CE.[99] In fact, there is not even any evidence that his suicide occurred on *duanwu*; the first known assertion of this date comes from the early Liang era, in a collection of marvel tales and "explanations" of the origins of festivals. That account seeks to explain contemporary *duanwu* practices for driving off evil spirits by citing a colorful but utterly suspect tale of an otherwise unknown man from Changsha in the late Han era, and his encounter with an evil water dragon and Qu Yuan's ghost. However, even this rather late text mentions only the traditional individual sacrifices to Qu Yuan, with no suggestion of any larger public spectacle such as the boat races, nor any association with the military garrisons at Jiangling and Xiangyang. If the boat races had been practiced at the time as a part of a double fifth celebration of Qu Yuan they would have been very difficult to ignore.[100] This evidence implies that the linkage of the boat races to Qu Yuan and the *duanwu* date came about no earlier than the sixth century.[101]

One likely source of influence for this linkage was the cultural pressure exerted by the Liang princes and their followers. Prince Gang is known to have actively discouraged the competitive tug-of-war exhibition while he was serving in Xiangyang, presumably a part of his general distaste for militaristic local traditions; the boat competition must have felt similar pressure.[102] At the same time, Prince Gang's entourage celebrated Qu Yuan as a moral as well as a poetic exemplar; the prince himself identified with Qu Yuan as a sensual, brilliant, but sadly misunderstood poet, and took him as his personal hero. The prince's literary clique was intent on equaling the brilliance of the *Chuci* 楚辭, the classic collection of Chu verses attributed to Qu Yuan, and undertook further efforts to elaborate and "refine" the folk song traditions of the western garrisons.[103] The group included some native "Chu" scholiasts from the Nanyang cluster based at Jiangling, who may have been especially supportive of this celebration of Chu's unique literary heritage.

A different but complementary source of inspiration for the association of the boat competition with Qu Yuan was the strong tradition in the lower Yangzi area of worshipping Wu Zixu 伍子胥, a powerful minister of the Warring States period kingdom of Wu who had been compelled to commit suicide, then thrown into a river. In literary parlance, Wu Zixu was very closely associated with Qu Yuan; both were considered exemplars of upright ministers who had suffered at the hands of unworthy rulers.[104] His tradition's close parallels with the boat competition were noted in the annotations to the festival calendar quoted previously:

> Handan Chun's *Stele for Cao E* says: "At the time of the fifth month fifth day, he went out to greet Lord Wu [Zixu]; making his way upstream against the waves he was engulfed by the waters." So this is also a custom of Eastern Wu, where the event is linked to Zixu, not connected to Qu Ping [Yuan].[105]

By comparison with Qu Yuan's rather weak popular legacy, the worship of Wu Zixu is very well attested in texts dating from the eastern Han period, and unquestionably associated with the double fifth date. By the fourth century there were temples to Wu Zixu as far away as the north China plains; an early collection of locality stories from Jing province notes his old family estate in Nanyang commandery, not far north of Xiangyang, so his lore would have circulated in that region as well.[106] Wu Zixu was revered for his tremendous military prowess, his success at gaining revenge, and eventually for his control over the forces of water; many accounts indicate that his often troublesome spirit was to be placated by sailing into the middle of a river on a boat and performing special dances.[107] The well-established ceremonies for Wu Zixu may have influenced the elaboration of a similar legacy for Qu Yuan, in order to explain a superficially similar waterborne ritual that in fact had quite different origins.

The sum of the evidence suggests that the boat races themselves were originally a form of competitive spectacle, one of numerous public mock-military exercises that were promoted by wealthy local men and higher officials of the garrison. Their elaboration into a festival to commemorate Qu Yuan on the double fifth date, however, is best seen as an effort to "sanitize" the more violent aspects of the festival by giving it a literary veneer pleasing to Prince Gang or other members of the Liang regime, either at that time or in subsequent years.[108] It may have been part a conscious effort to try to harmonize the traditions of military and literary elites of the western garrisons, using a distinctively "Chu" cultural exemplar as a binding motif. At the minimum, it would have been a way to gain favor, or at least avoid censure, from the imperial household. The festival is an especially clear illustration of the militant and public-minded traditions of Xiangyang local culture at this time, as well as its ongoing evolution in response to the pressure exerted by representatives of the southern court.

## CONCLUSION

The involvement of Xiangyang men in Xiao Yan's successful coup was a transformative event for those participants and their immediate lineages. All of them gained levels of prestige, wealth, and influence that had been simply unattainable for most Xiangyang men of prior generations. Even those men who were unable to take full advantage of this opportunity would have passed on some of their wealth and connections to their own clientelage networks back home, their brothers and other male relatives, and their sons. Those who did make the most of the opportunity, such as Wei Rui, managed to leap out of provincial obscurity into the ranks of the capital elite, intermarrying with families from all over the empire, and placing their offspring into lucrative mid-level civilian offices and princely staff positions.

The impact of Xiao Yan's coup on Xiangyang as a place is much less clear. In the short run, it received a good deal more attention that it might have otherwise; certainly, the patronage of Buddhist temple construction, the arrival of a large and prestigious community of capital literati, and the careful collection of local lore would not have happened if Xiangyang had not been the "cradle" of the dynasty. On the other hand, the emphasis of Xiao Yan's sons and other imperial agents on literati culture, on "civilizing" the rough customs of the region, appears to have made only superficial headway, while sacrificing the opportunity to develop new clientelage ties with the next generation of local fighting men. With the withering of this personal avenue of recruitment, the ties between Xiangyang and the court once again lapsed, as they had under the Qi regimes, leaving the area dangerously adrift and open to new patrons who could once again offer opportunities for advancement.

FIVE

# SUBLIMATION, 530–600

Xiao Yan's rule did not fundamentally change the relationship between the imperial court and the Xiangyang garrison. Those few local men who achieved wealth, status, and perhaps some trappings of Jiankang culture also relocated their families to the capital, leaving Xiangyang bereft of such leadership. By the later phase of Xiao Yan's rule, the most important figures in Xiangyang local society were representatives of the same, largely illiterate military culture that had distinguished the region for over a century. Though some of these men had experience in the entourage of an imperial prince, or perhaps even had a relative at court, the region had once again become only loosely tied to the throne.

The unprecedented length of Xiao Yan's reign gave the many would-be successors among his sons and grandsons ample time to develop personal cliques of supporters. Some, like Prince Gang or his younger brother Prince Yi, patronized mostly literary men; others were more alert to preparing for an armed succession struggle, and courted men experienced in fighting and leading troops. What none could have anticipated was the destruction of much of Jiankang itself in the years 548–552, which set off an unusually leaderless civil war where no man had a preponderance of "legitimacy" or troops, and in which the fluid, self-interested voluntarism of the patronage system was especially pronounced. Men routinely and almost cavalierly sold their allegiance to whoever seemed to offer the best prospects, resulting in an extremely tangled, violent, and deadly web of expediency, betrayal, and revenge. The northern regimes took this opportunity to intrude forcefully into southern affairs, and found it relatively easy to mop up the allegiance of the leaders of small, free-floating military bands whose quest for patrons knew no particular loyalty to the fractious scions of Jiankang, nor to their local regions. The fate of Xiangyang and Jiangling, both of which fell under northern dominion in this period, exemplified the absence of fixed loyalties, not just among military clients, but among members of the imperial Xiao family itself, who had few qualms about cutting deals with the regime at Chang'an in order to win advantage over perceived threats from within their own household.

The sublimation of Xiangyang under the rule of Chang'an did not bring radical change to the region, whose local culture was in many ways closer to that of Guanzhong than to Jiankang anyway. Increased opportunities for military service during the sweeping and ultimately successful campaigns against the northeastern Qi and southeastern Chen regimes probably compensated for more limited opportunities to attain very high office. The local Buddhist establishment enjoyed continued patronage, and appears to have gained substantially in stature by the early Sui period (581–617). The greater importance placed on family lineage and surname under the Chang'an regime worked to the advantage of those Xiangyang families, notably the Jingzhao Weis, whose distant kin already enjoyed high status in the north. The demise of the south was lamented in highly allusive and antiquarian terms by men from the well-educated cluster at Jiangling, but for prominent men from Xiangyang the new regime was, at least in the short run, almost certainly regarded as a success.

## FIGHTING BANDS AND FREE-FLOATING ALLEGIANCES

The largely illiterate military culture of the Xiangyang garrison was not much changed by the success of a small number of its members in the early Liang period. Evidence from the civil war of the mid-sixth century shows that many military men, of very much the same type as those that had once backed Xiao Yan, remained dominant in the area and were prepared to enlist under the banner of whoever offered the best prospect for success. These men were organized into small bands, often headed by an alliance of brothers together with their sons, nephews, and other close male relatives, and leading a group of anywhere from a few hundred to a few thousand men. Their power was often very localized, and their allegiance was essentially free-floating and available to the most promising patron. Prominent examples of such groups are those headed by Liu Zhongli, Du An, Du Shupi, and Xi Gu.

In 548 Xiao Yan's regime fell into a deep crisis usually termed "the chaos of Hou Jing 侯景之亂." The outlines of the disaster are well known. Xiao Yan by this time was in his early eighties and probably rather senile. In 548, in a misguided effort to gain advantage against the northern regime of Gao Huan, who controlled the "eastern Wei" court, one of two claimants to the Wei throne, Xiao Yan invited a rogue northern general named Hou Jing to come south as an ally. By the time Hou Jing arrived near Jiankang, however, he had marshalled a large ragtag army, and promptly undertook a highly destructive siege of the city, which laid waste to the fortunes of many of the capital elite, even as it attracted the allegiance of others.[1] Hou Jing's campaign is best viewed as a spark that lit the fuse of a far more fundamental, systemic problem that had plagued all of the southern regimes: imperial succession. For the princes ensconced in their provincial garrisons, the imminent demise of Xiao Yan's regime was a long-anticipated event, which they had been positioning themselves to take advantage of for years. Hou Jing's entry into the mix of possible contenders for the throne was an unexpected twist, but few thought him likely to succeed (which indeed he did not). As a result, the collapse of Xiao Yan's regime, and the obvious weakness of his anointed successor Prince Gang, was primarily viewed as an opportunity for personal advancement, for the princes themselves, but also for the many men who were, or hoped to become, their clients.

The most important local leader in Xiangyang in the 530s and 540s was Liu Zhongli 柳仲禮, the grandson of Liu Qingyuan. As noted in the previous chapter, Qingyuan mostly did not relocate to the capital, nor did he bring his eldest son Liu Jin there to be educated; indeed, Jin was noted for being "deficient" in the polite arts. Jin was finally recruited into Prince Gang's entourage in the 520s, and moved down to Jiankang to assume an honorary but otherwise insignificant post. Once again, his own sons did not follow him, but remained at Xiangyang, where they gained a great reputation and were even celebrated in a local ode called the "Song of the Four Young Men of the Liu Family" (*Liu si lang ge* 柳四郎歌).[2] The biography of Zhongli, the eldest, notes that he had great height and strength, flaring eyebrows and "gall spirit" (i.e., courage). "Fighting men with horses and weapons all followed him; he managed all of his former officials and clients (*gujiu* 古舊) and greatly gained the allegiance of the people."[3] His local leadership was critical in fighting off a campaign by northern forces in 532. Though based at Xiangyang, Zhongli nonetheless had much better connections with the court than the average local fighting man; he had been honored by Xiao Yan himself with a personal portrait, and eventually received a lucrative appointment as inspector of neighboring Si province.

Liu Zhongli was also ambitious. Anticipating the difficulties with Hou Jing early on, he had raised more than ten thousand troops from Yong and Si provinces, and proclaimed himself the "unequalled hero of the age."[4] When the Jing provincial inspector, Prince Yi, put out an initial call for troops to rescue the capital, Zhongli and his younger brother Jingli 柳敬禮 (who had another three thousand troops)[5] immediately moved into action, taking their forces down to Hengjiang 横江, about forty miles upriver from the capital, to meet up with their affinal cousin Wei Can, who had taken on the role of convening troops from the western regions in preparation for the relief of the capital. Can, the eldest son of Wei Rui's eldest son Fang, had been born and raised entirely in the capital, and served imperial princes most of his life, first Prince Gang, then (after Gang was elevated to heir-apparent) Prince Yi. Though he had ancestral roots in Xiangyang, there is no evidence, apart from his affinal relationship with the Lius, that he maintained any significant ties in the area. At a pivotal meeting on the last day of the year, and against some opposition, he nominated Liu Zhongli as the commander-in-chief of the combined expeditionary force, probably because Zhongli and his brother brought the largest contingent of fighting men into the fray, and also because they had some practical background leading troops, unlike most of Prince Yi's staff. The records suggest that Liu Zhongli and Wei Can initially intended to share authority over the division of forces. However, Wei Can's men were set upon by an advance unit of Hou Jing's forces the following day; though many of their men fled, Wei Can, his son, three younger brothers and a cousin all stood their ground and were killed.[6]

The relief army's subsequent efforts to defeat Hou Jing were beset by weak leadership and mistrustful calculations of personal interest among all the major parties. Since no elder imperial prince accompanied them, the leading subordinates of the various princes had multiple and often conflicting loyalties: to their own self-interests, to their immediate military commander, to their distant princely patron, and perhaps to "the Liang imperial house," whichever one of the many princes was thought to be its appropriate representative. There can be little doubt that Wei Can would have preferred to see Hou Jing defeated and either Prince Gang (his former patron) or Prince Yi (his current one) installed on the throne once their father passed away. Liu Zhongli, by comparison, had never had any close association with any member of the imperial house; he was essentially a free operator, watching the unfolding of events and judging where his best advantage lay. He delayed mounting any substantial attack for over two months, until the imperial palace fell and Hou Jing secured control over the emperor and Prince Gang, both of whom "accepted" the rebel under obvious duress. It was now plausible that Hou Jing might go on to found a new dynasty, as Liu Yu, Xiao Daocheng, and Xiao Yan had done before. Liu Zhongli, apparently estimating that there was no special merit in antagonizing a potential new emperor, or in getting himself and his hard-won followers killed, dissolved much of the "relief" forces and, along with his brother and several other top generals, submitted to Hou Jing.

Liu Zhongli's surrender is reviled in the official *Liang History*, which denies him a biography and seeks to make him look as depraved as possible, noting his drunkenness, his womanizing, and his wild, misbehaving troops, all favored criticisms of Xiangyang military commanders. Several surviving anecdotes particularly emphasize Zhongli's unfilial behavior toward his father Jin, who was in the imperial palace the entire time and supposedly urged his son to fight. In one account, Jin comments to Xiao Yan about their useless sons, "unfilial and unloyal." In another, Zhongli after his surrender comes to see the captive emperor, and Liu Jin, at the emperor's side, swears, "You are not my son; why trouble to even meet with you?"[7] Another anecdote, seeking to redeem the reputation of Zhongli's younger brother Jingli, has him uttering a deathbed curse of his brother as an "old whore" who "collapsed the state and destroyed the family."[8] The veracity of these anecdotes is dubious; their ideological purpose is to make Zhongli's betrayal more personal, a violation of the revered virtue of filial piety and thus, by parallelism, the virtue of loyalty.[9] Mere disloyalty was too common and too vague a fault in that troubled time; stronger censure was required.

In any event, what occurred next is every bit as revealing as the surrender itself. Hou Jing detained some of the submitted generals, including Liu Zhongli's younger brother, but he sent the two most important, Zhongli and Wang Sengbian 王僧辯, back to their original posts in the west. Despite their treasonous surrender to Hou Jing, Prince Yi immediately reemployed them as soon as they arrived. Their highly fungible loyalty was not an obstacle to their career advancement; the prince needed them much more than they needed him. Indeed, Prince Yi had become so embroiled in his own problems in the western lands that he called on all remaining forces to return to their posts, thereby allowing Hou Jing to continue holding the prince's father and brother captive, and to dominate Jiankang unchallenged for the next two years. Prince Yi's loyalty was clearly more to his own career than to that of the Xiao household in general, or to the welfare of the capital city.

Tensions between Jiangling and Xiangyang soon came to play a prominent role in the western region, as they so often had before. Prince Yi's garrison at Jiangling was effectively ringed by the posting of three of his nephews, the sons of Xiao Tong, the original Liang heir-apparent who had died two decades previously. At that time, Xiao Yan had passed over Xiao Tong's sons to nominate his own son Prince Gang as heir. The sons reportedly nursed a grievance about this; more to the point, they had a better than average prospective claim to the throne, certainly far better than Xiao Yan and his brothers had had when they staged their coup. Prince Yi, fearful that the three would band together against him, had the eldest of them (who was based at Badong) killed before he could return to his post, and sent a force to attack the second at Changsha. The third nephew, Xiao Cha, Prince of Yueyang 岳陽王詧, was Yong inspector, based at Xiangyang; when his brother sent a request for aid against Prince Yi, he immediately sprang into action.

Prince Cha was no innocent in the development of insubordinate and mutually suspicious relations between the brothers and Prince Yi. Like other princes, he had seen that a civil war to succeed Xiao Yan was imminent, and was quite pleased to be appointed to the extremely strategic and historically auspicious Xiangyang posting in 546, when he was only twenty-seven years old.[10] He had brought with him an impressive entourage of talented men from the capital, the most important of which was Cai Dabao 蔡大寶, who had been with him for many years and was known as a brilliant strategist, later compared favorably to Zhuge Liang.[11] Another of his entourage was Liu Xia 柳霞, Liu Qingyuan's nephew, who had grown up in Xiangyang and served several princes who were there on command before coming to the capital in the early 540s as part of the entourage of Xiao Lun, Prince of Shaoling 邵陵王綸. Liu Xia was a man of much different mettle than Qingyuan's own offspring; in fact, Qingyuan reportedly saw Xia as the hope of his family, carrying on the line of powerful Liu clan members that began with Liu Yuanjing and was passed down to Shilong and then to Qingyuan himself.[12] Prince Cha brought Xia back out to Xiangyang with his staff and made him the lieutenant inspector of Yong province (the same post Qingyuan had held under Xiao Yan).

At Xiangyang, Prince Cha worked assiduously to win over the populace and develop personal clientelage relations with its fighting men. He is recorded as having been a very upright man: a good writer, a devout Buddhist, uninterested in liquor, women, or other sensual pleasures, and devoutly filial. He was also ambitious, emotional, and a good judge of men, able to "hold generals and officials with bonds of gratitude, gaining their strength unto death."[13] The Xiangyang men who allied with him, such as Wei Yide 魏益德 and Yin Zheng 尹正, have only very brief biographies in a northern imperial history; described as local fighting men of no notable family background, they were almost certainly illiterate, just as were most of the men who had taken up with Xiao Yan.[14]

Prince Cha's best-documented local followers were several of nine brothers of the Jingzhao Du surname, the sons of Du Huaibao 杜懷寶. Huaibao was a distant relative of the Du family members who had intermarried closely with the Jingzhao Weis, but his own roots are described as entirely military. He had served Xiao Yan's younger brother Wei at Xiangyang during the coup that put Xiao Yan on the throne, and eventually became inspector of Liang province, a position often given to local military men. There he had engaged in valiant hand-to-hand combat to defend against an incursion by northern forces in the 530s. His sons carried on his tradition; for example, his third son Yi 杜嶷 was known for his great strength and his skill at mounted archery. While based in Liang province with his father, he developed a personal cohort of a hundred seventy fighting men who were known as "Du's Tigercats" (*Du biao* 杜彪).[15] By 549, leadership of the Du brothers and their corps of fighting men had fallen to the sixth son, Du An 杜岸, who "showed military skill and loved the art of strategy."[16] He was instrumental in aiding Prince Cha, first by quelling a rebellion of one of the prince's generals, then by deceiving and capturing Prince Yi's rival nominee for the office of Yong inspector, thereby sowing some of the seeds of mistrust between the two princes.

When Prince Cha sought to defend his brothers by launching a campaign against Prince Yi, he took Du An, two of An's younger brothers and their nephew with him at the head of one of his primary military units. His army of twenty thousand men and four thousand horses advanced to Jiangling in late autumn of 549 and attacked the city. A parley with Prince Yi is recorded: Prince Yi pointed out that a nephew attacking his uncle would give Prince Cha a bad reputation, and compared him to another recently rebellious Liang prince, while Prince Cha responded that he and his brothers were blameless and demanded that Prince Yi call off the attack on Changsha, promising to return to Xiangyang if he did so. Prince Cha then retreated and set up camp north of Jiangling. Heavy rains and flooding set in, swamping the encampment and causing a severe deterioration in morale over the next ten days.[17]

At this point, the Du brothers made a pivotal decision: they changed sides, taking their personal followers over to Prince Yi and leaving Prince Cha grossly exposed. The sources suggest several reasons for this. First, Xiao Cha's apparent irresolution did not inspire much confidence, and his followers' morale was low. Second, Du An's younger brother Ze 杜䂨 had previously served under Prince Yi while he was at Jiangling and thus had "old ties" (*jiu* 舊) to him.[18] These ties were not sufficient to command any unique loyalty, since Du Ze and his brothers also had such ties to Prince Cha, but they may have eased the negotiations between Prince Yi's side and the Du brothers. Third, the Du brothers were well rewarded by Prince Yi; each received the title of county marquis with a salary-fief of a thousand households, as well as the office of a provincial inspector and a generalship.[19] Unsurprisingly, this opportunity for personal advancement appears to have been a primary motivation in choosing a new patron.

The Du brothers nonetheless paid a high price for their decision. Du An immediately volunteered to take five hundred fast cavalry and strike Xiangyang the very next day, hoping to secure its surrender before Prince Cha could return. However, Cai Dabao, whom Prince Cha had left in charge of their garrison, was tipped off to the raid, and Prince Cha also made an especially quick retreat, so Du An and his forces circled north of Xiangyang to join up with his elder brother, who was governor of Nanyang.[20] Prince Cha appealed for aid from Yuwen Tai 宇文泰, who dominated the puppet "western Wei" emperor from his domain in the Guanzhong region. Yuwen Tai sent one of his generals with three thousand men to help defeat Du An, who was finally captured two months later.[21] In order to set an example to his men, Prince Cha had Du An's tongue cut out and his flesh chopped up and boiled. He also rounded up the Du brothers' mother, all of their wives, and any sons who were still in the area, and had them executed in front of the north gate of the town. The report continues: "He exhaustively exterminated all of the Du clan and their relatives; their young ones were castrated. He also excavated the gravesites of their ancestors, burned the bones to ash and scattered them, and made their skulls into lacquered bowls."[22] The Du brothers had presumably anticipated that the success of Du An's raid would lead to Prince Cha's surrender, thereby securing the safety of their families at Xiangyang, and perhaps even their own domination of the region. They had taken a tremendous risk, and lost badly.

Meanwhile, Prince Yi had enlisted the dubious help of Liu Zhongli and Wang Sengbian in fighting off his adversaries. Wang was sent south to complete the seizure of Changsha; Liu was ordered north to lead the assault on Xiangyang (see Map 5). Entrenched now in a bitter struggle with his

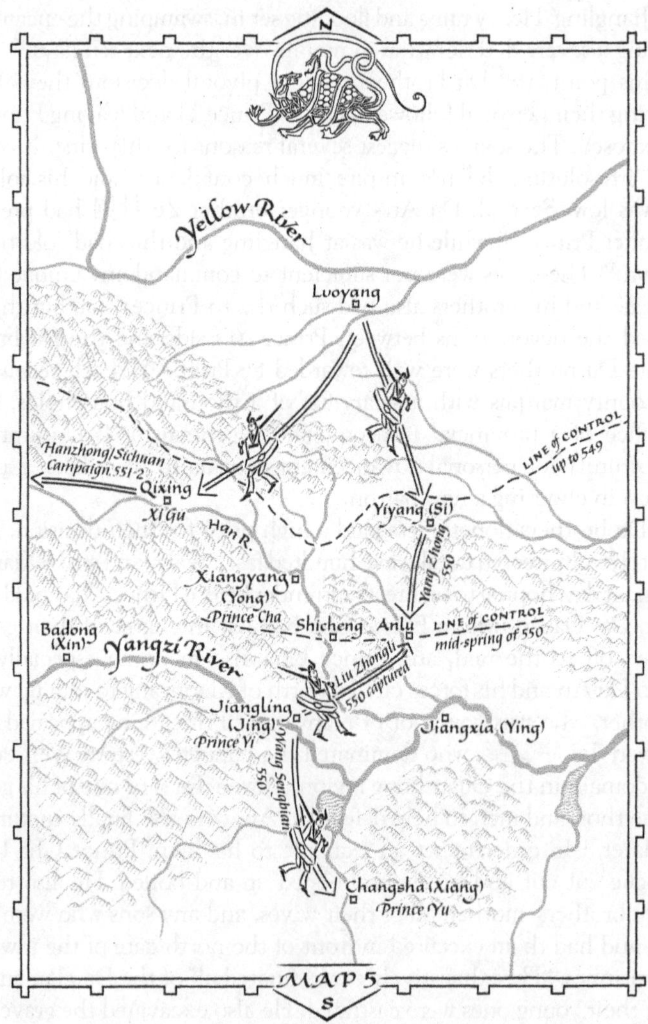


Map 5. Military campaigns in the central Yangzi, 550–552 CE

ambitious uncle, and apparently unable to raise much further local support, Prince Cha appealed again to the north. Yuwen Tai agreed to send one of his top generals, Yang Zhong 楊忠, to fight off the counterattack from Prince Yi, but required Prince Cha to send his wife and eldest son to Chang'an as security, which he did.[23] The arrangement was of course all to the benefit of Yuwen Tai, who would have happily seized the central Yangzi region anyway, and was more than pleased to gain the aid, or at least the neutrality, of the critical Xiangyang region.

Liu Zhongli proved to be no more disciplined in this campaign than in his previous one. Ignoring an appeal by Du An to aid in his defense against Prince Cha, he instead moved his main forces eastward to ensure control of Anlu, an important garrison north of the Han-Yangzi river junction, and sent his operatives to seize control of several other commandery administrations. His intent may have been to secure an independent stronghold for himself, perhaps anticipating an eventual return to his old base in Si and Yong provinces. He did not anticipate the rapid shift in events, however, especially the entry of northern forces. As he moved a squad to begin the attack on Xiangyang in the early spring of 550, Yang Zhong's forces moved directly south toward Anlu, gaining the surrender of key territories as they went, and laid siege to the town. After a brief skirmish, Liu Zhongli surrendered to Yang Zhong, and his subordinate forces quickly followed suit. Prince Yi promptly cut his own deal with Yuwen Tai's regime, sending his own son as a hostage and asking for peaceful relations, while formally relenquishing his claim over all the territory north of Shicheng and Anlu, a "border" roughly halfway between Jiangling and Xiangyang (see Map 5).[24]

The new geostrategic situation put enormous pressure on any holdout "southern" forces now trapped behind Yang Zhong's new frontier. Xi Gu 席固, descended from a northerner who had immigrated to the Xiangyang area in the early fifth century, was serving as the governor of Qixing 齊興 commandery, up the Han River west of Xiangyang. During Prince Yi's call for troops in 549 he had stayed put in his commandery, built up the allegiance of the locals, and personally controlled over a thousand troops. Prince Yi had eventually promoted him to be inspector of Xing 興 province, in the same area, and his forces swelled to more than five thousand. According to his biography, he intended to "control his own province and watch the times change." After Prince Yi assented to Yang Zhong's control of the north-central Yangzi region, Xi Gu concluded that Yuwen Tai's regime was considerably more competent (and more proximate) than Prince Yi's regime, and he offered his surrender. His timing and strategic position in the upper Han river valley were excellent, since Yuwen Tai was plotting to seize that region next, as a precursor to the conquest of Sichuan. As a result, Xi Gu did very well for himself, receiving a fief as a county lord with two thousand households, a position as a provincial inspector, and some of the highest honorary titles granted in the Yuwen regime's system.[25]

The Du brothers' second cousins, Du Shupi 杜叔毗 and his brothers and nephews, had a much less successful experience. Each of them had several hundred personal followers, and as a group they dominated the military staff positions of the Liang provincial garrison, farther up the Han River valley. In 552 forces from the Yuwen regime surrounded the Liang provincial seat at Nanzheng. While Shupi was on a diplomatic mission to the Chang'an court, the members of the inspector's personal staff decided to surrender, but, fearful that the Du brothers would not go along with the scheme, they struck and killed all of them, offering the excuse that they had been plotting to rebel. The inspector executed one of the ringleaders, but most escaped punishment, and all of them, as well as Du Shupi, wound up surrendering to the Chang'an court anyway.[26]

These sorts of local dramas occurred in provincial garrisons all over the western lands, as one by one their occupants calculated their personal advantage and, inevitably, were conquered and subsumed by the much more coherent and less fragmented forces of the north. The cases of Liu Zhongli, Du An, Du Shupi, and Xi Gu exemplify the significance of small groups, often bands of brothers and other close male relatives, each controlling a few hundred to a few thousand personal troops, whose allegiance was open to the highest bidder. The fragmentary effects of such voluntarism amongst these isolated fighting units allowed the Yuwen regime to pick them off with relatively little difficulty as they moved into the south.

## XIANGYANG UNDER THE YUWEN REGIME

Though Xiangyang remained nominally under the control of Prince Cha, the events of 550 placed it solidly under the military domination of the Yuwen regime. Over the next several years this de facto arrangement became de jure, as Xiangyang came under direct administration from Chang'an. The process was a smooth one, never requiring any military campaign against the city, nor provoking any local rebellion. In fact, one is hard-pressed to identify any drastic result from the transition to northern rule; only over the next generation or two do the contrasts with southern rule become somewhat more apparent.

The military grip of the Yuwen regime on the upper Yangzi region at this time was formidable. Yuwen Tai initially sought to anoint Prince Cha as the heir to the Liang throne, but the prince demurred. However, he did accept the title "King of Liang" (*Liang wang* 梁王), a precursor to the more elevated title, and he went to Chang'an in the fall of 550 to meet with Yuwen Tai in person.[27]

Meanwhile, Hou Jing failed to make much headway in his upriver campaign in 551, so he elected to kill the remaining members of the Liang imperial house who were under his control and make himself emperor. In response, Prince Yi had himself elevated as Liang Emperor Yuan 梁元帝, but at the same time he further mortgaged his future by acceding to the Yuwen regime's control over the upper Han river valley, in return for their pledge of support.[28] Yuwen Tai promptly moved his forces into the area and proceeded to seize all of Sichuan over the following year, eliminating another of Prince Yi's rival claimants to the much-weakened Liang imperial title.

In the summer of 552 Prince Yi's two strongest generals, Wang Sengbian and Chen Baxian 陳霸先, spearheaded a downriver campaign that re-took Jiankang, leading to the death of Hou Jing. By that time, it was evident that they were operating as much in their own interests as in Prince Yi's. Rather than relocate to the greatly damaged and depopulated old capital and effectively become their captive, Prince Yi elected to keep his "imperial" court upriver in Jiangling, where he had a strong base of local supporters amongst the Nanyang immigrant cluster. He apparently did not anticipate trouble from Yuwen Tai, perhaps believing that he had been a sufficiently pliant ally. This proved a fatal miscalculation. In 554 Yuwen Tai's forces moved south from Xiangyang and seized Jiangling easily. Much of the imperial library, which Prince Yi had moved upriver, was destroyed in the process, and the literati of the prince's court were taken captive and transported under grueling conditions to Chang'an. Prince Yi himself was executed, and Prince Cha, who had distinguished himself only by being even more thoroughly pliant than his uncle, was installed at Jiangling as the new Liang emperor, posthumously known as Emperor Xuan of the "later" Liang dynasty 後梁宣帝.

For the Xiangyang area, the reassignment of Prince Cha led to direct administration by the Yuwen regime, with the new title of Xiang province 襄州. It was a very smooth transition, for several reasons. Most immediately, Xiangyang avoided the wrenching destruction and subsequent forced relocation that the Jiangling elite experienced. The Jiangling elite had made a deep investment in their service to Prince Yi over several decades, and his slow surrender to the Yuwen regime seems to have been undertaken in a state of great denial, with catastrophic consequences. By comparison, Prince Cha's surrender was much more clear-sighted, and neither his initial collaboration, nor his later transfer to Jiangling, required any fighting at Xiangyang itself. The lack of any rebellion or other protest over these events suggests that most of the leading men of the region accepted the opportunity to work for a different regime.

The Yuwen regime also offered plentiful opportunities for fighting men. The core leadership of the regime consisted of about a dozen close associates of Yuwen Tai who had accompanied him on the conquest of the Guanzhong region in the 530s; it was much more strongly oriented toward military virtues than the Jiankang elite had been, and harbored far greater military ambitions than had any southern regime.[29] After working through the succession crisis that eventually put Yuwen Tai's son Yuwen Yong 宇文邕 on the throne as Zhou Emperor Wu 周武帝 (r. 560–577), the regime's leadership was engaged in almost continual warfare with the eastern Wei/northern Qi regime, and gradually developed the resources necessary to conquer the regime at Jiankang, which had been reconstituted by the general Chen Baxian.

The benefits of this investment in military affairs rapidly came home to the Xiangyang region. In 565 it was made the command headquarters for four provinces covering the entire northern part of the central Yangzi area, including Jiangling itself, with the emperor's only full brother, Yuwen Zhi, Lord of Weiguo 衛國公直, as local commander.[30] Though this administrative arrangement was discontinued in 572, it was effectively restored again in the period leading up to the seizure of the imperial title by the regent Yang Jian 陽堅 (enthroned as Sui Emperor Wen 隨文帝 in 581), when Xiangyang was the center for Yang Jian's "loyalist" forces who fought against the rebellion of Sima Xiaonan 司馬消難 in the Yangzi valley.[31] The arrangement was formally restored in 586, in the run-up to the campaign to conquer the Chen regime, when Yang Jian's third son, Yang Jun, Prince of Qin 秦王俊, was made the local commander and head of one of the three main wings of the Sui assault on Jiankang.[32] Xiangyang's centrality in the military plans of the Chang'an regime was aided by the unusual status of Jiangling, which remained under the nominal rule of Xiao Cha and his descendents until 587. As a result, it did not play its usual role as the administrative seat and primary military staging area for the central Yangzi; Xiangyang, which took on this role instead, thereby benefited from a much greater level of imperial attention than it otherwise might have.[33]

Broadened opportunities at the lower ranks of military service may have helped to compensate for a reduced opportunity to advance very high. The top generals of the Chang'an regime maintained a tight system of marital endogamy and heritable privilege, resulting in a relatively closed system which did not allow newcomers in readily. Moreover, they did not have significant personal armies; the military recruitment system, at least at the highest levels, was a good deal more impersonal than was the clientelage system of the southern princes.[34] As a result, it did not offer the same opportunity for rapid advancement into the upper ranks that the far more fluid, unstable southern regimes had. In practice, however, very few men from Xiangyang had ever benefited from the opportunities the southern system afforded; it had functioned more like a very limited lottery that was held only once per generation, upon imperial succession.

The men from Xiangyang who rose the highest in the Chang'an regime over this period were those who made timely and strategic surrenders from the south. A symbolic testament to the regime's appreciation of such men is represented by their move in 564 to build an elaborate tomb at Xiangyang for Xi Gu, whose fighting traditions and well-timed surrender made him the "right sort" of local man.[35] Still, many local men who pursued opportunistic routes of career advancement discovered only dead ends. Liu Zhongli, though reportedly respected in the north, gained no high office from his surrender, which northern sources describe unflatteringly as a "capture."[36] The Du brothers' fate after allying with Prince Yi was even more unfortunate. They soon attached themselves to the prince's most competent general, Wang Sengbian, sealing the alliance by marrying their nephew, Du Kan 杜龕, to Wang's daughter. Kan and his two remaining uncles were key participants in the campaign to take Jiankang in 552, in which both uncles died. In the subsequent struggle between Wang and Chen Baxian for control of the city and the throne Wang was also killed. Du Kan then rebelled against Chen Baxian's forces at the urging of his wife, and was also killed, thereby ending the fortunes of this entire branch of the Dus.[37]

Men with more education and less fighting potential tended to find the process of changing allegiance not quite as fraught with danger, but also less potentially rewarding. Many well-educated men who had served Prince Yi and were taken to Chang'an in 554 received acclaim and significant postings in the north, though they usually did not gain great power.[38] A similar fate befell the clients of Prince Cha, who had relocated to Jiangling and gained exalted, but largely powerless offices. After the regime (now headed by Xiao Cha's grandson) was finally eliminated in 587, some of the men serving it received office in the Sui regime. These men were typically the more educated men whom Prince Cha had originally brought out from the capital, or their descendents. Xiangyang fighting men such as Wei Yide and Yin Zheng, though they had gained noble titles and fiefs of a thousand households in their own lifetimes, left no noteworthy descendents.[39]

One educated Xiangyang man who succeeded in changing sides to his own advantage was Liu Xia. He had accepted high titles from Prince Cha when the prince was still "King of Liang" at Xiangyang, but when the regime moved to Jiangling he declined to follow, submitting the following memorial:

> My lord has restored the imperial fortunes, and made his dragon flight over the old [lands of] Chu. Your servant has met with good fortune, raising his name early on, guided by betrothing himself to his state, his beginning and end. Since the House of Jin moved south, your servant's family has been poor. My great-

> uncle [Yuanjing] was Defender-in-chief; my father [Jiyuan] was Unequalled [in Honor]; my uncle [Qingyuan] was Minister of Works; altogether through their official positions our fortunes were made great and our household was at the capital. Now all that remains is this servant in front of you, left alone to guard their graves. [You] have often enjoined your servant and others that, when in service, do not abandon this purpose. Now that Xiangyang has entered the Northern Court, if your servant were to accompany the imperial entourage, my promotion would not benefit common affairs, while my demotion would show the failure of the initial appointment. A bright mirror, that conceals desires and bends low—a good servant has a heart like this.[40]

The need to tend the familial graves may have been a reasonable sounding excuse, but Liu Xia was hardly the last surviving member of the Liu lineage; many of Qingyuan's grandchildren were alive, as were several grandsons of Liu Shilong; one was in service to Prince Cha at the time.[41] Nonetheless, Liu Xia remained in Xiangyang, studying the classics and refusing all appointments either from Prince Cha or from the Chang'an regime, until Prince Cha himself died in 562. Liu Xia went to Jiangling and publicly mourned at the funeral of his former patron, as a good client was expected to. He then promptly came out of retirement and accepted the high titles being offered to him by the northern court.[42] His well-timed retirement allowed him both to fulfill his duties to his former patron, yet also prepare the way to shift his allegiance honorably to a wholly new patron. His scrupulousness about these matters, especially when contrasted with the more bluntly self-interested approach of men such as his first cousin once removed, Liu Zhongli, suggests some of the capital polish that he had gained from his early upbringing.[43]

The transition of the Xiangyang region to northern control appears to have been a success for both sides. The Chang'an court gained tremendous strategic advantage and military resources for relatively little effort; Xiangyang men gained a more stable and much more active patron for military recruitment. The obvious bias of southern historians against the "treasonous" role of Prince Cha should not obscure the fact that his actions led to essentially the same result, with much less trauma, as the actions of his uncle Prince Yi, who is approvingly heralded as the "legitimate" last emperor of the Liang. The literary portrait of these events as a catastrophe, exemplified by Yu Xin's justifiably famous "Lament for the South" (*Ai Jiangnan fu* 哀江南賦), must be seen as reflecting the specific experience of the elite at Jiangling, as well as their literary and anti-military bias.[44] For Xiangyang, by comparison, the experience was neither especially dramatic nor tragic.

## VENGEANCE AND FAMILY TIES

The sublimation of Xiangyang into the northern regime highlights the social and cultural differences between different subregions of China, especially regarding family ties and social networks. Scholars routinely take the culture of Jiankang as representative of the "south," but as this study has emphasized, Jiankang culture was hardly typical for regions outside the capital itself. The military culture of Xiangyang may have been less similar to that of Jiankang than to the Guanzhong region. The heavy in-migration of families from Guanzhong had led the Xiangyang area to be called "Yong province (in exile)" or "south Yong province" in the first place. Observing the area's mixed ethnic groups and its fighting spirit, representatives from the southern court made the comparison explicitly, though since they usually had no direct experience of Guanzhong it must be seen primarily as reflecting their prevailing bias against such customs.

One distinctive feature of Xiangyang culture throughout the fifth and sixth centuries was the significance of revenge as a cornerstone of the upholding of personal and family honor. This hallmark remained just as strong in the late Liang period as it had been in the early Song. Prince Cha's bitter punishment of the Du family members shows how well he understood this aspect of the culture, and sought to set an example for his other followers. The Du brothers naturally responded by seeking revenge of their own. After they re-took the capital under the command of Wang Sengbian, they went to Prince Cha's father's gravesite at An'ning 安寧陵, dug up and burned the contents, in order to "requite the bitterness" brought upon their house by Prince Cha's actions. Prince Yi, in the usual manner of imperial princes, chose not to reprimand them for this action, even though the grave was that of his own brother.[45]

The case of their second cousin Du Shupi is equally graphic. As previously noted, Shupi's brothers had all been killed by rivals in the Liang provincial military staff immediately prior to the surrender to the north in 552. After one of the men responsible, Cao Ce 曹策, came to Chang'an, Shupi petitioned for him to be punished, but the Yuwen regime decided against it, since the actions had taken place prior to the garrison's surrender. According to a tale in Shupi's biography, he longed for revenge but feared the court's power. His mother, however, had no such qualms, telling Shupi, "If Cao Ce died in the morning, I could die in the evening and my heart would be sweet—how can you have doubts?" Spurred on by this twisted interpretation of Confucius's teachings, and by his reverence for his mother's wishes, Shupi attacked Cao Ce in the capital streets in broad daylight, stabbed him to death, cut off his head, ripped out his innards, and dismembered his body. He then presented himself bound at court, requesting punishment. Yuwen Tai was pleased with his spirit and pardoned him, in much the same manner as the Liang princes would have.[46]

While such obligations between fathers, sons, and brothers were strong, more extended family networks appear to have been uncommon among Xiangyang men. This contrasts with the situation not only at Jiankang, but also in the north, where both Chinese and non-Chinese worked to document their distant ancestries, and extended family ties and family rank became extremely important to the imperial status and recruitment system established by the Chang'an court. The resultant cultural difference is borne out by the following anecdote of Wei Ding 韋鼎, a grandson of Wei Rui who was admitted to the Sui court following the conquest of the Chen regime:

> The Minister of Personnel, Wei Shikang, and his brethren were extremely respected, and Sui Emperor Wen [Yang Jian] once leisurely asked [Wei] Ding, "Are you and Shikang close or distant relatives?" He answered, "My ancestral house moved to the south, and I am unacquainted with our ancestry (literally: spirit tablets)." The emperor said, "You have a noble ancestry of a hundred generations, how can you forget your origins!" He ordered him to oversee the offering of sacrificial wine and food, and had Shikang invite Ding to Duling. From the Grand Tutor of Chu [Wei] Meng on down, Ding turned out to be the twentieth generation. He researched and wrote about his ancestry, made the *Wei Clan Registry* (*Wei shipu* 韋氏譜) in seven scrolls to publicize it, and stayed for over ten days before returning.[47]

This anecdote tells us a good deal about the nature of southern provincial families. First, it is very revealing that Wei Ding did not know his distant ancestry. Though he probably could trace it back a generation or two prior to Wei Rui, he was clearly unaware of their lineage prior to the migration south in the early fifth century. His branch of the Jingzhao Weis was, along with some branches of the Hedong Lius, one of the best educated and most esteemed families to have lived in the Xiangyang region; if they could not trace their ancestry back more than a few generations, the virtually uneducated common fighting men of Xiangyang were even less likely to have done so. Their customs contrast sharply with that of a small number of very eminent Jiankang clans, who brought their genealogies south with them when they emigrated, or forged them later on, and could claim ancestry back for a dozen generations or more, to the western Jin, the Han dynasty, or even earlier. Not only could Wei Ding not do this, he also apparently did not feel compelled to act as if he could.

Second, Wei Ding was also not aware of how important and powerful his surname was in the north. In the south, the Jingzhao Wei surname may have been of some help in gaining status, but other factors were far more important. Wei Rui's well-timed participation in Xiao Yan's coup, and his subsequent efforts to get his sons a good education at court and place them on the staffs of imperial princes, were the cornerstone of his descendents' success. In the north, however, the possession of an exalted surname was a good deal more consequential. When Wei Ding moved to the northern court he suddenly found himself with a ready-made community of allies and patrons in the form of Wei Shikang and his extended family. These men were only very distant relatives; as it turned out, Wei Ding was an eighth cousin to Wei Shikang's father. Distance of relationship, however, was apparently not of great significance; what mattered was that Wei Ding had an exalted surname, and Wei Shikang and his clan—not to mention Yang Jian himself—believed that, in order to maintain proper social hierarchy, any man who shared that surname needed to be well respected.

The case of the Hedong Liu surname is less clear, but suggests the same phenomenon was at work. First, the southern branches of the Hedong Liu clan do not appear to have maintained significant political ties through an extended family network. Liu Xia, though patronized by his uncle Qingyuan, otherwise is not known to have forged any significant association with Qingyuan's son Jin or his four grandsons, including Liu Zhongli; in fact, the two men were on opposite sides of the civil war between Prince Yi and Prince Cha. Once in the north, however, Liu Zhongli paid more attention to his distant family ties. Failing to receive any official position in Chang'an after he was taken captive, he "returned his household to his ancestral lands" (復家本土) by settling in Hedong, where other men of the Liu surname were prominent and very powerful.[48] His son Yu 柳彧, perhaps guided by the influence of these distant relatives more than by his father, went on to be a scholar of classics and histories and served the northern Zhou and Sui regimes in a series of mid-level staff positions.[49]

Not all men who came under northern rule took advantage of this opportunity. Liu Xia's sons remained resolutely in the south for most of their lives; indeed, his eldest stayed in retirement at Xiangyang for the last ten years of his life rather than take office under the Sui. Du Shupi also chose retirement back to the upper Han River valley, where he had an extensive estate. Notably, his great-grandsons, scholars under the Tang dynasty, are recorded as "men of Xiangyang," their distant Jingzhao heritage no longer considered a central part of their identity.[50]

## THE FURTHER DEVELOPMENT OF BUDDHISM

The previous chapter argued that Buddhism, at least in its more scholarly forms, was not strongly rooted in Xiangyang in the early sixth century. Patronage of Buddhism by the Yuwen regime initially does not appear to have differed greatly from that of the Liang regime. However, during and after the repression of Buddhism in the years 574–577 there is evidence that a more scholarly, institutionalized Buddhism developed a stronger foothold in the region.

At the time of Hou Jing's rebellion, local men continued to have a reputation as hostile to court-sponsored Buddhism. An account in a Buddhist collection records that, when the Du brothers seized control of the capital as a part of Wang Sengbian's forces, their nephew Du Kan went into the Chongyun Hall, the most revered Buddhist temple in the inner palace, and had his men mount the dais, with the intent of chopping down the two giant Buddha statues there and melting them down into weapons. The story reports that the statues came to life, paralyzed the men, then beat them senseless and finally killed them. Though of dubious veracity, the tale conveys the assumption that provincial fighting men such as Du Kan were hostile to symbols of Buddhist power and reverence.[51]

Representatives of the Yuwen regime nonetheless supported the refurbishment of local Buddhist institutions, in much the same fashion as had the Liang princes. In 564 the local commander of the Xiangyang garrison, the Lord of Taiyuan, Wang Bing 太原公王秉, sponsored the enlargement of the Flourishing Effort Monastery (*xingye si* 興業寺) just outside of town to the northeast. A much later record suggests that the temple was already noted for having a magically long-lived tortoise in its pool, and a stele inscribed by a well-known calligrapher. Wang Bing added a seven-story pagoda and another stele, and renamed the compound the Perennial Happiness Monastery (*changle si* 常樂寺).[52] Ten years later, when the Zhou Emperor initiated a persecution of Buddhism, Wang Bing was again serving as the local commander. A story about this period offers the first evidence of a widespread popular Buddhist community in Xiangyang since the period of Dao'an's ministry in the fourth century. The account, recorded in the early seventh century, concerns a protest against the destruction of a particularly venerated statue of Amida Buddha, supposedly first commissioned by Dao'an:

> When Zhou [Emperor] Wu destroyed the dharma [starting] in the *jia-wu* year Jiande 3/574, the Lord of Taiyuan, Wang Bing, was inspector of Xiang province.[53] His assistant Zhangsun Zhe 長孫哲 did not believe in the dharma. He heard [that the Amida Buddha statue] had supernatural responsiveness, so he initially intended to destroy it utterly. The gentry and women of the town and the defrocked monks and nuns heard that he intended to destroy it, wailed with grief and overflowed the road. Zhe glared, brim-full of anger, at the monks & laity lamenting, and he compelled his subordinates to immediately order [the demonstration] broken up. He ordered one hundred people to be bound by their necks, but when pulled they would not move. Zhe spoke heartlessly, saying

> that those who had overseen the event should be beaten one hundred strokes each, starting with those who were being dragged. He added three hundred strokes, but they still would not move. Zhe's anger was further inflamed, and he added five hundred more strokes and had them dragged down to the ground, the sound shaking the earth. People all were terrified; only Zhe was leaping for joy, and further ordered them burned to death.[54] He raised his voice in happy song, then mounted his horse to go tell the inspector, but having gone only one hundred paces he suddenly fell from the horse, was struck dumb staring straight ahead, and could not be revived for four watches [i.e., eight hours]. By nightfall he was dead. The monks and laity sang a very happy song.[55]

Obviously much about this account is embellished for dramatic effect to further propagate the wonders of the Buddhist faith. At core, however, the account is predicated upon the existence of a substantial Buddhist community in Xiangyang which was capable of organizing against perceived threats. The theme of vengeance, in which local Buddhists fight off evil state representatives, is similar to the tale of Facong, from chapter 4, but this time the evidence suggests much more widespread participation.

Circumstantial evidence further suggests that Xiangyang's community of believers may not have been an especially learned or eminent one. Daoxuan's *Continued Biographies of Eminent Monks*, also assembled in the early seventh century, has four profiles of men who were born in the Xiangyang region and joined the sangha in the 550s to the early 570s. All four of them elected to leave the area to begin their careers elsewhere, which implies that the social and intellectual milieu in Xiangyang was still not very promising for ambitious young Buddhists.[56]

Things appear to have changed following the end of the Zhou persecution, when Yang Jian's regime returned to strongly promoting the Buddhist dharma. Around this time, several monks with local roots returned to the area and made substantial contributions to the local ministry. The monk Zhirun 智潤, for example, had been born in the Xiangyang area around 540 CE, but initially took no teacher and merely studied on his own. He finally went elsewhere to seek greater knowledge when he was twenty years old. After a long sojourn and a widely varied study in Huayan and other schools, he eventually returned to the Xiangyang area just after the Zhou persecution to preach and "transform the customs of the region." At least one local youth, originally surnamed Zhang 張, was persuaded to join the sangha under Zhirun's tutelage and took the name Zhiba 智拔 in 578, when he was only six years old.[57]

The very pious Yang Jian took particular notice of the Xiangyang area in the run-up to the conquest of Chen in the mid-580s. Recognizing the significance of the region in the career of his father Yang Zhong, Yang Jian personally commissioned the enlargement of the Phoenix Woods Monastery (*fenglin si* 鳳林寺), on the Gazing-at-Chu hills (*wang Chu shan* 望楚山) southwest of town, and had it renamed the Flourishing State Monastery (*xing'guo si* 興國寺) in 586.[58] The development enticed the return of Xiangyang's most influential Buddhist, the monk Huizhe 慧哲. Originally of a local family surnamed Zhao 趙, Huizhe had left home, probably in the 550s, and traveled to Jiankang, where he became very highly respected and was appointed by one of the Chen emperors as the grand chief of the Buddhist clergy (*dasengzheng* 大僧正). After the fall of the Chen regime in 589 he returned to Xiangyang, where he took up residence in the Dragon Spring Monastery (*longquan si* 龍泉寺), part of the Sui imperial Buddhist complex on the Gazing-at-Chu hills. There he had a ministry of more than three hundred disciples, including several other monks with local origins who eventually returned to the area to study with him.

Though Huizhe died in 597, the activity recorded in Xiangyang is thereafter a good deal more substantive and continuous than it was previously.[59] Three accounts profile local men who took monastic vows in the generation following the Zhou persecution; all of them stayed in the area for their initial careers, suggesting the local sangha had become a more promising venue for ambitious young monks.[60] By the end of the Sui period the local sangha was so powerful that local monks were able to join with local gentry and raise troops to try to overthrow the Xiang provincial military commander.[61] Such forthright intervention was never recorded during the southern regimes.

## CONCLUSION

The mid-sixth century was a time of tremendous trauma in most parts of the southern regime. Those not caught in the direct fighting were compelled to make life and death decisions about whom they would follow, and how to decide their often contradictory allegiances. For some, like the Du brothers, this decision led to the destruction of their clan. For others, like Xi Gu, it led to high office and tremendous posthumous honors. In either case, however, what we find is that men's allegiances beyond their immediate and often potent dedication to close male relatives were up for grabs. Xiangyang men had a powerful code of vengeance, which demanded a fierce and violent defense of one's father or brothers, and led to the development of small personal bands of a few hundred or a few thousand fighting men at most. By comparison, they had a highly fungible loyalty to everyone else, including their immediate patrons, and switched sides for the expedient purpose of personal survival and gain.

Given these circumstances, the sublimation of the Xiangyang area to the Chang'an regime was a fairly smooth operation. In fact, because the Chang'an regime was much more focused on military patronage than the southern regime had been, it probably dispersed more benefits to more local men, and knitted them more tightly into its ranks. The process was greatly aided by the Chang'an regime's eventual focus on retaking the south, which brought a vigorous and well-connected military command center to Xiangyang, a pattern that echoed the Jin conquest of the south in the late third century. The process even appears to have finally accomplished at least some part of the "transformation" of local culture along Buddhist lines, which had earlier been attempted, with no evidence of success, by the Liang princes.

# SIX

# CONCLUSION

Having looked at southern dynasties history from a provincial *hanmen* perspective, what have we learned? First, we have found that personal patronage is an exceedingly effective model for understanding the military and political system of the southern dynasties, especially as viewed from the perspective of provincial elites. Second, we have seen that provincial *hanmen* society was quite different from that of the imperial court, which is commonly thought to be representative of "southern" culture. Third, since patronage relationships were personal and voluntary, bridging cultural differences was a critical part of their success, and thus to the ability of the southern dynasties system to function at all. In this conclusion I will review what we have learned about the nature of Xiangyang provincial society and culture, and then explore its implications for the operation of the patronage system in the wider political realm.

## LOCAL COMMUNITY AND LOCAL CULTURE

In the introduction to this work I offered a distinction between communities with "hard" boundaries and those with "soft" boundaries. "Hard-boundaried" communities show a strong, self-generated sense of identity and political cohesion, and make explicit demands on members' loyalty and allegiance. For the Xiangyang area, evidence of this sort of community is extremely scarce. The brief accounts of widespread community activism in the 450s, as a response to the Daming-period residence determination, are the only substantive testimony, but this evidence is overwhelmed by the many, many instances of local men serving outside the community in ways that were clearly driven by their own proximate interests, not in the service of larger regional loyalties.

A more plausible idea is that "hard" local communities formed a basis for political identity on a scale smaller than "Xiangyang" as a whole, perhaps at the level of immigrant clusters. Here the evidence is better, but still scanty. The families of the Jingzhao cluster may have practiced some form of marital endogamy, and conceived of one another as associates and peers in ways that sharply distinguished others from outside the cluster. The leadership of the immigrant cluster that formed Huashan commandery was passed down among the scions of the Kang lineage, suggesting something akin to kingship and perhaps entailing a significant level of political allegiance and subordination. We have no record of who their supposed "subjects" were, however, nor the membership of anyone within such a community. The records of the leaders of these local groups show them working outside of the community, even relocating far away, with no clear indication that their primary loyalty was to community interests rather than to their own advancement. Liu Qingyuan and his descendents are the only example where local men deliberately forsook significant opportunities to advance themselves in order to cultivate their local base instead. The case for a tight, "hard-boundaried" political identity in these smaller-scale communities therefore seems unproven, though suggestive.

By comparison, there is substantial evidence for a regional community with a "soft" boundary, which created an indistinct emotional tie but did not command political allegiance or identity. Communities of this sort readily admit outside members, and accept that their members will work outside the community for their own personal ends, though this may cause some conflicting interests or a twinge of regret. The Xiangyang region as a whole had a distinctive, if heterogeneous, cultural mix that on occasion served as a source of pride and resistance when contrasted with the culture and power of the Jiankang court; this ethos is reflected most clearly in the tales recorded by Bao Zhi, and in the role of the monk Facong. This did not develop into an overriding sense of political loyalty among local men, but it did have an effect on the personal, emotional, and social aspects of relations between the court and the province. Because these personal and social relations were the cornerstone of the patron-client system that staffed the southern military, they had significant political ramifications. We cannot understand history from the provincial *hanmen* perspective, therefore, unless we first attempt to imagine the provincial society and culture that bred the *hanmen*, and to which they felt emotionally, if not politically, bound.

The most obvious and defining characteristic of the society of the Xiangyang area at this time was the use of violence. The leading men of this region typically hunted in the hills and wild lands when they were young, fought on campaigns (often against hill people) by the time they were in their teens, and gained fame and prestige by the number they were able to kill. They served in the local garrison as line troops, rose in prestige to command divisions, and, if they were lucky, caught the attention of an imperial prince and got taken up as a personal client, with a position on his personal military staff and an opportunity to follow him to other postings. Local men's ability to engage in personal combat was valued and rewarded by imperial princes and other potential patrons all through the fifth and sixth centuries.

There were certainly other career tracks open to local men that did not involve personal combat, especially in trade. Such trade would often have been linked to the garrison itself, which, in addition to recruiting troops, also developed large stockpiles of supplies that would have required purchasing agents, boatmen, warehouse managers, and other tradesmen who did not ordinarily engage in combat. Virtually none of these men made it into the historical record, but they were part of local society just the same. Cai Na's elder brother Ju, for example, was wealthy but apparently did not fight for the garrison, instead using his money to patronize local clients, probably fighting men. Cao Yizong's eventual father-in-law, surnamed Xiang, was quite wealthy (much more so than the Cao brothers), presumably from commercial ventures. The fact that he anxiously sought to marry his daughter into the Cao family suggests, however, that the culture of the garrison was widely admired and a source of high status within local society, even among those who did not themselves serve in the military.

Closely tied to the centrality of violence was the importance of vengeance and personal honor. There are numerous accounts of men with murdered fathers seeking out the man responsible and cutting him down in broad daylight in the market square, sometimes elaborating the deed by hacking off his limbs and cutting out his internal organs. Du Ze and his brothers took this so far as to violate the tomb of a former heir-apparent to the imperial throne, in order to avenge the brutal destruction of their own clan members and their graves. Fathers were not the only relatives who deserved such dedication; other accounts record similar responses to the violation of brothers and even cousins. This familial "Confucian revenge ethic" is best illustrated in the account of Du Shupi, whose mother egged him on to exact revenge by paraphrasing the *Analects*.[1] The tale of Xue Andu and Liu Yuanjing at the capital further illustrates that, while provincial men often assumed that violent revenge was right and proper, others understood that the culture of the capital was different, and likely to disapprove of such violent feuds. Nonetheless, agents of the imperial court who were posted to the provinces routinely chose not only to forgive acts of revenge, but to promote the perpetrators, recognizing that their sense of honor, and their willingness to kill for it, were valuable assets in fighting men. Such an outcome was facilitated if the perpetrator went through the ritual of presenting himself bound and ready for punishment, thereby clearly demonstrating that his crime was a personal one, not an act of disloyalty to the regime.

The range of relationships considered to justify revenge-taking highlights a third characteristic of Xiangyang society: exceedingly narrow family ties.

Given the wealth of scholarship on the supposedly "aristocratic" nature of the medieval elite, and their preoccupation with genealogy, this is perhaps the most unexpected element of local culture. Accounts of Xiangyang men show them associating in bands of close male relatives, usually brothers (often six, seven, or ten of these) and their sons, and occasionally cousins. By comparison, more distant relatives are rarely mentioned as political associates, and were probably not known or recorded. In several cases, groups of male relatives who were separated by only two or three generations of ancestry made political decisions quite independently of one another, winding up on different sides of civil wars. It might be argued that having family members ally with different men and different courts was a survival strategy for an extended family network, but the evidence does not suggest that they operated this way. For example, Du An and his brothers were based in Xiangyang, first allied with Prince Cha, then with Prince Yi, in whose service they fought their way to Jiankang before all of them were killed. Their second cousins, Du Shupi and his brothers, emigrated into Liang province; Shupi threw his lot in with the Chang'an regime and did quite well for himself, eventually retiring back to his substantial estates in Liang province. There is no evidence whatsoever that he "continued the line" of Du An, Du Ze, and their offspring, or that his strategy had been in any way coordinated with theirs.

The most telling evidence for limited family ties comes from Wei Rui and his offspring, who were the best-educated, most "cultured" family line to emerge from Xiangyang in the Liang period. The evidence from Wei Ding's biography testifies that even this lineage was unable to trace its ancestry back prior to Rui's great-grandfather's emigration to the south in the early fifth century, if that far; their ancestral ties to powerful men in the late Han, Wei, and western Jin period, as well as to contemporary high-status lineages in the north, only became known to them when they gained access to the far better records of northern lineages after the conquest of the Chen regime in 589. Other local lineages were probably no more aware of their ancestry, which would only have been reconstructed by Tang-era historians as a result of the records preserved in the north (and perhaps a bit of imagination).

The narrowness of familial ties tends to support other evidence for the essentially personal, face-to-face nature of Xiangyang society. Xiangyang men developed enduring ties to brothers and cousins because they grew up together and served closely together. By comparison, they were unlikely to feel a strong tie to men they had barely met, even if they happened to be related by blood; blood ties alone were a rather abstract concept that had little hold on local men's conception of loyalty. In other words, though ties with blood relatives are ordinarily thought of as ascribed, in the Xiangyang case they might equally well be conceived of as personal and at least somewhat a matter of environmental circumstance, and even choice.

The social system based on violence, vengeance, and narrow, personalized family ties was reflected in a variety of other local cultural practices that are more difficult to reconstruct, for several reasons. First, Xiangyang society was very heterogeneous, with recent immigrant groups and resettled hill peoples forming perhaps the majority of the population, so it is hazardous to make any sort of blanket assertion about local cultural practices. More critically, local men left no written record of their culture; besides a few tombs, the information we have about it comes entirely through the eyes of outsiders, often unsympathetic ones. Nonetheless, what they report tends to complement what we have already found from the evidence of local men's political and social behavior.

The most salient characteristic of local culture was the very limited literacy of most local men. Many of the most successful are explicitly identified as having been barely literate, if at all; none are noted for scholarly works. Classical literacy appears to have survived only in isolated pockets: Wei Rui and his brothers and affinal relatives in the Jingzhao cluster, perhaps, or the so-called three lords who supposedly hid out west of town to make classical music during the late Song period. Such men are characterized as gaining little or no local fame or status, and deliberately refusing to associate with the "common folk" of the area, or to compare themselves to them. They certainly did not set the cultural tone of the region as a whole.

Local men's lack of classical education means that they would not have appreciated the cultural history of the region in the way that most surviving local history texts do. The anecdote in which Zhang Jing'er is unaware of the legacy of Yang Hu and the "Stele of Falling Tears" is especially revealing, for it shows that local fighting men were believed to be ignorant of their own local past. Without the ability to read, most of that past would have been opaque to them. Furthermore, many of them came from elsewhere, and probably had little or no investment in local legends and lore; others, such as Zong Yue, came from quite poor households and cannot be presumed to have been very concerned with such abstractions. The antiquarian corpus of stories from the Han, Three Kingdoms, and Jin periods, preserved and celebrated by narrow communities like the Nanyang immigrant cluster at Jiangling, and adapted into texts such as the *Annotations to the Classic of Waterways*, bore little or no relevance to contemporary Xiangyang culture and society. Bao Zhi was exceptional for recording local tales that were current in his own day and age; notably, they show little engagement with the body of lore passed down from earlier times.

Instead, local society was based on an oral and physical culture quite unlike that of antiquarian lore, or of the literate elite at Jiankang. As discussed in chapter 2, the best-known hallmark of this oral culture was the "western lyric" tradition, which involved dancing girls, rhythmic percussion, and lyrics drawn from experiences in commercial life. Known from the early fifth century, and still popularly patronized by wealthy local men such as Cao Jingzong early in the sixth, we have a record of this tradition only because imperial princes and their clients from the Song period onward found much to appreciate in it, and adapted it with more classical language and allusive poetic purpose. We have little or no evidence of how widespread or popular it really was in Xiangyang itself, or of the many varieties of local music that went unexplored and unrecorded by the literate capital elite. By all accounts it was a rich tradition, now almost entirely lost.

Another distinctive local cultural tradition was the staging of competitive spectacles, such as boat races, ball games, and tug-of-war competitions. It is difficult to be sure just when these traditions began, but, as discussed in chapter 4, the evidence for them begins to appear only in the late sixth and early seventh centuries. These spectacles demonstrate the development of a military-oriented local elite that was actively engaged in patronizing the lower classes, using their material and organizational resources to stage elaborate coordinated competitive events for popular entertainment. Such a role would have been quite uncharacteristic of the detached, socially disengaged ethos of the late Han elite (which persisted locally into the fourth century), but fits very well with what we know to have been an extremely combative, ostentatious, and honor-bound style among the Xiangyang local elite in the fifth and sixth centuries. Like the western lyric tradition, some of these customs were eventually taken up into "high" court culture and dressed up in classical guise. In the best-known case of the boat races, an association with Qu Yuan was developed probably no earlier than the 520s, in response to Prince Gang, and perhaps not until the end of the century.

The evidence regarding local Buddhism also shows the mark of this illiterate oral and physical culture. Collected biographies of eminent monks, which favor monks of the scholarly Buddhist establishment, show little evidence of activity in Xiangyang in the fifth and early sixth century.[2] Locally born men who went on to become "eminent" monks in the early to mid-sixth century got their start by going somewhere else to study, suggesting that the region did not support an educated Buddhist establishment, despite the efforts of Prince Gang and others to develop one. Indeed, accounts of local men such as Guo Zushen and Du Kan show outright hostility to the Buddhist establishment. Even the faithful, such as Wei Rui, are supposed to have had a relatively heterodox approach to the faith, one that is also evidenced by local tombs. The most prominent local Buddhist in the early sixth century, the monk Facong, was a recluse and local miracle worker, not tied to any larger Buddhist establishment; he served not as an advocate but an opponent of the more institutionalized sort of Buddhism promoted by court representatives. Based on such limited evidence, Buddhism in Xiangyang appears to have been comparable to the Buddhism seen at Chang'an in the mid-fourth century under Fotudeng, a faith which appealed to a largely illiterate populace that was most readily impressed by miracles and other evidence of supernatural efficacy that could bring immediate and tangible benefits.

The social and cultural system of the Xiangyang region contrasts sharply with Jiankang's literate and refined culture, which left us far more evidence of its values and practices, and which has received the vast bulk of scholarly attention. Yet it was Xiangyang, and garrisons like it, that bred the provincial *hanmen* that dominated the military system of the southern courts, and shaped their political order and their destiny. We cannot understand the southern regimes without taking this provincial *hanmen* culture into account; it was every bit as much a part of "southern" culture as was the high literary tradition of Jiankang.

## PATRONAGE AND THE EVOLUTION OF COURT-PROVINCIAL RELATIONS

What bridged the difference between the imperial court and this fractious provincial society was personal patronage ties between local fighting men and imperial princes or other imperial agents who were posted to the region. Such personal patronage ties may have been the primary social structure within Xiangyang local society as well, though there also may have been ascribed or bound ties with little or no voluntarism to them; the evidence is quite slight, either way. What we can say is that the stratum of local society that interacted with the imperial court operated by a set of social presumptions dominated by voluntary and often shifting personal ties, not fixed and abstract loyalties.

As discussed in the introduction, the voluntary nature of patronage ties leads to a very fluid, unpredictable social system, in which men can and do change sides based on emotional ties and calculations of self-interest. This fluidity is demonstrated repeatedly in Xiangyang men's career choices. Perhaps the clearest example is the episode when many Xiangyang local men who had served under Liu Hu in the 450s and early 460s wound up fighting against him in the civil war of 465–466. Liu Hu tried to woo them back by appealing to the emotions of their old local ties, a strategy that presumably was thought to have a reasonable chance of success. However, they stayed firmly allied with their new patron, whom they judged (correctly, as it turned out) to be a more promising source of career advancement. The episode neatly illustrates the significance of both emotional and careerist approaches to personal loyalty and the possibility of tension between them.

The shifting nature of these highly personal, idiosyncratic calculations had enormous implications for court-provincial relations and the system of military recruitment. Imperial princes and other potential patrons recruited fighting men by developing personal, face-to-face relations with them, attempting to secure their allegiance primarily through material rewards and promotions. These were costly, however, and could quickly be outbid in a crisis, so princes also sought to cultivate an emotional bond of *en* 恩, or gratitude, a bond sometimes referred to in the literature simply as *jiu* 舊, "old ties." Prince Yigong kept Liu Yuanjing's allegiance throughout his life, not only by ensuring that he got ample promotions and rewards, but also by treating him as a comrade and drinking partner. Xiao Yan is noted for having carefully cultivated his personal relationships with his Xiangyang military clients, even after he became emperor, by humoring their embarrassing social habits and flattering them with personal portraits. His grandson, Prince Cha, is also noted for holding on to his local clientelage network, even as he took the region over to the north, due to his tremendous camaraderie with local fighting men, who were able to recognize in him a relatively kindred soul, just as they had surely been able to recognize in Prince Gang a decidedly un-kindred soul. In other words, the interpersonal skills and flexibility of individual imperial princes would have made a significant difference in their ability to recruit military support.

One of the hallmarks of such a system is that it is incapable of generating a stable, self-regenerating power structure at the center. An aristocratic system, in which power and status relationships are ascribed by birthright, can last many generations; by comparison, a system based upon patronage relationships expires with the death of the patron, sometimes before, as men search out a new and more promising patron. Sometimes personal ties were passed on to a designated heir, but, as the violent cycle of the southern regimes makes abundantly clear, this happened rather rarely. Xiangyang men certainly never demonstrated any evidence of a higher, abstract loyalty to the "dynasty" at Jiankang. Even in the Liang period, when their sense of "loyalty" to the imperial house might have been expected to be strongest, local men shopped around for the most promising patron, among the warring Liang imperial princes, the military strongmen of the south, and eventually the rulers of northern regimes as well. The fratricidal mania of the Liang princes was partly to blame for this, of course; even so, the fact that Xiangyang men were willing to benefit from throwing their allegiance to obvious enemies of the Liang court, such as Hou Jing and Yuwen Tai, demonstrates that abstract loyalty to the dynastic house did not figure prominently in their calculations.

The other result of patronage as a social system is the prevalence of vertical over horizontal ties, and the corresponding weakness of class or regional solidarities. In other words, though the system does not generate stability at the center, it also tends to undermine the development of strong and coherent opposition in the provinces. To some extent, this part of the argument is also justified by Xiangyang's example, since men's career choices were not affected by a strong sense of local identity either, despite their distinctive local culture.

The lack of local identity cannot be attributed exclusively to the workings of the patronage system, however, since (as highlighted especially in chapter 3) the society was fragmented due to many other factors as well: the presence of large populations of hill people and discrete immigrant clusters; language and dialect differences; differing levels of education; and vertical institutional affiliations. The lack of a significant literate upper class, which might have taken the lead in developing a local cultural identity, was probably also a factor.

Nonetheless, the historical development of the Xiangyang region in the fifth and sixth centuries does suggest that the imperial patronage system exacerbated the fragmentation that was already present. Shen Yue's history of the Song dynasty consistently suggests the idea that Xiangyang had been a more cohesive society prior to its first and ultimately very disruptive engagement with imperial power and politics in the 450s and 460s. His account of the region under Liu Daochan's tenure in the 430s is quite idealized, and cannot be taken at face value, but it is instructive that the period before local men began to serve at the capital was already being viewed as a kind of golden age of harmony and solidarity.[3] Equally telling is Shen Yue's account of the region's resistance to the imperial imposition of new household registration and tax requirements in 457, which "caused poor and rich to talk to one another; none in the territory were not enraged."[4] This is a portrait of a society up in arms, in which preexisting social divisions were bridged by a common cause of opposition to the imperial court and its impositions. Moreover, the region benefited in this case by having clear leadership from Liu Yuanjing and his brothers and cousins, who had been local military leaders for decades. Their coordination of the resistance was instrumental in forcing the court to back down, recall their hardline representative, restructure local administration and household registration in a manner more to the locals' liking, and eventually offer an amnesty for all crimes and unpaid taxes.

The irony of this campaign was that Liu Yuanjing's leadership role was due as much or more to his success in the imperial system as to his local accomplishments. In the highly fragmentary and loose-boundaried society of the Xiangyang area, authority flowed most readily to men who could demonstrate their ability to bring in external approval and resources. Thus, in the local civil strife of 461, locals took control and "nominated" a new leader of the garrison, but chose an outsider whom they knew would be acceptable to the court. As I argued in chapter 2, they were certainly mindful of the terrifying punishment of the Guangling garrison in 459, which signaled to all of the garrisons that excessive insubordination would have drastic consequences. Rather than put forward a local strongman with the unifying ability and the courage (or foolhardiness) to take an oppositional approach to the Jiankang regime, the garrison leaders preferred to cooperate and accept an outside appointee.

The fruits of this cooperation for particular individuals were quite significant. Liu Yuanjing had already blazed the trail, opening up the patronage system of the imperial court to men from the Xiangyang area, and showing very concrete benefits in his high titles and his ample estate at the capital. In the wake of the general civil war of 465–466 local military men saw more clearly than ever that pleasing the representatives of the imperial court was their most profitable route for advancement. Zhang Jing'er, Cao Xinzhi, his son Cao Jingzong, and many others accepted clientelage status under imperial princes in pursuit of wealth and rank in the imperial system. It was perilous, to be sure, but no more so than hand-to-hand combat with local hill tribes or the armies of the north, and the rewards were far richer.

So long as the imperial court was generously forthcoming with patronage positions, this fluid relationship worked relatively well. When the avenues of advancement were blocked, however, the Xiangyang area became more rebellious, and its allegiance more free-floating and "biddable." For example, following the execution of Zhang Jing'er in 483, few local men achieved significant status at the imperial court for a generation; this is also a period when there was a definite upswing in local rebellions, such as that of Huan Tiansheng in 487, or the civil war that ended Wang Huan's tenure in office in 493. The renewal of the patronage pipeline under Xiao Yan relieved this tension, but it again became apparent in the late Liang period, as the benefits that accrued to the founding generation were not renewed, or at least not expanded upon, for the subsequent one. The pattern suggests that, had the imperial recruitment system been less open and fluid, the Xiangyang area would have been more rebellious, and potentially a good deal more autonomous, as it had been back in the fourth century when it was dominated by a series of local strongmen.

By comparison, the arc of the region's development in the fifth and sixth centuries suggests that the imperial patronage system, by drawing men's attention and allegiance up out of their local society, continuously undermined the development of an indigenous local elite stratum that was committed to defending the locality and maintaining popular local support. This is clearly the case with Cao Jingzong, who had been ready to take an imperial post and relocate away from Xiangyang in his twenties; what local support he developed subsequently was in some ways a result of his frustrated imperial career. This is also the case with Liu Zhongli, who, though he built up local support, clearly envisioned it as a stepping stone to higher office, not an end in itself. He was no longer the leader of an isolated, and thereby (if only by default) somewhat cohesive society, as his great-granduncle Yuanjing had been; his eyes had been trained up toward something larger. As a result, he and others from his society, such as Du Shupi, Xi Gu, and Liu Xia, were well primed to be brought into the orbit of the highest bidder, the strongest center of power available: not Jiankang, but Chang'an.

# APPENDIX A

# GENEAOLOGICAL CHARTS

# Appendix A
## Diagram #1

### Selected descendents of Liu Zhuo 柳卓
Originally from Jie 解 county in Hedong 河東 commandery
first settled in Xiangyang in the early eastern Jin (320s-330s)

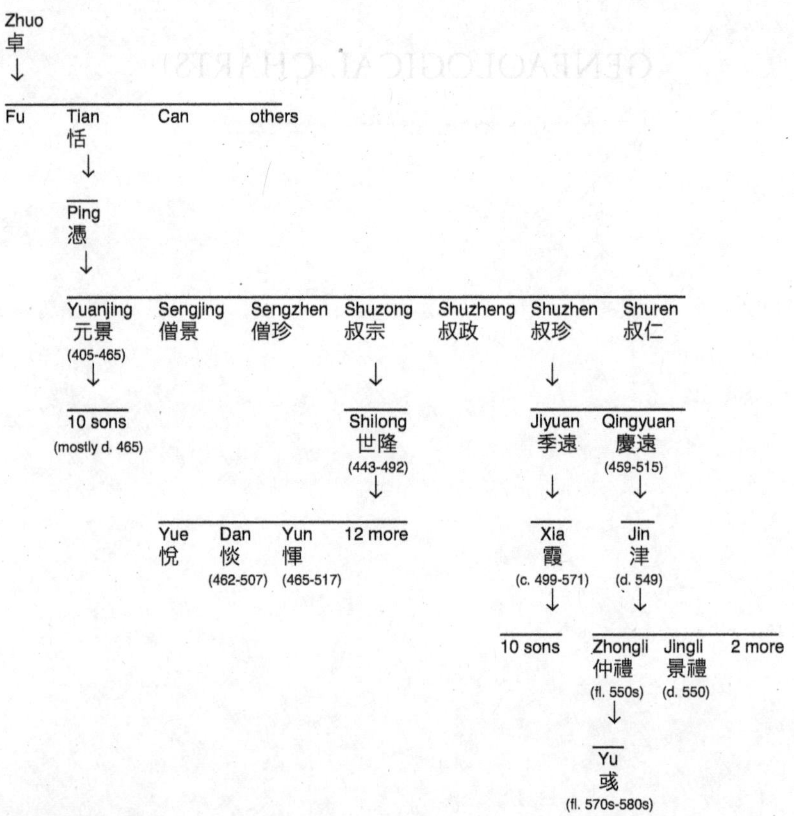


References:
NS 28: 977-995
ZS 42: 765-7/ BS 70: 2441 (Jiyuan, Xia)
SuiS 62: 1481-4/ BS 77: 2622-25 (Yu;
*Yuanhe xingji* 7.226-30: 1111-16
XTS 73A: 2850-54

# Appendix A
## Diagram #2

### Selected descendents of Wei Hua 韋華
Originally from Duling 杜陵 county in Jingzhao 京兆 commandery
who settled in Xiangyang ca. 418
showing affinal relatives surnamed Du 杜 and Wang 王
who were also a part of the Jingzhao immigrant cluster at Xiangyang

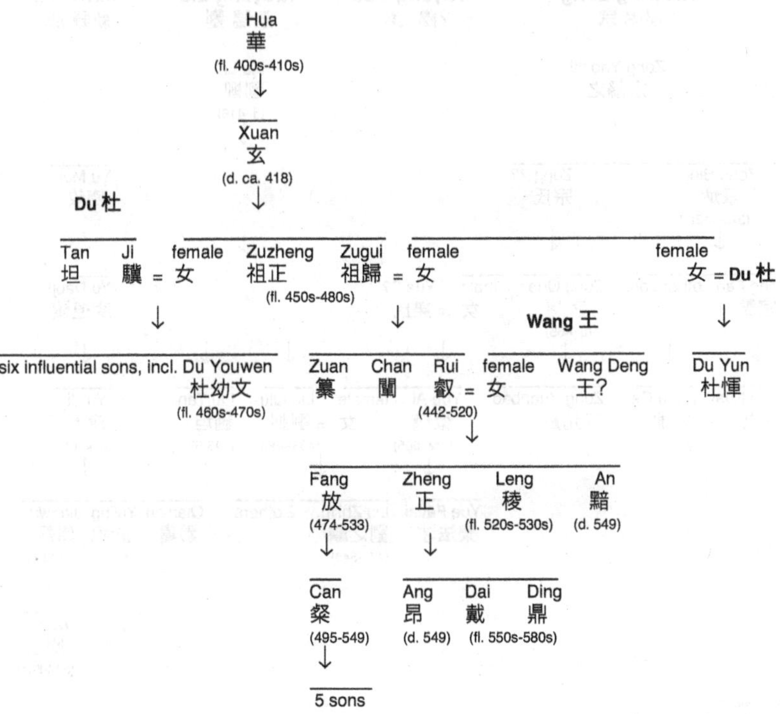


References:
LS 12: 220-27, 28: 423-4, 43: 605-8
NS 58: 1425-37
SS 65: 1720-23 (Du Tan & Ji and sons)
*Yuanhe xingji* 2.205-212: 182-86
XTS 74a: 3310

# Appendix A
## Diagram #3

### Relationships among selected members of the Nanyang cluster
All descended from families which emigrated from Nanyang commandery and settled in Jiangling in the eastern Jin period

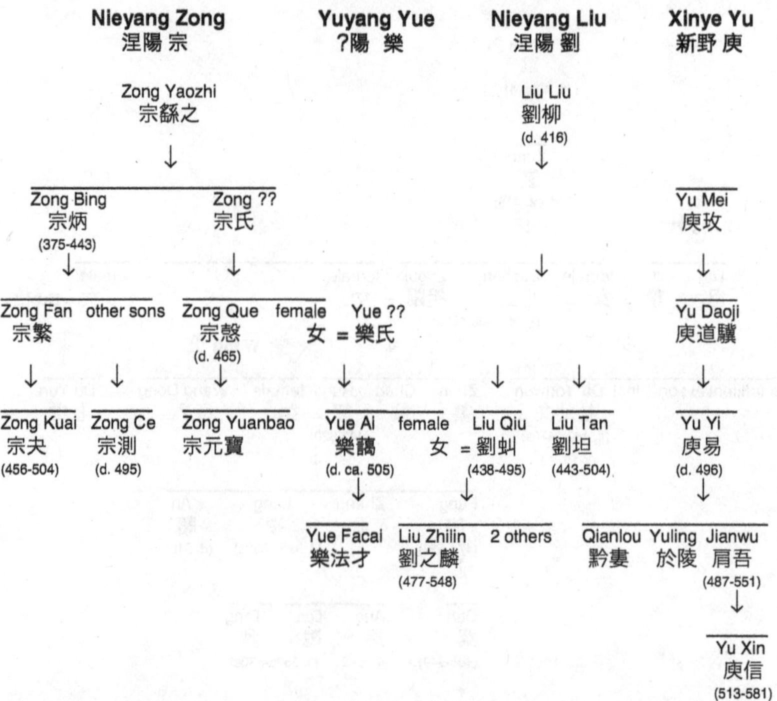


References:
- SS 93:2278-79 (Zong Bing)
- SS 76: 1971-72 (Zong Que)
- NQS 54: 939-41 (Liu Qiu, Yu Yi, Zong Ce); on p. 939 they are noted as having associated with one another as a "study clique."
- LS 19 (Zong Kuai, Yue Ai, Liu Tan); on p. 299 they are noted as being supported by local people and recruited by Xiao Yingzhou.
- LS 40: 572-4/NS 50: 1249-53 (Liu Zhilin)
- LS 47: 650-1; LS 49: 689-92 (sons of Yu Yi)
- XTS 71a: 2255 (profile of Nanyang-Nieyang Liu descendents)

# NOTES

## CHAPTER ONE. INTRODUCTION

1. A summary of attempts to characterize the medieval social order is provided in Albert Dien's introduction to his edited volume, *State and Society in Early Medieval China* (Hong Kong University Press, 1990), 1–29.

2. Patricia Ebrey, *The Aristocratic Families of Early Imperial China: A Case Study of the Po-ling Ts'ui Family*. (Cambridge University Press, 1978); David Johnson, *The Medieval Chinese Oligarchy* (Boulder: Westview, 1976); Nakamura Keiji 中村圭爾, "Liuchao guizuzhi lun 六朝貴族制論," in *Riben xuezhe yanjiu Zhongguoshi lunzhe xuanze*日本學者研究中國史論者選擇, vol. 2 (Beijing: Zhonghua shuju, 1992): 359–91.

3. Dennis Grafflin, "The Great Family in Early Medieval China," *Harvard Journal of Asiatic Studies* 41, no.1 (1981): 65–74, demonstrates the extreme turnover in high-status families of the southern court. Robert Somers, "The Society of Early Imperial China: Three Recent Studies," *Journal of Asian Studies* 38, no.1 (1978): 132–37, emphasizes the existence of other hierarchies of status and influence besides officeholding, suggesting a diverse and pluralistic social order, rather than a monolithic one.

4. Tang Changru 唐长孺, *Wei-Jin Nanbeichao shi lun cong xubian* 魏晋南北朝论丛续编(Beijing: Sanlian shudian, 1959), 92–93. Individual family studies are noted in Helwig Schmidt-Glintzer, "The Scholar-Official and His Community: The Character of the Aristocracy in Medieval China," *Early Medieval China* 1 (1994): 64.

5. Scott Pearce, Audrey Spiro, and Patricia Ebrey, in the introduction to their edited volume, *Culture and Power in the Reconstruction of the Chinese Realm, 200–600* (Cambridge and London: Harvard University Press, 2001), 25–26, 28.

6. Wolfram Eberhard, *Conquerors and Rulers: Social Forces in Medieval China* (Leiden: E. J. Brill, 1952); Tanigawa Michio 谷川道雄, "Prominent Family Control in the Six Dynasties," *Acta Asiatica* 60 (1991): 92–3. See also Tanigawa Michio, *Medieval Society and the Local "Community,"* trans. Joshua Fogel (Berkeley: University of California Press, 1985); Ochi Shigeaki 越智重明, "The Southern Dynasties Aristocratic System and Dynastic Change," *Acta Asiatica* 60 (1991): 54–77. The economic side of this formulation is often associated with the term *haozu* 豪族 or "powerful families," as in Nakamura, "Liuchao guizuzhi," 359–61. Schmidt-Glintzer, "Scholar-Official," essentially equates the "communitarian" ideal with the idea of "aristocracy."

7. Dien, "Introduction," 7, also raises the issue of whether families sharing the same surname and place name of origin, or choronym, can be considered of one cohesive clan; the evidence from this study suggests that, without further supporting evidence, they should not be.

8. The criticisms are summarized in Joshua Fogel's introduction to Tanigawa, *Medieval Society*, and more extensively in Kubozoe Yoshifumi 窪添慶文, "Japanese Research in Recent Years on the History of Wei, Chin, and the Northern and Southern Dynasties," *Acta Asiatica* 60 (1991): 104–34.

9. Evidence of the charitable ideal is gathered in Tanigawa, *Medieval Society*, 102–12, and "Prominent Family Control," 92–93; Miranda Brown, *The Politics of Mourning in Early China* (Albany: State University of New York Press, 2007), 105–26, also discusses the occasional promotion of this ideal in late Han epitaphs.

10. Andrew Chittick, "The Development of Local Writing in Early Medieval China," *Early Medieval China* 9 (2003): 35–70; Patricia Ebrey, "Estate and Family Management in the Later Han as Seen in the *Monthly Instructions for the Four Classes of People*," *Journal of the Economic and Social History of the Orient* 17 (1974): 173–205, notes that Cui Shi's conception of the local circle deserving one's charity was quite narrow, and his engagement with the local community relatively limited.

11. Benedict Anderson, *Imagined Communities: Reflections on the Origin and Spread of Nationalism* (London and New York: Verso, 1991); Harold Isaacs, *Idols of the Tribe: Group Identities and Political Change* (Cambridge: Harvard University Press, 1989); Rupert Emerson, *From Empire to Nation: The Rise to Self-Assertion of Asian and African Peoples* (Cambridge: Harvard University Press, 1960).

12. Prasenjit Duara, "De-Constructing the Chinese Nation," *The Australian Journal of Chinese Affairs* 30 (1993): 20–21, further elaborated in Prasenjit Duara, *Rescuing History from the Nation: Questioning Narratives of Modern China* (Chicago: University of Chicago Press, 1997).

13. Anderson, *Imagined Communities*; Duara, "De-Constructing the Chinese Nation."

14. Charles Holcombe, *In the Shadow of the Han: Literati Thought and Society at the Beginning of the Southern Dynasties* (Honolulu: University of Hawaii Press, 1994), and "Re-imagining China: The Chinese Identity Crisis at the Start of the Southern Dynasties Period," *Journal of the American Oriental Society* 115, no.1 (1995): 1–14; Michael Loewe, "China's Sense of Unity as seen in the Early Empires," *T'oung Pao* 80 (1994): 6–26.

15. David Knechtges, "Sweet-peel Orange or Southern Gold? Regional Identity in Western Jin Literature," in *Studies in Early Medieval Chinese Literature and Cultural History*, ed. Paul Kroll and David Knechtges (Provo, UT: T'ang Studies Society, 2003): 27–79, discusses the sharp cultural distinctions made between northerners and men of the lower Yangzi area following the end of the Three Kingdoms period; Teng Ssu-yu, tr., *Family Instructions for the Yen Clan: Yen-shih Chia-hsun*, by Yen Zhitui (Leiden: E. J. Brill, 1968) offers numerous examples from the late sixth century on roughly the same cultural divide; see for example the chapter, "Customs and Manners," 22–45. Local history writing sometimes reflects nascent elements of such regional sub-identities; see Chittick, "Local Writing."

16. Andrew Chittick, *Pride of Place: The Advent of Local History in Early Medieval China* (University of Michigan Doctoral Dissertation, 1997).

17. Holcombe, "Re-Imagining China," 14, characterizes the "narrowly privileged elite" of the post-Han period as clinging to this formulation.

18. Patricia Ebrey, "Patron-Client Relations in the Later Han," *Journal of the American Oriental Society* 103, no.3 (1983): 533–42; however, she suggests that it declined in significance thereafter, as a more rigid class-based "aristocratic" social system took hold. See also Brown, *Politics of Mourning*, 85–103; Christopher Leigh Connery, *The Empire of the Text* (Lanham, MD: Rowman and Littlefield, 1999), 111–39.

19. Gan Huaizhen 甘懷真, *Huangquan, liyi yu jingdian quanshi: zhongguo gudai zhengzhi shi yanjiu* 黃權, 禮儀與經典詮釋：中國古代政治史研究 (Taibei: Lexue shuju, 2003): 249–98; Tang, *Xubian*, 93–123; Pearce, Spiro, and Ebrey, "Introduction."

20. Terry Johnson and Christopher Dandeker, "Patronage: Relation, and System," in *Patronage in Ancient Society*, ed. Andrew Wallace-Hadrill (London and New York: Routledge, 1989).

21. The most extensive theoretical and comparative approach to patronage is S. N. Eisenstadt and L. Roniger, *Patrons, Clients, and Friends: Interpersonal Relations and the Structure of Trust in Society* (Cambridge: Cambridge University Press, 1984); the basic characteristics of such relationships are summarized on pp. 43–50. These ideas are elaborated with relationship to the Roman Empire in numerous articles in Wallace-Hadrill, *Patronage*, including those by Saller, Drummond, and Garnsey and Woolf, and summarized at the beginning of Johnson and Dandeker, "Relation and System," 221–22.

22. Eisenstadt and Roniger, *Patrons, Clients, and Friends*, 49–50; Johnson and Dandeker, "Relation and System," 234–37.

23. Johnson and Dandeker, "Relation and System," 230–31; Eisenstadt and Roniger, *Patrons, Clients, and Friends*, 29–42; Scott Silverman, "Patronage as Myth," in *Patrons and Clients in Mediterranean Societies*, ed. Ernest Gellner and John Waterbury (London: Center for Mediterranean Studies of the American Universities Field Staff, 1977).

24. Ebrey, "Patron-Client Relations"; Gan, *Huangquan*, 259–67; Tang, *Xubian*, 102–107.

25. Gan, *Huangquan*, 274–79.

26. This strategy has been applied quite profitably to the study of the Roman Empire and late antiquity; for example, Patrick Amory, *People and Identity in Ostrogothic Italy, 489–554* (Cambridge and London: Cambridge University Press, 1997). Some efforts have also been made in rather narrow studies of medieval China, e.g., Howard Goodman, *Ts'ao P'i Transcendent: The Political Culture of Dynasty-Founding in China at the End of the Han* (Seattle: Scripta Serica, 1998).

27. Johnson and Dandeker, "Relation and System," 223–24.

28. NS 58: 1436–37; this episode is discussed at greater length on pp. 130–31.

29. Johnson and Dandeker, "Relation and System," 223–24.

30. Connery, *Empire of the Text*.

31. On bound retainers, see Tang Changru, "Clients and Bound Retainers in the Six Dynasties Period," in Dien, *State and Society*, 111–38. In my work I do not speculate as to how local men recruited and held onto their even lower-status personal followers; my guess is that these ties were also relatively fluid, but they may have been substantially more tightly bound than those at a higher level.

32. The Bai River used to be called the Yu (or Yuan) River in Han and Six Dynasties times, while the nearby Gun River system was called the Bai. This can be quite confusing, since the two rivers are in the same area.

33. See notes by Yang Shoujing 楊守敬 and Xiong Huizhen 熊會貞 to the *Shuijing zhu shu* 水經注疏, by Li Daoyuan 酈道元 (Nanjing: Jiangsu guji chubanshe, 1999), 2385–86.

34. Barry Blakely, "The Geography of Chu," in *Defining Chu: Image and Reality in Ancient China*, ed. Constance Cook and John Major (Honolulu: University of Hawai'i Press, 1999), 10–13.

35. For general reference on the expansion and collapse of Chu, see Luo Yunhuan 罗运环, *Chuguo babai nian* 楚国八百年 (Wuhan: Wuhan University Press, 1992).

36. Paul L.-M. Serruys, *The Chinese Dialects of Han Time According to Fang-yen* (Berkeley: University of California Press, 1959), 91–94; W. South Coblin, "Migration History and Dialect Development in the Lower Yangtze Watershed," *Bulletin of the School of Oriental and African Studies* 65, no. 3 (2002): 529–31.

37. Population figures: HHS-Z 28a: 1563–64. The annotation indicates that the population of Wan County was 47,547 households, which would be almost 240,000 people by the usual reckoning of about five persons per household. Not all of them can safely be considered "urban" residents of Wan city, however.

38. Hans Bielenstein, "Wang Mang, the restoration of the Han dynasty, and Later Han," in *Cambridge History of China vol. 1: The Ch'in and Han Empires 221 B.C.–A.D. 220*, ed. D. Twitchett and M. Loewe (Cambridge and London: Cambridge University Press, 1986).

39. Andrew Chittick, "The Life and Legacy of Liu Biao: Governor, Warlord, and Imperial Pretender in Late Han China," *Journal of Asian History* 37, no. 2 (2003): 155–86; Ueda Sanae 上田早苗, "Go-Kan makki no Joyo no gozoku," *Toyoshi kenkyu* 28, no. 4 (1970): 31–36.

40. John W. Killigrew, "The Reunification of China in AD 280: Jin's Conquest of Eastern Wu," *Early Medieval China* 9 (2003): 1–34.

41. JS 104: 2712; JS 5: 121 (on plague among Shi Le's troops and at Xiangyang); JS 27: 805–806; SS 32: 934; SGZ 28: 783 (on fire at Xiangyang). Chittick, *Pride of Place*, 176, 180, 196 quotes passages from a Xiangyang local history noting the extermination of prominent family lineages at this time. See also Yasuda Jiro 安田二郎, "Jin-Song geming he Yongzhou (Xiangyang) de qiaomin," in *Riben qingnian xuezhe lun Zhongguoshi: Liuchao Sui-Tang juan* (Shanghai: Shanghai guji chubanshe, 1995): 118.

42. Yasuda, "Jin-Song geming," 118. NQS 15: 281–82 notes the typical condescending attitude of Jiankang officials in the mid-fourth century, as well as the predominance of immigrant clans by the century's end.

## CHAPTER TWO. DEVELOPMENT

1. NQS 15: 281–82.

2. JS 117: 2980.

3. William Crowell, "Northern Émigrés and the Problems of Census Registration under the Eastern Jin and Southern Dynasties," in *State and Society in Early Medieval China*, ed. Albert Dien (Hong Kong: Hong Kong University Press, 1990),

171–209; Xia Rixin 夏日新, "Guanyu Dong Jin qiao zhou-jun-xian de jige wenti," *Wei Jin Nanbeichao Sui-Tang shi ziliao*, vol. 11 (Wuhan: Wuhan daxue chubanshe, March 1993): 36–49.

4. JS 63: 1712–14.

5. JS 81: 2115–17; Xia, "Qiao zhou-jun-xian," 42.

6. Crowell, "Northern Émigrés," 191–99.

7. SS 74: 1922 (account of Lu Zongzhi and his descendents); SS 51: 1472–74 (account of Liu Daogui); SS 2: 31–33.

8. JS 117: 2980; the event is dated to the twelfth month of Long'an 2/398 in JS 10: 251.

9. Du: see LS 46: 641–42/NS 64: 1556. Wang: LS 12: 220; NS 74: 1843 . Xi: see ZS 44: 798/BS 66: 2338–39. Kang: see LS 18: 290/NS 55: 1373.

10. SS 65: 1720–21; NS 70: 1698–99.

11. Crowell, "Northern Émigrés"; Xia, "Qiao zhou-jun-xian."

12. SS 83: 2109. The Henan Zongs may have benefited from their surname, which was the same as that of a powerful Nanyang clan, in originally gaining exempt status.

13. JS 14: 432; SS 37: 1138; Yasuda Jiro 安田二郎, "The Changing Aristocratic Society of the Southern Dynasties and Regional Society: Particularly in the Hsiang-yang Region," *Acta Asiatica* 60 (1991): 32; Yasuda, "Jin-Song geming," 121–33; Xia, "Qiao zhou-jun-xian," 42–43.

14. SS 52: 1504–1505; SS 45: 1379–80; SS 51: 1480; SS 46: 1393–95; SS 65: 1718–19 (biographies of five consecutive men in the office, showing the extent of their command authority); SS 40: 1255 (office of Commandant for Pacifying the Man).

15. See list in prior footnote.

16. Yasuda, "Jin-Song geming," 120–21.

17. SS 44: 1347–62.

18. SS 65: 1718–19. This account was written (or at least assembled) by Shen Yue, who had direct personal experience in the Xiangyang area in the 470s; see fn. 41.

19. It is important to keep in mind that the scale of northern migration may not have been very overwhelming. In later Han times, when the census was relatively reliable, Nanyang commandery alone supported a population of more than a half-million households (HHS-Z 22: 3476–77), and the greater Xiangyang/Yong province region probably could support twice this. During the chaotic fourth century, when the city was decimated by fire, disease, and civil war, it is likely that a high percentage of the local population either died or fled to other regions. By comparison, even the largest immigrant groups recorded are on a much smaller scale: for example, the ten thousand households under Wei Hua who left to return to the north in 398, or the three thousand led by Kang Mu who came to settle around 420. Thus, it is quite possible that northern immigration alone had not fully repopulated the region. Although census figures throughout the early medieval period are not at all reliable, the massive collapse (more than 90 percent) of officially registered population and the continued reports of immigration and new settlement in the area can only mean that a good deal of land lay fallow. See also Li Hu, "Liuchao shiqi Jingzhou diqu de renkou," *Wei Jin Nanbeichao shi lunwen ji* (Jinan: Qi-Lu sushe, 1991), 32–55.

20. See SS 77: 1981; XTS 73A: 2835; JS 6: 156, 160; JS 55: 1499 (all for references to Liu Chun). SS 37: 1122 notes South Hedong commandery-in-exile, though it is recorded under Jing province.

21. SS 77: 1891.

22. Ibid.

23. NS 38: 981. This anecdote is not in the surviving edition of Song Yue's *Song shu.*

24. Yigong's three promotions were in 439, 440, and 444; see SS 61: 1644; also SS 77: 1981.

25. SS 97: 2396.

26. For convenience, however, I will continue to refer to these movements as "Man rebellions," since, whatever the ethnic background of the people on the Man side, they were commonly referred to by this term.

27. Li, "Jingzhou diqu de renkou," 34–41.

28. Rapid natural population growth in peacetime (families with seven to ten sons are frequently mentioned), along with settlement by northerners and "Man" people, is the likely explanation; see Li, "Jingzhou diqu de renkou."

29. SS 6: 109.

30. SS 77: 1982, 1996–97; SS 97: 2396.

31. SS 77: 1997.

32. SS 76: 1971–72.

33. SS 88: 2215–16.

34. SS 77: 1986. Xue Andu was taken onto Prince Dan's staff and followed him when he was reassigned elsewhere.

35. SS 6: 110–11; SS 77: 1986–88.

36. SS 77: 2001; SS 74: 1914. As an example of a lesser reward, Huang Hui, an aide to Zang Zhi who was born into a military household in Jingling, south of Xiangyang, was relieved of military household status; SS 83: 2122.

37. SS 77: 1988.

38. He refers to this hope in a secret letter to Prince Yixuan, recorded in ZZTJ 128: 4012. Abbreviated texts of this letter, without this part, are noted in SS 68: 1800 and SS 74: 1915.

39. JS 44: 1250.

40. SS 77: 1989.

41. The compiler of the *Song shu*, Shen Yue, had firsthand experience with the society and the kind of men he was writing about. His father had been a military man, executed during Liu Jun's coup in 453 when Shen Yue was twelve years old. Shen Yue's career included an early stint in provincial service, including a posting as magistrate of Xiangyang county. In writing imperial history he sought to illustrate some of the dangers, both of military service, and of having too close an association with the imperial clan. His biographies of Xiangyang military men should be seen in this light. See Richard Mather, *The Poet Shen Yue(441–513): The Reticent Marquis* (Princeton: Princeton University Press, 1988), 19–22 (early career in the provinces), 11 (influences on his historical perspective).

42. SS 83: 2112–13; NS 40: 1030. See also SS 77: 1989 for a reference to his role as Yuanjing's general.

43. TPYL 180: 878, quoting *Xiang-Mian ji.*

44. SS 83: 2113.

45. SS 83: 2109.

46. NQS 25: 464.

47. SS 83: 2110.

48. A similar anecdote is told of a sixth-century man from Xiangyang, Zhang Jingren 張景仁, who is celebrated in the section of the Southern *History* on "Filial & Righteous Exemplars" for killing the man who had killed his father. After humbly turning himself in, his crime was forgiven by the imperial prince then in charge of the Xiangyang command, who went on to praise him and instruct the local officials to remit his tax and corvee payments. See NS 74: 1843.

49. NS 37: 971; the parallel section in SS 76: 1971 says only that his cousin Qi did not blame him, which makes little sense.

50. These practices of Xiangyang men in the medieval period bear many parallels to those of men in pre-Han China; see Mark Edward Lewis, *Sanctioned Violence in Early China* (Albany: State University of New York Press, 1990), especially 39–42 and 80–94.

51. SS 88: 2216.

52. SS 83: 2110–12.

53. Jui-lung Su, "Patron's Influence on Bao Zhao's Poetry," in *Studies in Early Medieval Chinese Literature and Cultural History in Honor of Richard B. Mather and Donald Holzman*, ed. Paul Kroll and David Knechtges (Provo: T'ang Studies Society, 2003), 303–30, offers a good portrait of the influence on courtly poetry due to imperial patronage of this tradition.

54. Chan Man Sing, *The Western Songs (Xiqu) of the Southern Dynasties: A Critical Study* (Canberra: Australian National University Dissertation, 1984), 97–146.

55. Chan, *Western Songs*, 141–42. Cao Jingzong, another Xiangyang man from a military background whom we will hear more of in chapters 3 and 4, is known to have kept several hundred such women in his personal retinue; see LS 9: 181.

56. See discussion of the preface to the "Xiangyang yue" in Chan, *Western Songs*, 36–38. The earliest reference to Prince Dan's association with this piece is in SS 19: 552, and the primary reference to this connection is cited from the *Gujin yuelu* 古今樂祿, composed in 568; see Chan, *Western Songs*, 7. Though one cannot say for sure that the poem was not composed anonymously and merely attributed to Prince Dan, the connection is plausible and attested to early on. Even if it was written by someone a generation later, it still is evidence of courtly attitudes toward Xiangyang and its music from around that time.

57. Guo Maoqian, *Yuefu shiji* (Beijing: Zhonghua shuju, 1979), 703.

58. Chan, *Western Songs*, 77–78.

59. Chan, *Western Songs*, 16.

60. For an example of the similar exoticization and sexualization of provincial minority populations in present-day China, see Dru Gladney, "Representing Nationality in China: Refiguring Majority/Minority Identities, *Journal of Asian Studies* 53, no. 1 (February 1994): 92–123.

61. SS 79: 2042; specific dates in SS 6: 116–17. I translate the term *wang* 王 as "king" here, instead of "prince," because, together with the taking of a reign title,

and the selection of Chu (which did not correspond to any fief) as a title, Prince Hun clearly intended to signal his sovereignty, not merely his royal lineage.

62. SS 76: 1975–76.

63. Quote from SS 76: 1975; additional information on the residence determination from SS 6: 120; SS 37: 1138; *Jiankang shilu*, by Xu Song, ed. Zhang Chenshi (Beijing: Zhonghua shuju, 1986), 13: 478; and ZZTJ 128: 4031. The last two sources specify that the objective was to "merge two provinces, three commanderies, and sixteen counties of the Yong area, and found a single commandery with four counties." Based on the evidence in SS 37 of which counties were abolished in Daming 1 and which ones were shifted to new jurisdiction later in the Daming period (a distinction noted in Yasuda, "Changing Aristocratic Society," 41), and the discussion of the broader scope of the reform included under the subheading of Jingzhao commandery, it seems likely that the intended "new" commandery was to be Jingzhao, which was the home of the most powerful immigrant clans. Likely candidates for the four counties would be Duling, Guangping, Shiping, and Mei (from Fufeng), which would have preserved the leading counties from the four most prominent immigrant commanderies. In the ultimate settlement of this issue, all of these districts were clustered geographically to the north and west of Xiangyang; since this presumably corresponded roughly to the location of the settlers, a merger of them into a single jurisdiction with contiguous territory would have been plausible.

64. SS 76: 1975.

65. SS 76: 1975 is explicit that the locals "were not willing to be put on the registers."

66. There is no one source for this assertion, but the fact that the ultimate settlement of the issue allowed for so many jurisdictions to be retained, and even expanded upon, suggests that this was one of the local's concerns.

67. SS 76: 1975.

68. See the discussion of the province in the Song treatise on administrative geography, SS 37: 1135–44, which was primarily based on the situation as of 464, soon after the residence determination campaign had ended. Two of the commanderies listed there were added after that time.

69. SS 79: 2043–45.

70. SS 79: 2044.

71. SS 81: 2073–75.

72. SS 81: 2075–76.

73. SS 6: 127.

74. SS 6: 130.

75. SS 77: 1990.

76. Notably his nephew Liu Shilong, who will be profiled in the next chapter.

77. SS 77: 1990; SS 61: 1651.

## CHAPTER THREE. FRAGMENTATION

1. SS 7: 144–46; SS 88: 2218–21.

2. Wang Zhongluo 王仲荦, *Wei Jin Nanbeichao shi* 魏晋南北朝史 (Shanghai: Shanghai renmin chubanshe, 1994), 395–96.

3. SS 84: 2147.
4. SS 84: 2138; SS 83: 2112–13; NQS 25: 464.
5. SS 77: 1990; SS 84: 2131, 2137.
6. NQS 24: 445; NS 38: 982.
7. SS 84: 2138.
8. SS 83: 2113.
9. SS 6: 125, 132; SS 77: 1991.
10. SS 76: 1972.
11. NQS 25: 465; SS 88: 2221; SS 8: 161.
12. NQS 25: 464.
13. SS 59: 1607; SS 83: 2113.
14. SS 51: 1466; SS 83: 2113.
15. SS 74: 1927–29.
16. NQS 1: 3–7.
17. SS 50: 1452–55.
18. NQS 1: 3. An unknown rivalry or enmity with Shen Youzhi and/or Zhang Xingshi might also explain the decision.
19. SS 79: 2051; NQS 25: 465.
20. NQS 25: 465.
21. NQS 25: 465–66, 472.
22. NQS 25: 473–75.
23. NQS 25: 475.
24. NQS 35: 627 (Xiao Qiang); NQS 24: 453 (Zhang Gui); LS 9: 178 (Cao Jingzong).
25. LS 9: 178/NS 55: 1353–54. The son's name may have been Daowen 道文; see LS 9: 184, n. 6, and NQS 25: 474–75.
26. Pearce, Ebrey, and Spiro, *Culture and Power*, 29–31, discuss the southern court's efforts to "gentrify" military men. They highlight one potential problem with the strategy: a gentrified *hanmen* is no longer any good for fighting. Here I emphasize a much more important problem with the strategy: its outright failure, due to the limited opportunities and even worse incentives to gentrify.
27. We know Shuzong died when Shilong was still young, suggesting the 440s. We also know that Shuzong's highest office was as an aide to a Jianwei general (NS 38: 982), a title Shen Qingzhi held for most of the 440s until he relinquished it to Yuanjing in the 450 campaign. Shuzong might have served under his elder brother in that campaign, but even so he probably had fought under Qingzhi in the anti-Man campaigns as well.
28. NS 38: 983; NQS 24: 445.
29. Ibid.
30. NS 38: 985; NQS 24: 452.
31. NS 38: 986–90; also LS 12: 217-9; LS 21: 331–32.
32. SS 83: 2114.
33. NS 44: 1099.
34. LS 9: 178/NS 55: 1353; LS 10: 193/NS 55: 1364; NQS 44: 1099.
35. NS 55: 1357.
36. NQS 26: 484–85.

37. Jennifer Holmgren, "The Making of an Elite: Local Politics and Social Relations in Northeastern China during the Fifth Century A.D.," Papers *on Far Eastern History* 30 (1984): 1–79.

38. On the fluidity of "ethnic" distinctions and their relationship to immigrant groups, compare the modern case of Subei people, in Emily Honig, *Creating Chinese Ethnicity: Subei People in Shanghai, 1850–1980* (New Haven: Yale University Press, 1992). The Xiangyang situation is complicated by the fact that none of the well-established, higher-ranking, educated local families from the late Han and Three Kingdoms period, families who might have been good marriage prospects for high-status migrants from Jingzhao and Hedong, are known to have survived the turbulent fourth century. By comparison, the social gulf between those high-status migrant families and the low-status, illiterate local military men would have been much more difficult to bridge.

39. LS 18: 290/NS 55: 1373.

40. This does not necessarily mean that they lack any basis; for example, the Di 氐people from farther up the Han River appear to have had a more clearly demarcated identity than the Man, with their own "king" and a significant state; see NQS 30: 559/NS 46: 1152. The point is simply that the epithets used by Han imperial historians do not necessarily demarcate groups that had any stronger sense of self-identity than other groups to which such epithets were not applied.

41. Dialect differences are discussed in Serruys, *Chinese Dialects*, 91–94; Coblin, "Migration History," 530–31. An example of this segregation in modern times for a disadvantaged, but ethnically "Han" group, is found in Honig, *Creating Chinese Ethnicity*.

42. The phenomenon of self-segregation by immigrant groups, including (perhaps especially) those with relatively better status and financial resources, is common in later periods of Chinese history (e.g., Jiangxi settlers in Xiangtan, in Purdue, Peter, "Insiders and Outsiders: The Xiangtan Riot of 1819 and Collective Action in Hunan," *Modern China* 12, no. 2 (1986): 166–201), as well as in immigration patterns worldwide (e.g., Cuban exiles in Florida).

43. LS 12: 220; NS 58: 1425. Information on Zhang Yue is from SS 59: 1607.

44. LS 12: 220; also SS 65: 1722. The Liang inspectorate position was known for its tremendous opportunities for corruption, and Youwen was said to be particularly greedy. Rui (who has an exemplary biography) remained pure and honest, of course, but Youwen built up a mighty fortune, with thousands of gold pieces, dozens of female slaves, and silk and bamboo in abundance. After relocating to the capital he associated closely with several other relative parvenus, and eventually was executed along with most of his brothers, sons, and nephews in 476.

45. LS 12: 220/NS 58: 1425.

46. The Wangs originally hailed from Bacheng, a county in Jingzhao commandery. Their first recorded member is Wang Tuo 王堉, who served under the former Qin regime (JS 112: 2880), and another is Wang Xiu 王脩 (NS 13: 364); they are known to have been a prominent Xiangyang-area family in the early sixth century (NS 74: 1843).

47. Information on Wei Rui's estate is from *Xiang-Mian ji*, as quoted in TPYL 180: 878. Zugui's sons are profiled in LS 12: 220 and NS 58: 1430.

48. LS 12: 226–27.

49. LS 12: 220–21; NS 58: 1425–26.

50. NS 58: 1430.

51. The Jingzhao Luo surname is otherwise unknown. I suspect that "Luo Huidu" may be a mis-writing for "Wei Huidu 韋惠度," who was known to have lived in Xiangyang and served in provincial positions during the Song period. After he returned to the north his highest office was as Inspector of Luo 洛 province, and the title and surname may have gotten confused. See ZS 39: 693; BS 64: 2275.

52. TPYL 576: 2601, quoting the *Xiang-Mian ji*.

53. The text writes "Zhaoling 邵陵" instead of "Baling" throughout, but this is clearly an error.

54. TPYL 576: 2601.

55. NS 38: 985. The *Nan Qi shu* does not have this anecdote in Shilong's bio, nor does it have any other mention of Wei Zuzheng or Zugui. The effort to promote Zuzheng's eminence here, and in Wei Rui's bio (LS 12: 220/NS 58: 1425), suggests that Wei Rui and his family had some influence over the historical record in the interim.

56. This is known from a reference to Liu Zhongli 柳仲禮, Qingyuan's grandson, as the "younger affinal cousin (*waidi* 外弟)" of Wei Can 韋粲, Wei Rui's grandson; see LS 43: 606. This means either that Wei Rui's eldest son Fang 韋放 was married to one of Qingyuan's daughters, or that Qingyuan's eldest son Jin 柳津 was married to one of Wei Rui's daughters. The former is more likely, since Wei Rui was seventeen years older than Qingyuan, and his children were probably also correspondingly older. Since men usually married younger (sometimes much younger) women, it is more likely that Wei Fang (born in 474) married one of Qingyuan's young daughters no later than 494, prior the birth of his first son Can. However, the opposite is also possible, in which case the marriage would have occurred after Xiao Yan's coup and the rise of both men to national prominence.

57. TPYL 180: 878, quoting the *Xiang-Mian ji*. The event probably occurred in the 460s, prior to Cai Na's death in 472. It is worth noting that, like Rui, Cai Na's son Daogong also followed the future Liang Emperor Wu and gained high office, so the Cai estate's aura should have been pretty good too.

58. SS 93: 2278–29; SS 93: 2291; NQS 54: 940–41.

59. The three are profiled in sequence in NQS 54: 939–41 and NS 50: 1244–45, 50: 1248–49, and 75: 1860–62. Their close association is referred to in the bios of Ce, Qiu, and Yu Yi's son Heilou (LS 47: 650–51 and NS 50: 1245).

60. Buddhism and local history are recorded as interests for Zong Bing and both of his descendents, Zong Ce and Zong Shangzhi, as well as for Yu Shen 庾詵, an unspecified member of the Xinye Yu clan at Jiangling (LS 51: 750–52); Buddhism is also noted as significant for Liu Qiu, and local history and culture was an area of interest for Yue Ai, Qiu's brother-in-law.

61. SS 76: 1971; also NS 37: 971.

62. Profiled in LS 19: 299–304, and NS 37: 972, NS 50: 1253–54, and NS 56: 1397–98.

63. Examples include men of the Tianshui Yangs 天水楊 (LS 10: 195–97/NS 55: 1365), the Guangping Fengs 光平馮 (LS 18: 286–89/NS 55: 137), the Fufeng Mas 扶風馬 (SS 45: 1378; LS 17: 279/NS 26: 714), and the Liyang Changs 歷陽昌 (LS 18: 293/NS 55: 1376–77).

64. NS 40: 1021.

65. NS 38: 982, 990.

66. XTS 73A: 2835–54.

67. SS 77: 1991.

68. NQS 30: 553–55.

69. XTS 71A: 2179–2244; NS 33: 862–67; LS 28: 413/NS 58: 1438.

70. NQS 51: 869–72; WS 71: 1565–67/BS 45: 1645–53.

71. Shilong's father married a woman surnamed Guo 郭, a very common and thus untraceable surname, while Shilong's own wife was surnamed Yan 閻 (NS 38: 983). There was a Hedong Yan lineage (BS 84: 2828), but Shilong's wife was more likely to have been one of the Tianshui Yans, who had probably settled in the Xiangyang area (WS 71: 1579).

72. In addition to Wei Hua's lineage, there is also the lineage of Wei Gui 軌 (Hua's third cousin), and that of Wei Huidu 惠度, his fourth cousin once removed, both of whom emigrated to Xiangyang; Huidu later returned north. Wei Lang 閬, Hua's third cousin once removed, stayed in the north, as did the ancestors of Wei Zhishan 直善, Wei Rui's sixth cousin. See LS 12: 226–27 (on Wei Ai and his grandfather Gui); BS 64: 2275–77 (on Wei Tian 瑱 and his great-grandfather Wei Huidu); WS 45: 1009–18 and BS 26: 955 (on Wei Lang); ZS 31: 535 and BS 64: 2259 (on Wei Xiaokuan 孝寬 and his grandfather Zhishan). These various branches of the Weis are all linked to a common ancestor, Wei Mu 穆 and his elder brother Wei Qian 潛, in *Yuanhe xingji*: 126–91.

73. NS 58: 1436.

74. SS 77: 1990.

75. It may be only a coincidence that, just a few years prior to this, robbers in the area had broken into the tomb of an ancient King of Chu and discovered jade artifacts and an ancient manuscript. The brief report of this is first quoted in a {Zhao} Song-dynasty text, but it may have originated with earlier local history. See *Leishuo* 2/8.

76. Account of the campaign pieced together from NQS 26: 490; NQS 30: 556, 562; NQS 57: 989. See also ZZTJ 136: 4274–76, 4279–80.

77. NQS 26: 488–89 (biography of Chen Xianda). Chen is recorded as being from south Pengcheng commandery, an immigrant jurisdiction subordinated to south Xu province and lodged at Jingkou; see NQS 14: 246–48.

78. NQS 40: 708 (biography of Xiao Zimao).

79. NQS 49: 848–51 (biography of Wang Huan).

80. NQS 40: 708 (biography of Xiao Zimao); NQS 30: 561–62 (biography of Cao Hu). Cao Hu is of no relation to the local Xiangyang Cao family.

81. NQS 57: 993 (account of the northern Wei regime).

82. NQS 57: 996–97 (account of the northern Wei regime).

83. NQS 51: 873–74 (biography of Cui Huijing); NQS 30: 561–64 (biography of Cao Hu). See also ZZTJ 141: 4412–20.

84. NQS 6: 90 indicates that "all commanderies north of the Mian {Han} had been taken." The region is in some places referred to as "the five commanderies north of the Mian [Han] River" (*mianbei wu jun* 沔北五郡); for example, in NQS 57: 998, the principal account of the campaign. A note in ZZTJ 141: 4420 identifies the five as Nanyang (at Wan), Xinye, Shunyang (at Nanxiang), North Xiangcheng (at Zhuyang), and West Runan and North Yiyang (both at Wuyin). Given what we know of the Wei

campaign, however, it is clear that all of the territory north of the Han River was taken; these five probably represented merely the most important garrisons to have fallen.

85. NQS 57: 996–97; NQS 26: 491 (biography of Chen Xianda); WS 98: 2169–70 (account of southern regimes). See also ZZTJ 142: 4433–38.

86. Zhang Canhui 張燦輝, "Yongzhou shili yu Liangdai zhengzhi 雍州勢力與梁代政治," *Wenshi* 文史 56, no. 3 (2001): 81–89.

87. NQS 51: 869–72; Wei 71: 1565–67 (biographies of Pei Shuye); Wei 71: 1587–88 (biography of Xi Fayou).

88. NQS 57: 997 (account of the northern Wei regime). For an earlier example of this trope, see TPYL 417: 1925, quoting Xi Zuochi's fourth-century local history of Xiangyang, in which one of Zuochi's late Han ancestors, in service to Liu Bei but surrounded by forces from Wu, says, "I must become a ghost of Han, not a servant of Wu, and you cannot compel me!"

89. WS 43: 973; NQS 57: 997–98. Both accounts record an interesting exchange between Fang Boyu and northern representatives leading up to his surrender.

90. LS 12: 221 (Wei Rui dismisses Chen's cause).

## CHAPTER FOUR. ZENITH

1. Zhang Canhui, "Yongzhou shili," 81–83.

2. The core of this group is described as the "eight friends," of which Xiao Yan is one, but the epithet may very well have been coined later in order to link the group to earlier groups of "eight" (notably from the late Han period), and to give Xiao Yan's role more prominence. In any event, Prince Ziliang had far more than eight clients. See Richard Mather, *The Age of Eternal Brilliance: Three Lyric Poets of the Yung-ming era (483–493)* (Leiden: Brill Academic Publishers, 2003).

3. NQS 51: 873–74; compare LS 1: 2–3.

4. NQS 26: 491; see also NQS 57: 996–97; WS 7B: 185; ZZTJ 142: 4433–38.

5. LS 9: 175–77; LS 11: 205–14.

6. LS 9: 182–84/NS 38: 991–92. Qingyuan's career began on the civilian staff of Ying province, but thereafter he served in several central court positions, including on the staff of the Defender-in-Chief (*dasima*), most likely Yuzhang Prince Xiao Yi, younger brother of the emperor, who held the post from 487–492 and was quite a powerful figure. In other words, Qingyuan was decently connected at court, which is why he was known to Xiao Yan.

7. LS 28: 423.

8. LS 9: 178–81.

9. LS 12: 221.

10. LS 12: 217–19; LS 18: 286–93.

11. LS 7: 160.

12. LS 1: 4. The blame for Xiao Yi's death is placed on Baojuan's minions in the official history of Xiao Yan's own regime, certainly not an unbiased source. Others may have been responsible; indeed, Xiao Yan himself had some motivation for seeing his elder brother out of the way.

13. LS 10: 187–93; LS 12: 217–19.

14. LS 10: 193–201; LS 12: 219.

15. LS 19: 299–304.

16. LS 10: 187. Xi Chanwen's role is also referred to in LS 12: 219 and NS 35: 1558. Virtually the same quote is also attributed to Xiao Yan himself, in LS 1: 4.

17. LS 1: 9.

18. LS 1: 10–13.

19. NQS 38: 673.

20. LS 1: 25–34; Lance Eccles, "The Seizure of the Mandate: Establishment of the Legitimacy of the Liang Dynasty (502–557)," *Journal of Asian History* 23, no. 2 (1989): 169–80. Mather, *Shen Yueh*, 126–30 discusses the guilt that Shen Yue felt for recommending the execution of Xiao Baorong, but the fact that he felt compelled to do so only highlights how widely accepted a practice it was.

21. Men from the Xiangyang clique are profiled primarily in LS chapters 9 and 11, with lesser military men in 18; from Jiangling, in chapter 10, with men from the Nanyang cluster in 19; from Jiankang, in chapters 13–16, with military men at court in 17. Chapter 12 alone is mixed, profiling Wei Rui and his relatives (from Xiangyang), Xi Chanwen (at Jiangling), and three of the sons of Liu Shilong (who were in all three cliques).

22. All of these fiefs are noted in the participants' respective biographies, previously noted. I do not count the sons of Liu Shilong as men from Xiangyang, since they had essentially emigrated to the capital. They managed to position themselves in all three cliques, and profited quite handsomely.

23. LS 12: 225/NS 58: 1430.

24. TPYL 180: 878; LS 9: 179, 181.

25. LS 9: 178–81/NS 55: 1353–57.

26. LS 18: 293, 288–89, 291; LS 10: 197.

27. LS 24: 368–69 and LS 4: 109 (Cao Yizong); LS 3: 70 and LS 28: 423 (Cao Zhongzong); LS 18: 292 (Cao Shizong). In all cases we have references only by name, with no relationship to Cao Jingzong specified. I surmise the fraternal relationship based on the fact that the men served in the Xiangyang area and shared with Cao Jingzong both the surname and the second syllable of the given name, as did the one man specifically identified as his brother, Cao Yizong (see NS 55: 1357). It is possible that they were only cousins.

28. Wei Rui and his offspring are profiled together in NS 58: 1425–34.

29. NS 58: 1436–37.

30. LS 9: 182–84.

31. NS 38: 992.

32. Livia Kohn, *Daoism and Chinese Culture* (Cambridge, MA: Three Pines Press, 2001), 74–75.

33. Michel Strickmann, "The Mao Shan Revelations: Taoism and the Aristocracy," *T'oung Pao* 63, no. 1 (1977): 37.

34. Michel Strickmann, "A Taoist Confirmation of Liang Wu Ti's Suppression of Taoism," *Journal of the American Oriental Society* 98, no. 4 (1978): 467–75.

35. John Marney, *Liang Chien-wen ti* (Boston: Twayne Publishers, 1976), 65–69.

36. Chittick, *Pride of Place*.

37. Chittick, *Pride of Place*, 39; see also Huang Huixian 黄惠贤, ed., *Jiaobu Xiangyang qijiu ji* 校补襄阳耆旧记 by Xi Zuochi 习凿齿 (Zhengzhou: Zhongzhou guji chubanshe, 1987), 116–42.

38. *Shuijing zhu shu* 28: 2345–2422. In his discussion of Li Daoyuan's methods (pp. 18–25), Yang Shoujing notes that, though he was able to travel widely in the north, he was not able to do so in the south, and so was largely reliant on written material for those sections. The one post-420 comment (on p. 2369) regards Liu Jun, who renamed some hills south of town; it probably derives from Guo Zhongchan.

39. JS 34: 1020. The anecdote about his exchange with Zuo Zhan dates from no later than the fourth century; it is cited to Xi Zuochi's *Xiangyang qijiu ji* in YWLJ 35: 625 and 79: 1358 and TPYL 886: 3936, as well as in the partial Xinzhai edition of the text; see Chittick, *Pride of Place*, 23–27. My translation is indebted to Stephen Owen, *Remembrances: The Experience of the Past in Classical Chinese Literature* (Cambridge: Harvard University Press, 1986), 23.

40. Owen, *Remembrances*, 22–32.

41. NQS 25: 473.

42. Zhang Zhongxin 張仲炘, "Hubei jinshi zhi 湖北金石志," in *Shike shiliao xinbian* 石刻史料新編, series #3 vol. 16. (Taibei: xinwenfeng chubanshe, 1986), 11840; LS 40: 572/NS 50: 1249–53.

43. NS 62: 1531; NS 50: 1246–47; SuiS 33: 985.

44. This argument requires a somewhat lengthy but very plausible chain of presumptions. First, according to the Southern Song scholar Chen Zhensun 陳振孫, *Zhizhai shulu jieti* 直齋書錄解題 in *Siku quanshu* v.674 (Taibei: Shangwu chubanshe, 1981), 684, the material in six different local histories of Xiangyang was edited into a single work, the *Xiang-Mian ji* 襄沔記, in the early eighth century. Because this work is described as condensing approximately thirty *juan* of material into only three *juan*, I presume that it added essentially no new material. Only two of the six source texts were written as late as the sixth century, and the other, the *Jing-Chu suishi ji* 荆楚歲時記, is extant. I therefore presume that any tale attributed to the *Xiang-Mian ji* which is not from the *Jing-Chu suishi ji*, but which includes figures or historical events dating from the period between Guo Zhongchan's death (in 453) and Bao Zhi's time (the early- to mid-sixth century) was drawn from Bao Zhi's text. Finally, it appears that both the *Nan Yongzhou ji* and the *Xiang-Mian ji*, as well as some earlier works such as Xi Zuochi's, may be cited as the *Xiangyang ji* 襄陽記 in later compilations; again, I presume that, if the tale addresses material dateable to the period 453–530, its ultimate source was Bao Zhi.

45. TPYL 185: 897, citing the *Xiang-Mian ji*; TPYL 178: 869, citing the *Nan Yongzhou ji*. For the compilation of the *Wen xuan*, see Knechtges, *Wen Xuan* vol. 1.

46. For example, see HHS/XHZ 22: 3481, n. 9.

47. TPGJ 296: 2359, citing *Xiangyang ji* (a common alternate title for the *Nan Yongzhou ji* or the *Xiang-Mian ji*).

48. See Huang, *Jiaobu*, 54–55 for a list of other references to Xi Zuochi's version of this tale; the earliest and clearest is in YWLJ 49: 885.

49. It is possible that the quote from Guo should comprise only the first sentence, about the posture of the deer, in which case all of the supernatural elements of

the tale come from Bao. I have broken it after the second sentence because the section beginning with the specific date clearly stands apart as a separate tale.

50. TPGJ 296: 2355, citing the *Han-Mian ji* 漢沔記 (clearly an error for *Xiang-Mian ji*).

51. TPGJ 469: 3866, citing the *Nan Yongzhou ji*. Xiuqian may have been a relative of Lü Sengzhen, who was a close associate of Xiao Yan's in the initial coup.

52. TPGJ 469: 3866–67, citing the *Nan Yongzhou ji*.

53. Information on these tombs is drawn from Annette Juliano, *Teng-hsien: An Important Six Dynasties Tomb* (Ascona, Switzerland: Artibus Asiae Publishers, 1980); Cui Xinshe 崔新社 and Pan Jiefu 潘杰夫, "Xiangyang Jiajiachong huaxiang zhuanmu 襄阳贾家冲画像砖墓," *Jiang-Han kaogu* 江汉考古1986.1: 16–33; Zheng Yan 郑岩, *Wei-Jin-Nanbeichao bihuamu yanjiu* 魏晋南北朝壁画墓研究 (Beijing: Wenwu chubanshe, 2002).

54. Juliano, *Teng-hsien*, 5–11.

55. Juliano, *Teng-hsien*, 49.

56. Juliano, *Teng-hsien*, 7–8, also plate 145.

57. Cui and Pan, "Jiajiachong."

58. Juliano, *Teng-hsien*, 52.

59. In mirror inscriptions from the Eastern Han Ziqiao is often paired with Master Redpine (Chi Songzi 赤松子), who is known to have had a local shrine in southern Nanyang area since Han times; Juliano, *Teng-hsien*, 55, n. 266.

60. Audrey Spiro, *Contemplating the Ancients: Aesthetic and Social Issues in Early Chinese Portraiture* (Berkeley: University of California Press, 1990), 34–35 notes that images of the "four greybeards of Shang mountain" conveyed similar ideals to the Seven Sages; they are, however, an older motif.

61. Cui and Pan, "Jiajiachong."

62. Keith Knapp, *Selfless Offspring: Filial Children and Social Order in Medieval China* (Honolulu: University of Hawaii Press, 2005).

63. Zheng, *Bihuamu yanjiu*, 84–85 emphasizes the "heterodoxy" of these tombs, but I would not presume that sharp delineations were made between "Daoist" and "Confucian" icons (nor always between them and Buddhist ones), and prefer to emphasize their shared significances.

64. The tale is recorded in a highly abbreviated form, with only a brief mention of the cypress tree episode, and none of the swallows, in TPHYJ 145: 299. Another, less abbreviated version is recorded in TPGJ 270: 2117, this one without the cypress tree, but with a full account of the swallows. Both of these are credited to the *Nan Yongzhou ji*, signifying Bao Zhi's edition. An unsourced but otherwise much more complete version of the tale, with both the cypress tree and the swallow stories, and the note about Xiao Zao erecting a pavilion, is in NS 74: 1843; it is probably taken from Bao Zhi's original, or shares a common source with it.

65. Juliano, *Teng-hsien*, 73. The explicitly Jin-era "Seven Sages of the Bamboo Grove" are notably absent at Xiangyang, however.

66. Juliano, *Teng-hsien*, 74; Cui and Pan, "Jiajiachong," 31–32; Zheng, *Bihuamu yanjiu*, 80, 84–85.

67. LS 12: 225/NS 58: 1430.

68. The only "eminent" monk known to have stayed at Rosewood Creek is Daowen, noted as having sojourned there for no more than a few years in the 420s; *Gaoseng zhuan* 7: 287–90.

69. LS 1: 4; LS 11: 212.

70. NS 52: 1291.

71. Xia Rixin, "Wei Jin Nanbeichao shiqi Jingzhou diqu fojiao de chuanbo yu fazhan 魏晋南北朝时期荆州地区佛教的传播与发展," in *Ri-Zhong guoji gongtong yanjiu: diyu shehui zai Liuchao zhengzhi wenhua shang suo qi de zuoyong* 日中国际共同研究：地域社会在六朝政治文化上所起的作用 (Xuanwen she, 1989): 214 records every known Buddhist establishment in the Xiangyang area in the Eastern Jin and Southern Dynasties.

72. Zhang, "Hubei jinshi zhi," 11840.

73. YWLJ 76: 1303–1304; NS 39: 1013.

74. In Yan Kejun 嚴可均, ed., *Quan Shanggu sandai Qin-Han sanguo liuchao wen* 全上古三代秦漢三國六朝文. (Beijing: Zhonghua shuju, 1958), ch. 17: 3051–53.

75. TPYL 178: 869, citing the *Xiang-Mian ji*.

76. TPYL 180: 878, citing the *Xiang-Mian ji*.

77. NS 70: 1720–21.

78. *Xu Gaoseng zhuan* 16: 555–56.

79. Guo, *Yuefu shiji*, ch. 48: 708; translation by author.

80. Guo, *Yuefu shiji*, ch. 48: 708; translation by author, noting Chan, *Western Songs*, 165–66.

81. Guo, *Yuefu shiji*, ch. 48: 705; translation adapted from Marney, *Liang Chien-wen ti*, 29.

82. YWLJ 76: 1303–1304; Marney, *Liang Chien-wen ti*, 29–30, 35.

83. YWLJ 52: 949; Marney, *Liang Chien-wen ti*, 31. Xi Zuochi's local history had an entire chapter dedicated to eminent local governors; it may have provided the basis for Prince Gang's choice of portraits. See Chittick, *Pride of Place*: 119–21, 213–20.

84. YWLJ 50: 900; Marney, *Liang Chien-wen ti*, 29–30, 35.

85. YWLJ 50: 900; Marney, *Liang Chien-wen ti*, 30.

86. Marney, *Liang Chien-wen ti*, 32–34.

87. No date for Xiao Gong's appointment, or for this memorial, is specified. Marney, *Liang Chien-wen ti*, 36 suggests that Xiao Gong succeeded Prince Gang in 526. However, Prince Gang is clearly indicated to have been kept in the Xiangyang post that year (LS 4: 104), and he was still Yong inspector in 530, when he was transferred back to the capital and succeeded at Xiangyang by Prince Xu (LS 3: 74). Xiao Gong's biography says he was sent out to Xiangyang to aid in suppressing the Man rebellion of Wen Dao (LS 22: 349), which is elsewhere dated to 532 CE (ZS 14: 218), but may have had subsequent flare-ups. The 532 date conflicts with several places where Prince Xu is indicated as having been Yong Inspector throughout the years 530-535 (LS 3: 74, 79; LS 29: 431). Xiao Gong's removal from Yong provincial office is noted as being instigated by Prince Xu while he was serving as Jing inspector, which began in 539 CE (LS 22: 349; LS 29: 430–31). On balance of this evidence, Xiao Gong's tenure in Xiangyang was probably in the mid- to late 530s.

88. LS 22: 349; translation by author, noting Marney, *Liang Chien-wen ti*, 36.

89. LS 4: 104.

90. NS 38: 992.

91. YWLJ 52: 948–49; NS 38: 992.

92. Derk Bodde, *Festivals in Classical China: New Year and other annual observances during the Han Dynasty, 206 B.C.-A.D. 220* (Princeton: Princeton University Press, 1975), 289–316.

93. *Jing-Chu suishiji jiaozhu*, 163. The original *Jing-Chu ji* was written by Zong Lin 宗懍, a member of the Nanyang immigrant cluster in Jiangling, no later than 565 CE. The annotated version, called *Jing-Chu suishiji*, by Du Gongzhan 杜公贍, was compiled in the Sui or early Tang period; see JTS 59: 1538.

94. Alan Berkowitz, *Patterns of Disengagement: The Practice and Portrayal of Reclusion in Early Medieval China* (Stanford: Stanford University Press, 2000); Chittick, "Local Writing."

95. Wolfram Eberhard, *The Local Cultures of South and East China* (Leiden: E. J. Brill, 1968), 396 describes the boat race as "a fight between two parties, and the losing party is sacrificed" by drowning in the river. However, his evidence for this is widely scattered across space and time, mostly from Song and late imperial times, and must be treated with extreme caution. There is no evidence of human sacrifice being involved in the sixth century.

96. SuiS 31: 897.

97. *Jing-Chu suishiji jiaozhu*: 67–76, 118–23; SuiS 31: 897.

98. Laurence Schneider, A *Madman of Ch'u: The Chinese Myth of Loyalty and Dissent* (Berkeley: University of California Press, 1980), 2–6.

99. Accounts of the temple are found in *Shuijing zhu shu* 38; also in *Yiyuan*, as quoted in YWLJ 79: 1349. Neither makes any reference to a more widespread cult, nor to the double fifth date or to boat races. Prior local histories of Jing province refer to Qu Yuan's familial estate and his tomb, and repeat Han dynasty tales about him, but add little else.

100. Wu Jun (469–520), *Xu Qixie ji*, as quoted in YWLJ 4: 74. Wu Jun's biography and other works are recorded in LS 49: 698 and NS 72: 1780; he was from the lower Yangzi area and assembled several works of local and imperial history, as well as this collection of anomaly tales. I discount a highly suspect linkage of Qu Yuan to the 5-5 date, apparently appended to a quote from the second-century *Fengsu tongyi*, cited in YWLJ 4: 75 and later in TPYL 31: 147.

101. The tug-of-war event also developed an obviously spurious "backstory," for it was supposed to have been passed down from a general of the Warring States period; see SuiS 31: 897; *Jing-Chu suishiji jiaozhu*: 72–76.

102. SuiS 31: 897.

103. Marney, *Liang Chien-wen ti*, 77–81.

104. Evidence of such linkage abounds; for example, in *Lun Heng* 4/5b, (translated by Alfred Forke, *Lun Heng* [New York: Paragon Book Gallery, 1962], vol. II: 248), where Wang Chong pairs the two men as famous riverine suicides, emphasizing that Qu Yuan's death did *not* cause supernatural events, as it was said Wu Zixu's did. In a much later example, JS 94: 2428 records a fascinating tale about a shaman from Wu who is coaxed to perform songs and dances on a boat in the Luo River south of Luoy-

ang; he gathers a large and appreciative crowd, who sigh and exclaim, "It's as if [Wu] Zixu and Qu Ping [Yuan] are standing to the left and right of us!"

105. *Jing-Chu suishiji yizhu* 22: 92. Cao E's biography, and the record of the stele inscription by Handan Chun, is described in HHS 10/84: 2794, where the stele is dated to 151 CE. The same version of the tale is widely cited from the western Jin–period *Kuaiji dianlu*, the likely source; see *Shishuo xinyu* 11/3: 579–80; YWLJ 4: 74–75; TPYL 31: 147.

106. See WS 106A: 2459 and 106B: 2519 for Wu Zixu temples in the north. His estate is noted by Fan Wang (mid-fourth century) in his *Jingzhou ji* 荊州記, cited in CXJ 24: 578.

107. David Johnson, "The Wu Tzu-hsu *Pien-wen* and Its Sources: Part II," *Harvard Journal of Asiatic Studies* 40, no. 2 (1980): 472–80.

108. Another account of the festival, probably from the mid-Tang period, details a further effort by local officials to recast the "purpose" of the competition, this time as a celebration of the *Classic of Filial Piety*; see TPYL 66: 316, citing the Poyang ji 鄱陽記. That particular approach did not catch on.

## CHAPTER FIVE. SUBLIMATION

1. Scott Pearce "Who, and What, Was Hou Jing?" *Early Medieval China* 6 (2000): 49–61.

2. NS 38: 994.

3. NS 38: 992, 994.

4. NS 38: 992–93.

5. NS 38: 994.

6. LS 37: 605–608 (Wei Can); also NS 58: 1432–34; ZZTJ 161–62: 4997–5000.

7. ZZTJ 162: 5008, 5012; NS 38: 992 has an abbreviated version of the former.

8. NS 38: 994.

9. Gan, *Huangquan*, 279–88.

10. ZS 48: 856.

11. ZS 48: 868–69.

12. ZS 42: 765–67; also BS 70: 2441–42, where his given name is written 遐. Interestingly, this conception of the Liu clan "succession" is not from father to son; the torch is passed first to a nephew, then a first cousin, then another nephew.

13. ZS 48: 862.

14. ZS 48: 870–71.

15. NS 64: 1556.

16. LS 46: 643.

17. ZZTJ 162: 5028.

18. LS 46: 642. This is the primary reason cited by Sima Guang, in ZZTJ 162: 5028. NS 64: 1557 attributes the old ties to Du An.

19. LS 46: 642–44; NS 64: 1557–58.

20. NS 64: 1557–58.

21. ZS 28: 478 notes the participation of northern forces in this effort; ZZTJ 162: 5031 suggests the date.

22. NS 64: 1558; ZS 48: 858. ZZTJ 162: 5031 clarifies the use of the head for the lacquered bowl.

23. ZS 48: 858.

24. ZZTJ 163: 5035–36.

25. ZS 44: 798; BS 66: 2338–39. See Albert Dien, "The Role of the Military in the Western Wei/Northern Chou State," in Dien, *State and Society*, 331–67, for the use of titles in the Western Wei/Northern Zhou regime.

26. ZS 46: 829/BS 85: 2851. Though it is not specified in the sources, it is likely that their father Jian 漸 came out to Liang province when his first cousin Huaibao was the inspector in the 530s, and subsequently stayed there.

27. ZS 48: 858–59; ZZTJ 163: 5047, 5049.

28. ZZTJ 164: 5073–74.

29. Dien, "Role of the Military."

30. ZS 5: 71, 80; also ZS 13: 202 (biography of Yuwen Zhi).

31. ZS 21: 354–55 (biography of Wang Yi 王宜) profiles the man who was Xiangyang commander at the time and led the campaign for Yang Jian. See also ZS 36: 641 for his successor.

32. BS 11: 412; SuiS 1: 24; SuiS 45: 1239–41 (biography of Yang Jun).

33. The situation is very similar to the period from 265–280, when the Sima regime of western Jin had conquered Sichuan and was preparing for the campaign to take over the Wu regime based at Jiankang. There again, because Jiangling was under the control of Wu, Xiangyang became the primary staging area for the campaign, and a series of very high-level officials (Yang Hu and Du Yu) ruled the area and lavished attention on it.

34. Dien, "Role of the Military," 332.

35. ZS 44: 798/BS 66: 2338–39.

36. NS 38: 992–94; ZS 2:32, 19: 317.

37. NS 64: 1557–59.

38. Examples include Yan Zhitui, discussed in Teng, *Family Instructions*, xx–xxv, and Yu Xin, profiled in William T. Graham, *The Lament for the South: Yu Hsin's Ai Chiang-nan Fu* (Cambridge and London: Cambridge University Press, 1980), 11–20.

39. ZS 48: 868–71.

40. ZS 42: 766–67.

41. ZS 48: 874.

42. ZS 42: 767.

43. His sons showed similarly reserved and careful allegiance strategies. His eldest son at first followed his father in serving Zhou, then retired back to Xiangyang after Yang Jian rose to power and, despite repeated entreaties, never took office again. His younger brother Zhuang served Xiao Cha at Jiangling; after being sent several times as an emissary to the Chang'an court, he developed good relations with Yang Jian and laid the groundwork for gaining high office once the later Liang court was finally eliminated. See ZS 42: 767–68; BS 70: 2442–44.

44. Graham, *Lament*.

45. NS 64: 1558. LS 8: 169 identifies An'ning as the burial mound of Prince Cha's father, Xiao Tong, the Zhaoming heir.

46. ZS 46: 829–30; BS 85: 2851. Though "twisted" in this particular application of the *Analects*, the "Confucian revenge ethic" was well rooted in classical commentaries and histories; see Lewis, *Sanctioned Violence*: 80–94. The permissive response by officials was by no means guaranteed, however; see ZS 22: 369–72 for a counterexample.

47. NS 58: 1436–37.

48. SuiS 62: 1481. The local power of the extended Liu clan is exemplified in the biography of Liu Chong 柳崇 and his relatives, in WS 45: 1029–31.

49. SuiS 62: 1481–84; see also BS 77: 2622–25.

50. JTS 190B: 5054; XTS 201: 5735 does note that he is a "distant descendent" of Du Yu, from the western Jin period . One of Xi Gu's Tang-dynasty descendents is also recorded as a "man of Xiangyang"; see JTS 190b: 5035; XTS 128: 4467.

51. *Fayuan zhulin jiaozhu* 法苑珠林校注, by Shi Daoshi 釋道世, edited by Zhou Shujia 周叔迦 and Su Jinren 蘇晉仁 (Beijing: Zhonghua shuju, 2003), j. 14: 478, citing from the *Ji shenzhou sanbao gantong lu* 集神州三寶感通錄.

52. Zhang, "Hubei jinshi zhi," 11841–42, items under both temple names; also TPGJ 472: 3886–87, quoting the *Xiang-Mian ji* (and probably from Bao Zhi) on the lore surrounding the temple. Wang Bing, sometimes also written as Wang Kang 康, has a brief biography in BS 62: 2209, which notes him taking the office of Xiang province commander in 562.

53. ZS 6: 91 indicates that Wang Bing (here written as Kang) was appointed Xiang province commander in 575. In ZS 5: 89, note 17, the editors state that BS 62: 2209 must be incorrect in dating this appointment to 562. However, the inscriptional material noted above confirms the 562 date, and the tale here roughly confirms the 575 date (since the Zhou Emperor's destruction of the dharma was a four-year-long event, not just in 574), so I presume that he served as Xiangyang commander two different times.

54. I interpret the term *ronghui* 融毀 as the graphically similar *ronghui* 熔燬, "smelt and destroy by fire."

55. *Fayuan zhulin* 13: 457, citing from the *Ji shenzhou sanbao gantong lu.*

56. See bios in *Xu Gaoseng zhuan* 9: 493–94 (Huizhe); 10: 502 (Zhirun); and 15: 539 (Huitiao and Huixuan).

57. *Xu Gaoseng zhuan* 10: 502 and 14: 537.

58. Zhang, "Hubei jinshi zhi," 11843. The local commander at the time was Liu Zhige 柳止戈, a descendent of the Si province Lius, distant relatives of the ones at Xiangyang; see reference at BS 64: 2281.

59. *Xu Gaoseng zhuan* 9: 493–94 (Huizhe).

60. *Xu Gaoseng zhuan* 14: 536–37 (Huileng and Zhiba); 25: 660–61 (Ceng Sheli).

61. *Fayuan zhulin* 13: 458.

## CHAPTER SIX. CONCLUSION

1. On the "Confucian revenge ethic" see Lewis, *Sanctioned Violence*, 80–94.

2. See Kieschnick, John, *The Eminent Monk: Buddhist Ideals in Medieval Chinese Hagiography* (Honolulu: University of Hawai'i Press, 1997), 112–38, on the predilection for scholarly monks in such works.

3. SS 65: 1719.

4. SS 76: 1975.

# BIBLIOGRAPHY

## EARLY CHINESE SOURCES CITED BY TITLE

*Chinese Encyclopedias. Abbreviated as follows:*

BTSC: *Beitang shuchao* 北棠書超, by Yu Shinan 虞世南, ed. Beijing: Zhonghua shuju, 1962.
CXJ: *Chuxue ji* 初學記, by Xu Jian 徐堅, ed. Beijing: Zhonghua shuju, 1962.
TPGJ: *Taiping guangji* 太平廣記, by Li Fang 李昉, ed. Beijing: Zhonghua shuju, 1961.
TPYL: *Taiping yulan* 太平御覽, by Li Fang 李昉, ed. Beijing: Zhonghua shuju, 1960.
YWLJ: *Yiwen leiju* 藝文類聚, by Ouyang Xun 歐陽詢, ed. Shanghai guji chubanshe, 1999.

*Dynastic History Series, Published in Beijing: Zhonghua shuju, 1959–. Abbreviated as follows:*

SJ: *Shi ji* 史記, by Sima Qian 司馬遷.
HS: *Han shu* 漢書, by Ban Gu 班固.
HHS: *Hou Han shu* 後漢書, by Fan Ye 范曄.
HHS-Z: *Hou Han shu zhi* 後漢書志, by Sima Biao 司馬彪.
SGZ: *Sanguo zhi* 三國志, by Chen Shou 陳壽, annotations by Pei Songzhi 裴松之.
JS: *Jin shu* 晉書, by Fang Xuanling 房玄齡.
SS: *Song shu* 宋書, by Shen Yue 沈約.
NQS: *Nan Qi shu* 南齊書, by Xiao Zixian 蕭子顯.
LS: *Liang shu* 梁書, by Yao Silian 姚思廉.
CS: *Chen shu* 陳書, by Yao Silian 姚思廉.
NS: *Nan shi* 南史, by Li Yanshou 李延壽.
WS: *Wei shu* 魏書, by Wei Shou 魏收.
BQS: *Bei Qi shu* 北齊書, by Li Baiyao 李百藥.
ZS: *Zhou shu* 周書, by Linghu Defen 令狐德棻.
SuiS: *Sui shu* 隨書, by Wei Zheng 魏徵.
BS: *Bei shi* 北史, by Li Yanshou 李延壽.
JTS: *Jiu Tang shu* 舊唐書, by Liu Xu 劉昫.
XTS: *Xin Tang shu* 新唐書, by Ouyang Xiu 歐陽脩.
ZZTJ: *Zizhi tongjian* 資治通鑑, by Sima Guang 司馬光.

*Other Early Chinese Sources*

*Fayuan zhulin jiaozhu* 法苑珠林校注, by Shi Daoshi 釋道世, edited by Zhou Shujia 周叔迦 and Su Jinren 蘇晉仁. Beijing: Zhonghua shuju, 2003.
*Gaoseng zhuan* 高僧傳, by Shi Huijiao 釋慧皎, edited by Tang Yongtong 湯用彤. Beijing: Zhonghua shuju, 1992.
*Gaoshi zhuan* 高士傳, by Huangfu Mi 皇甫謐. Shanghai: Shangwu, 1937.
*Jiankang shilu* 建康實錄, by Xu Song 許嵩, edited by Zhang Chenshi 張忱石. Beijing: Zhonghua shuju, 1986.
*Jing-Chu suishiji jiaozhu* 荊楚歲時記校注, by Zong Lin 宗懍, edited by Wang Yurong 王毓榮. Taibei: Wenjin chubanshe, 1988.
*Leishuo* 類說, by Zeng Zao 曾慥, in *Siku quanshu*, v. 873. Taibei: Shangwu, 1981.
*Lun Heng jijie* 論衡集解, by Wang Chong 王充, edited by Liu Pansui 劉盼遂. Beijing: Zhonghua shuju, 1959. See also translation by Alfred Forke.
*Shishuo xinyu jianshu* 世說新語箋疏, by Liu Yiqing 劉義慶, edited by Yu Jiaxi 余嘉錫. Shanghai guji chubanshe, 1993. See also translation by Richard Mather.
*Shuijing zhu shu* 水經注疏, by Li Daoyuan 酈道元, edited by Yang Shoujing 楊守敬 and Xiong Huizhen 熊會貞. Nanjing: Jiangsu guji chubanshe, 1999.
*Taiping huanyu ji* 太平環宇記, by Yue Shi 樂史, ed. Taibei: Wenhai chubanshe, 1963.
*Wen xuan* 文选, by Xiao Tong 萧统. Beijing: Zhonghua shuju, 1977. See also partial translation by David Knechtges.
*Xu gaoseng zhuan* 續高僧傳, by Shi Daoxuan 釋道宣. Jiangbei kejing chu, 1890.
*Yanshi jiaxun jijie* 顏氏家訓集解, by Yan Zhitui 顏之推, edited by Wang Liqi 王利器. Beijing: Zhonghua shuju, 1993. See also translation by Teng Ssu-yu.
*Yuanhe xingji* 元和姓簒, by Lin Bao 林寶. Beijing: Zhonghua shuju, 1994.
*Yuefu shi ji* 樂府詩集, by Guo Maoqian 郭茂倩. Beijing: Zhonghua shuju, 1979.

## SECONDARY SOURCES CITED BY AUTHOR

Amory, Patrick. *People and Identity in Ostrogothic Italy, 489–554*. Cambridge and London: Cambridge University Press, 1997.
Anderson, Benedict. *Imagined Communities: Reflections on the Origin and Spread of Nationalism*. London and New York: Verso, 1991.
Armstrong, John. *Nations before Nationalism*. Chapel Hill: University of North Carolina Press, 1982.
Balazs, Etienne. *Chinese Civilization and Bureaucracy: Variations on a Theme*. New Haven: Yale University Press, 1964.
Berkowitz, Alan. *Patterns of Disengagement: The Practice and Portrayal of Reclusion in Early Medieval China*. Stanford: Stanford University Press, 2000.
Bielenstein, Hans. "The institutions of Later Han." In. *Cambridge History of China vol. 1: The Ch'in and Han Empires 221 B.C.–A.D. 220*, ed. D. Twitchett and M. Loewe. Cambridge and London: Cambridge University Press, 1986.
———. *The Restoration of the Han Dynasty, with Prolegomena on the Historiography of the Hou Han Shu*. Stockholm, 1953.

———. "Wang Mang, the restoration of the Han dynasty, and Later Han." In *Cambridge History of China vol. 1: The Ch'in and Han Empires 221 B.C.–A.D. 220*, ed. D. Twitchett, D. and M. Loewe. Cambridge and London: Cambridge University Press, 1986.

Blakely, Barry. "The Geography of Chu." In *Defining Chu: Image and Reality in Ancient China*, ed. Constance Cook and John Major. Honolulu: University of Hawai'i Press, 1999.

Bodde, Derek. *Festivals in Classical China: New Year and Other Annual Observances during the Han Dynasty, 206 B.C.–A.D. 220*. Princeton: Princeton University Press, 1975.

Brown, Miranda. *The Politics of Mourning in Early China*. Albany: State University of New York Press, 2007.

Chen, Kenneth. "On Some Factors Responsible for Anti-Buddhist Persecution under the Pei-chao." *Harvard Journal of Asiatic Studies* 17, no. 1–2 (1954): 261–73.

Chen Shi 陳詩. "Hubei jinshi tongzhi 湖北金石通志." In *Shike shiliao xinbian* 石刻史料新編, series #3 vol. 13. Taibei: xinwenfeng chubanshe, 1986.

Chen Zhensun 陳振孫. *Zhizhai shulu jieti* 直齋書錄解題 in *Siku quanshu* v.674. Taibei: Shangwu chubanshe, 1981.

Chen Zhong'an 陳仲安 and Wang Su 王素. *Han-Tang zhiguan zhidu yanjiu* 漢唐職官制度研究. Beijing: Zhonghua shuju, 1993.

Chittick, Andrew. "The Development of Local Writing in Early Medieval China." *Early Medieval China* 9 (2003): 35–70.

———. "The Life and Legacy of Liu Biao: Governor, Warlord, and Imperial Pretender in Late Han China." *Journal of Asian History* 37, no. 2 (2003): 155–86.

———. *Pride of Place: The Advent of Local History in Early Medieval China*. UMI, University of Michigan Doctoral Dissertation, 1997.

Coblin, W. South. "Migration History and Dialect Development in the Lower Yangtze Watershed." *Bulletin of the School of Oriental and African Studies* 65, no. 3 (2002): 529–43.

Connery, Christopher Leigh. *The Empire of the Text*. Lanham, MD: Rowman and Littlefield, 1999.

Crowell, William. "Northern Emigres and the Problem of Census Registration under the Eastern Jin and Southern Dynasties." In *State and Society in Early Medieval China*, ed. Albert Dien. Hong Kong: Hong Kong University Press, 1990.

Cui Fuzhang 崔富章 and Li Daming 李大明, eds. *Chuci jijiao jishi* 楚辭集校集釋. Wuhan: Hubei jiaoyu chubanshe, 2000.

Cui Xinshe 崔新社and Pan Jiefu 潘杰夫. "Xiangyang Jiajiachong huaxiang zhuanmu 襄陽賈家沖畫像磚墓." *Jiang-Han kaogu* 江漢考古1986.1: 16–33.

De Crespigny, Rafe. *Generals of the South: The Foundation and Early History of the Three Kingdoms State of Wu*. Canberra: Australian National University Faculty of Asian Studies Monographs, 1990.

———. "Politics and Philosophy under the Government of Emperor Huan 159–168 A.D." *T'oung Pao* 66 (1980).

Dien, Albert, ed. *State and Society in Early Medieval China*. Hong Kong: Hong Kong University Press, 1990.

———. "The *Yuan-hun Chih* (Accounts of Ghosts with Grievances): A Sixth-Century Collection of Stories." In *Wen-lin: Studies in the Chinese Humanities*, ed. Chow Tse-tsung. Madison, Milwaukee, and London: University of Wisconsin Press, 1968.

Duara, Prasenjit. "De-Constructing the Chinese Nation." *The Australian Journal of Chinese Affairs* 30 (1993): 1–26.

———. *Rescuing History from the Nation: Questioning Narratives of Modern China*. Chicago: University of Chicago Press, 1997.

Eberhard, Wolfram. *Conquerors and Rulers: Social Forces in Medieval China*. Leiden: E. J. Brill, 1952.

———. *The Local Cultures of South and East China*. Leiden: E. J. Brill, 1968.

Ebrey, Patricia. *The Aristocratic Families of Early Imperial China: A Case Study of the Po-ling Ts'ui Family*. Cambridge and London: Cambridge University Press, 1978.

———. "Estate and Family Management in the Later Han as Seen in the Monthly Instructions for the Four Classes of People." *Journal of the Economic and Social History of the Orient* 17 (1974): 173–205.

———. "Later Han Stone Inscriptions." *Harvard Journal of Asiatic Studies* 40, no. 2 (1980): 325–53.

———. "Patron-Client Relations in the Later Han." *Journal of the American Oriental Society* 103, no. 3 (1983): 533–42.

Eccles, Lance. "The Seizure of the Mandate: Establishment of the Legitimacy of the Liang Dynasty (502–557)." *Journal of Asian History* 23, no. 2 (1989): 169–80.

Eisenstadt, S. N., and L. Roniger. *Patrons, Clients, and Friends: Interpersonal Relations and the Structure of Trust in Society*. Cambridge and London: Cambridge University Press, 1984.

Emerson, Rupert. *From Empire to Nation: The Rise to Self-Assertion of Asian and African Peoples*. Cambridge: Harvard University Press, 1960.

Farmer, Michael. "What's in a Name? On the Appellative 'Shu' in Early Medieval Chinese Historiography." *Journal of the American Oriental Society* 121, no. 1 (2001): 44–59.

Forke, Alfred, trans. *Lun Heng*, by Wang Chong. New York: Paragon Book Gallery, 1962.

Gan Huaizhen 甘懷真, *Huangquan, liyi yu jiangdian quanshi: zhongguo gudai zhengzhi shi yanjiu* 黃權, 禮儀與經典詮釋：中國古代政治史研究. Taibei: Lexue shuju, 2003.

Gernet, Jacques. *Buddhism in Chinese Society: An Economic History from the Fifth to the Tenth Centuries*. Trans. Franciscus Verellen. New York: Columbia University Press, 1995.

Gladney, Dru. "Representing Nationality in China: Refiguring Majority/Minority Identities." *Journal of Asian Studies* 53, no. 1 (1994): 92–123.

Goodman, Howard. *Ts'ao P'i Transcendent: The Political Culture of Dynasty-Founding in China at the End of the Han*. Seattle: Scripta Serica, 1998.

Graff, David. *Medieval Chinese Warfare, 300–900*. London and New York: Routledge, 2002.

Grafflin, Dennis. "The Great Family in Early Medieval China." *Harvard Journal of Asiatic Studies* 41, no. 1 (1981): 65–74.

———. "Reinventing China: Pseudobureaucracy in the Early Southern Dynasties." In *State and Society in Early Medieval China*, ed. A. Dien. Hong Kong: Hong Kong University Press, 1990.

Graham, William T. *The Lament for the South: Yu Hsin's Ai Chiang-nan Fu*. Cambridge and London: Cambridge University Press, 1980.

Hawkes, David. *Songs of the South: An Ancient Chinese Anthology*. Oxford: Clarendon Press, 1959.

Henry, Eric. "Chu-ko Liang in the Eyes of His Contemporaries." *Harvard Journal of Asiatic Studies* 52, no. 2 (1992.): 589–612.

———. "The Motif of Recognition in Ancient China." *Harvard Journal of Asiatic Studies* 47, no. 1 (1987): 5–30.

Holcombe, Charles. *In the Shadow of the Han: Literati Thought and Society at the Beginning of the Southern Dynasties*. Honolulu: University of Hawaii Press, 1994.

———. "Re-imagining China: The Chinese Identity Crisis at the Start of the Southern Dynasties Period." *Journal of the American Oriental Society* 115, no. 1 (1995): 1–14.

Holmgren, Jennifer. "The Making of an Elite: Local Politics and Social Relations in Northeastern China during the Fifth Century A.D." *Papers on Far Eastern History* 30 (1984): 1–79.

Honey, David. "Sinicization as Statecraft in Conquest Dynasties of China: Two Early Medieval Case Studies." *Journal of Asian History* 30, no. 2 (1996): 115–51.

Honig, Emily. *Creating Chinese Ethnicity: Subei People in Shanghai, 1850–1980*. New Haven: Yale University Press, 1992.

Huang Huixian 黃惠賢, ed. *Jiaobu Xiangyang qijiu ji* 校補襄陽耆舊記 by Xi Zuochi 習鑿齒. Zhengzhou: Zhongzhou guji chubanshe, 1987.

Hucker, Charles. *A Dictionary of Official Titles in Imperial China*. Stanford: Stanford University Press, 1985.

Isaacs, Harold. *Idols of the Tribe: Group Identities and Political Change*. Cambridge: Harvard University Press, 1989.

Johnson, David. *The Medieval Chinese Oligarchy*. Boulder: Westview, 1976.

———. "The Wu Tzu-hsu *Pien-wen* and Its Sources: Part I," *Harvard Journal of Asiatic Studies* 40, no. 1 (1980): 93–156.

———. "The Wu Tzu-hsu *Pien-wen* and Its Sources: Part II," *Harvard Journal of Asiatic Studies* 40, no. 2 (1980): 465–505.

Johnson, Terry, and Christopher Dandeker. "Patronage: Relation and System." In *Patronage in Ancient Society*, ed. Andrew Wallace-Hadrill. London and New York: Routledge, 1989.

Juliano, Annette. *Teng-hsien: An Important Six Dynasties Tomb*. Ascona, Switzerland: Artibus Asiae Publishers, 1980.

Kawakatsu Yoshio 川勝義雄. "Hou Jing zhi luan yu Nanchaode huobi jingji H侯景之亂與南朝的貨幣經濟." In *Riben xuezhe yanjiu Zhongguoshi lunzhe xuanze* 日本學者研究中國史論者選擇, vol. 4 (Beijing: Zhonghua shuju, 1992): 247–93.

Kieschnick, John. *The Eminent Monk: Buddhist Ideals in Medieval Chinese Hagiography*. Honolulu: University of Hawai'i Press, 1997.

Killigrew, John W. "The Reunification of China in AD 280: Jin's Conquest of Eastern Wu." *Early Medieval China* 9 (2003): 1–34.

Kleeman, Terry. *Great Perfection: Religion and Ethnicity in a Chinese Millenial Kingdom.* Honolulu: University of Hawai'i Press, 1998.

Knapp, Keith. *Selfless Offspring: Filial Children and Social Order in Medieval China.* Honolulu: University of Hawaii Press, 2005.

Knechtges, David. *The Han Rhapsody: A Study of the Fu of Yang Hsiung (53 B.C.–A.D. 18)*. Cambridge and London: Cambridge University Press, 1976.

———. "Sweet-peel Orange or Southern Gold? Regional Identity in Western Jin Literature." In *Studies in Early Medieval Chinese Literature and Cultural History*, ed. Paul Kroll and David Knechtges. Provo: T'ang Studies Society, 2003.

———, ed. *Wen Xuan, or Selections of Refined Literature, Volume One: Rhapsodies on Metropolises and Capitals*, by Xiao Tong. Princeton: Princeton University Press, 1982.

———, ed. *Wen Xuan, or Selections of Refined Literature, Volume Three: Rhapsodies on Natural Phenomena, Birds and Animals, Aspirations and Feelings, Sorrowful Laments, Literature, Music, and Passions*, by Xiao Tong. Princeton: Princeton University Press, 1996.

Kohn, Livia. *Daoism and Chinese Culture.* Cambridge, MA: Three Pines Press, 2001.

Kubozoe Yoshifumi 窪添慶文. "Japanese Research in Recent Years on the History of Wei, Chin, and the Northern and Southern Dynasties." *Acta Asiatica* 60 (1991): 104–34.

Lewis, Mark Edward. *Sanctioned Violence in Early China.* Albany: State University of New York Press, 1990.

Li Hu 黎虎. *Wei Jin Nanbeichao shi lunwen ji* 魏晉南北朝史論文集. Jinan: Qi-Lu sushe, 1991.

Loewe, Michael. "China's Sense of Unity as Seen in the Early Empires," *T'oung Pao* 80 (1994): 6–26.

Luo Yunhuan 羅運環. *Chuguo babai nian* 楚國八百年. Wuhan: Wuhan University Press, 1992.

Marney, John. *Liang Chien-wen ti.* Boston: Twayne Publishers, 1976.

Mather, Richard. *The Age of Eternal Brilliance: Three Lyric Poets of the Yung-ming era (483–493)*. Leiden: Brill Academic Publishers, 2003.

———. *The Poet Shen Yueh (441–513): The Reticent Marquis.* Princeton: Princeton University Press, 1988.

———, tr. *Shih-shuo Hsin-yu: A New Account of Tales of the World*, by Liu Yiqing. Ann Arbor: Center for Chinese Studies, University of Michigan, 2002.

Nakamura Keiji 中村圭爾. "Liuchao guizuzhi lun 六朝貴族制論," in *Riben xuezhe yanjiu Zhongguoshi lunzhe xuanze* 日本學者研究中國史論者選擇, vol. 2, 359–91. Beijing: Zhonghua shuju, 1992.

Ochi Shigeaki 越智重明. "Liang-Chen zhengquan yu Liang-Chen guizuzhi 梁陳政權與梁陳貴族制," in *Riben xuezhe yanjiu Zhongguoshi lunzhe xuanze* 日本學者研究中國史論者選擇, vol. 4, 294–314. Beijing: Zhonghua shuju, 1992.

———. "The Southern Dynasties Aristocratic System and Dynastic Change," *Acta Asiatica* 60 (1991): 54–77.

Owen, Stephen, *Remembrances: The Experience of the Past in Classical Chinese Literature.* Cambridge: Harvard University Press, 1986.

Pearce, Scott. "Who, and What, was Hou Jing?" *Early Medieval China* 6 (2000): 49–73.

Pearce, Scott, with Patricia Ebrey and Audrey Spiro, eds. *Culture and Power in the Reconstruction of the Chinese Realm, 200–600*. Cambridge and London: Harvard University Press, 2001.

Purdue, Peter. "Insiders and Outsiders: The Xiangtan Riot of 1819 and Collective Action in Hunan." *Modern China* 12, no. 2 (1986): 166–201.

Schneider, Laurence. A *Madman of Ch'u: The Chinese Myth of Loyalty and Dissent*. Berkeley: University of California Press, 1980.

Schmidt-Glintzer, Helwig. "The Scholar-Official and His Community: The Character of the Aristocracy in Medieval China," Early *Medieval China* 1 (1994): 60–83.

Serruys, Paul L.-M. *The Chinese Dialects of Han Time According to Fang-yen*. Berkeley: University of California Press, 1959.

Shu Fen 舒焚, ed. *Chuguo xianxian zhuan jiaozhu* 楚國先賢傳校注. Wuhan: Hubei renmin chubanshe, 1986.

Silverman, Scott. "Patronage as Myth." In *Patrons and Clients in Mediterranean Societies*, ed. Ernest Gellner and John Waterbury. London: Center for Mediterranean Studies of the American Universities Field Staff, 1977.

Somers, Robert. "Review Article: The Society of Early Imperial China: Three Recent Studies." *Journal of Asian Studies* 38, no. 1 (1978): 127–42.

Spiro, Audrey, *Contemplating the Ancients: Aesthetic and Social Issues in Early Chinese Portraiture*. Berkeley: University of California Press, 1990.

Strickmann, Michel. "The Mao Shan Revelations: Taoism and the Aristocracy," *T'oung Pao* 63, no. 1 (1977): 1–64.

———. "A Taoist Confirmation of Liang Wu Ti's Suppression of Taoism." *Journal of the American Oriental Society* 98, no. 4 (1978): 467–75.

Su Jui-lung. "Patron's Influence on Bao Zhao's Poetry." In *Studies in Early Medieval Chinese Literature and Cultural History: In Honor of Richard B. Mather and Donald Holzman*, ed. Paul Kroll and David Knechtges. Provo: T'ang Studies Society, 2003.

Sukhu, Gopal. "Monkeys, Shamans, Emperors, and Poets: The *Chuci* and Images of Chu during the Han Dynasty." In *Defining Chu: Image and Reality in Ancient China*, ed. Constance Cook and John Major. Honolulu: University of Hawai'i Press, 1999.

Tan Qixiang 譚其驤, ed. *Zhongguo lishi ditu ji* 中國歷史地圖集 (*The Historical Atlas of China*). Beijing: China Cartographic Publishing House, 1990. In eight volumes.

Tang Changru 唐長孺. "Clients and Bound Retainers in the Six Dynasties Period." In *State and Society in Early Medieval China*, ed. Albert Dien. Hong Kong: Hong Kong University Press, 1990.

———. *Wei-Jin Nanbeichao shi lun cong* 魏晉南北朝史論叢. Shijiazhuang: Hebei jiaoyu chubanshe, orig. 1955, reprint 2000.

———. *Wei-Jin Nanbeichao shi lun cong xubian* 魏晉南北朝史論叢續編. Beijing: Sanlian shudian, 1959.

Tang Yongtong 汤用彤. *Han Wei Liang-Jin Nanbeichao fojiao shi* 漢魏兩晉南北朝佛教史. Beijing: Beijing daxue chubanshe, 1938; reprint 1997.

Tanigawa Michio 谷川道雄. *Medieval Society and the Local "Community."* Trans. Joshua Fogel. Berkeley: University of California Press, 1985.

———. "Prominent Family Control in the Six Dynasties," *Acta Asiatica* 60 (1991): 78–103.

Teng Ssu-yu, tr. *Family Instructions for the Yen Clan: Yen-shih Chia-hsun*, by Yen Zhitui. Leiden: E. J. Brill, 1968.

Tsuzuki Akiko 都築晶子. "Guanyu nanren hanmen, hanshi de zongjiao xiangxiangli 關於南人寒門寒士的宗教想象力." In *Riben qingnian xuezhe lun Zhongguoshi: Liuchao Sui-Tang juan* 日本青年學者論中國史:六朝隋唐卷, 174–211. Shanghai: Shanghai guji chubanshe, 1995.

Ueda Sanae 上田早苗. "Go-Kan makki no Joyo no gozoku 後漢末期の襄陽の豪族." *Toyoshi kenkyu* 東洋史研究 28, no. 4 (1970): 31–36.

Vervoorn, Aat. Men *of the Cliffs and Caves: The Development of the Chinese Eremitic Tradition to the End of the Han Dynasty*. Hong Kong: Chinese University Press, 1990.

Wallace-Hadrill, Andrew, ed. *Patronage in Ancient Society*. London and New York: Routledge, 1989.

Wang Wanfang 王万芳. "Xiangyang jinshi zhi 襄陽金石志." In *Shike shiliao xinbian* 石刻史料新編, series #3 vol. 13. Taibei: xinwenfeng chubanshe, 1986.

Wang Zhongluo 王仲犖. *Wei Jin Nanbeichao shi* 魏晉南北朝史. Shanghai: Shanghai renmin chubanshe, 1994.

Xia Rixin 夏日新. "Guanyu Dong Jin qiao zhou-jun-xian de jige wenti 關於東晉僑州郡縣的幾個問題." In *Wei Jin Nanbeichao Sui-Tang shi ziliao* 魏晉南北朝隋唐史資料, vol. 11, 36-49. Wuhan: Wuhan daxue chubanshe, 1993.

———. "Wei Jin Nanbeichao shiqi Jingzhou diqu fojiao de chuanbo yu fazhan 魏晉南北朝時期荊州地區佛教的傳播與發展." In *Ri-Zhong guoji gongtong yanjiu: diyu shehui zai Liuchao zhengzhi wenhua shang suo qi de zuoyong* 日中國際共同研究：地域社會在六朝政治文化上所起的作用, 204–15. Xuanwen she, 1989.

Xiao Difei 蕭滌非. *Han Wei Liuchao yuefu wenxue shi* 漢魏六朝樂府文學史. Beijing: Renmin wenxue chubanshe, 1984.

Yan Kejun 嚴可均, ed. *Quan Shanggu sandai Qin-Han sanguo liuchao wen* 全上古三代秦漢三國六朝文. Beijing: Zhonghua shuju, 1958.

Yasuda Jiro 安田二郎. "The Changing Aristocratic Society of the Southern Dynasties and Regional Society: Particularly in the Hsiang-yang Region." *Acta Asiatica* 60 (1991): 25–53.

———. "Jin-Song geming he Yongzhou (Xiangyang) de qiaomin 晉宋革命和雍州（襄陽）的僑民," In *Riben qingnian xuezhe lun Zhongguoshi: Liuchao Sui-Tang juan* 日本青年學者論中國史：六朝隋唐卷, 116–44. Shanghai: Shanghai guji chubanshe, 1995.

Zhang Canhui 張燦輝. "Yongzhou shili yu Liangdai zhengzhi 雍州勢力與梁代政治." *Wenshi* 文史 56, no. 3 (2001): 81–89.

Zhang Zhongxin 張仲炘. "Hubei jinshi zhi 湖北金石志." In *Shike shiliao xinbian* 石刻史料新編, series #3 vol. 16. Taibei: xinwenfeng chubanshe, 1986.

Zheng Yan 鄭岩. *Wei-Jin-Nanbeichao bihuamu yanjiu* 魏晉南北朝壁畫墓研究. Beijing: Wenwu chubanshe, 2002.

# INDEX

Note: entries for individuals who are known to have been part of an extended clan are listed under their clan name, then alphabetized by given name.